Sociology and Interpretation

SOCIOLOGY AND INTERPRETATION

FROM WEBER TO HABERMAS

CHARLES A. PRESSLER
AND FABIO B. DASILVA

STATE UNIVERSITY OF NEW YORK PRESS

Published by
State University of New York Press, Albany

© 1996 State University of New York

For information, address State University of New York Press,
State University Plaza, Albany, NY 12246

Production by M. R. Mulholland
Marketing by Bernadette LaManna

Library of Congress Cataloging-in-Publication Data

Pressler, Charles A.
    Sociology and interpretation : from Weber to Habermas / Charles A. Pressler and Fabio B. Dasilva.
      p. cm.
    Includes bibliographical references and index.
    ISBN 0-7914-3043-X (hc : acid-free). — ISBN 0-7914-3044-8 (pb : acid-free)
    1. Sociology—Methodology. I. Dasilva, Fabio B. II. Title.
HM24.P735 1996
301'.01—dc20   95-40977
                                             CIP

10 9 8 7 6 5 4 3 2 1

"All the work of culture is *interpretation*—clarification, explanation, or exegesis—of life. Life is the eternal text, the burning bush beside the road where God cries out. Culture—art or science or politics—is the commentary, that mode of life in which life itself acquires polish and neatness through internal refraction."

—Jose Ortega y Gasset

CONTENTS

PREFACE

As has been argued frequently, interpretation is a central aspect of human life, whatever might be the life-horizons in which the person is engaged, e.g., dealing with nature, dealing with history, or dealing with others. Even in the most "exact" fields, such as the physical sciences, when we examine such activities from a social viewpoint, we immediately realize that they necessarily depend upon the live human beings who are intrinsically bound up in that activity. In any scientific experiment, it is the case that human beings have to constantly interpret what is going on, even under laboratory conditions. Thus, whenever we are in the context of human life, interpretation is essential. Nevertheless, one can argue that there are contexts in which interpretation becomes even more significant, and that is certainly the case with the social sciences, and among them sociology. As a consequence, when one looks at the history of sociology, and of social thought in general, one must always face the question of interpretation. Accordingly, interpretation has played a significant role in the thought of a number of major authors.

From a sociological perspective, we might consider that interpretation emerges historically as a crucial problem in particular social contexts. If we appeal to a simple differentiation of two models of society, for instance Tönnies' classic formulation of *Gemeinschaft* and *Gesellschaft,* it seems clear that in the first case interpretation does not emerge as a radically important problem; it remains underground and breaks through only when the harmony and stability of life found in such societies is broken. In a *Gemeinschaft* society, there is an appearance of a clarity of life, of nonmediated knowledge, of a taken-for-granted reality, of a familiarity, which is fundamentally a result of the stability of the roots that persons have in such a life-context. In its most common case, a *Gemeinschaft* style of living is the situation of an isolated agricultural village, in which time is circular, and goes through the repetitions of the agricultural year, with its defined tasks, festivals, and so on. There is a predominance of face-to-face relationships, a close-knit, interactional life, and a dependence upon tradition and custom, so that life seems to repeat itself over and over again. In such a situation, everything seems to be known, so there are no questions, there is no need to investigate phenomena of life or nature further, since stories of passing encounters told by the elders serve as much as anything else to help the population understand and unveil present problems.

The situation is quite different in the case of *Gesellschaft.* Now, instead of "savages" (Lyotard), we find the civilized, the rootless, who no longer can fall back into custom and tradition. They find themselves by themselves, without established links with others, so that every process of any relationship must be worked out in different contexts, and the only hope is to appeal to transcendental criteria, those of a constructed, "civilized" world that seems to be universal and ahistorical. Certainly even these objectives must be bargained with others because it is not especially clear that such criteria can be found. In other words, for the life-world to become livable, at least an artificial community must be established, a system of life that could be at least a simulacra of the previous *Gemeinschaft.* Such "community" must be worked out by means of a process of interaction based on communication among actors. And it is in the to and fro of such communication that the question of interpretation emerges in its most clear and compelling form, such as in the commonplace, "what do you mean?" It is through this process of dialogical communication that a community of shared-meaning systems can reestablish a link of meaning between coparticipants.

In this volume, we are concerned with such a problematic, and we address it through the analyses of certain key social thinkers. Out of the classical tradition, we have selected Max Weber. He is the sociologist *sine qua non* of that classical period who was concerned with the question of interpretation. As a matter of fact, and as is well known, he was also concerned with the question of establishing causal explanations following the quasi-model of the exact sciences. To the program of the natural sciences, Weber added a significant requirement, the demand for undertaking a process of interpretation, which is called for by virtue of the fact that we are dealing with human phenomena — thus, his advocacy for an interpretative sociology. We will analyze both the salience of such issues in his work and the tension that his work brings about by virtue of his additional quest for causal analysis.

Following Weber, we discuss some of his immediate followers, who were in different ways even more concerned with the question of interpretation, although they tended to leave behind the interest in causal explanation. In this section, three authors are considered: Karl Mannheim, Alfred Schutz, and Max Scheler. The question of interpretation plays a somewhat different role in the work of each of these authors.

For Schutz, interpretation enters his system within his sociological approach to phenomenology. Although influenced by Husserl and especially by Bergson, Schutz has two fundamental aims: first, to present a critique and reformulation of Weber's position in order to sort out and go beyond the tension between explanation and interpretation. He attempts to do this by shifting Weber's position away from the analysis of a theory of hypothetical ideal types seen as purely intellectual constructs and towards the emergence of types within human consciousness as cognitive structures of understanding. Secondly, after effecting these epistemological shifts, he engaged in the delineation of some of the myriad of cognitive structures present in human life. It is to the appeal of such cognitive structures that the process of human understanding, for him, emerges.

Whereas Schutz' work addresses particularly the question of interpretation at the interactional level, Mannheim deals with a different facet of interpretation, referring instead to global structures of meaning. Starting originally from a Marxist approach, Mannheim sets up his frame on the relationship between base and superstructure and centers his analysis on the character of superstructures as involving spheres of knowledge, ideology, and utopia. His immediate problem becomes that of how to find a mediative category that might be the ground for the establishment of a "community" of meaning, given the multiplicity of groups and subsectors in any complex society. Mannheim discovers such a "ground" in the free-floating intelligentsia, which has become a much-criticized conception. Although that may very well be a flawed conclusion, Mannheim's theoretical contribution to interpretation at a macro-level presents us with a wealth of insights, such as those found in his analysis of the human mind, that are still quite pregnant.

Finally, in this section we look at the contributions of Max Scheler. Scheler is also classified as a phenomenologist, but one who is quite different from Schutz or Husserl. Scheler develops his own personal kind of phenomenology, which is centered on his interest in the investigation of human values. The question of interpretation and values is a crucial one, because interpretation never occurs in an aseptic context. Every time human beings interpret something, they necessarily place what is being interpreted into a context of meaning, which is simultaneously a context of valuation. As has been analyzed elsewhere, words are never simply words, and concepts are never simply concepts. We learn them in an experiential context, infused with values. Of course, that is very simple to understand; right and left are never simply directions — think about persons who are right- or left-handed, and one immediately unveils a value-dimension of each classification. Among other things, it is this dimension of interpretation in which we are particularly interested with our review of Scheler.

In the third part of this volume, we move to an analysis of contemporary trends in interpretation. Recently, we have witnessed in sociology what has been called the "turn into language," which has brought into focus the significance of language for contemporary thought, and has also stimulated a major concern with questions of interpretation in the larger frame of hermeneutic theory. This contemporary concern has led to a renewal and a reanalysis of the hermeneutic tradition and the redrawing of positions today regarding hermeneutic issues. We think that in this critical renewal we may note three major positions: positivist, humanist, and critical. Accordingly, we have selected one or two major authors to investigate the bearing of each one of these three orientations toward interpretation. They are: Emilio Betti, an Italian legal historian; Hans-Georg Gadamer, a German philosopher; and Theodor Adorno and Jürgen Habermas, two major exponents of the Frankfurt School of Critical Theory, one early and one later.

Betti is one of the contemporary scholars who has dedicated a substantial amount of his career to the question of hermeneutics and interpretation. He follows in a sense the classical path opened by Schleiermacher and aims at establishing a general theoretical interpretation that will remain effective across disciplinary lines. His two-volume work on the topic, *Teoria Generale della Interpretazione,* remains one of the major contributions toward that goal. Moreover, what is specific to Betti is that in contradistinction to other thinkers in the domain of hermeneutics, he argues for the possibility of reaching a canonic interpretation, that is, one that will be closer to the true meaning of the text than those that appeal to any multiplicity of other meanings. It is this positivistic concern, a quasi-intention toward the exactness of result, that is simultaneously appealing and questionable in his work.

Gadamer operates within a humanist interpretive tradition. As a philosopher, he is fundamentally concerned with texts of different authors and different ages, and his context is the interaction between reader and text, a classic, although quite specific, interpretative situation. Moreover, Gadamer is not particularly concerned with the question of procedural techniques involved in the process of interpretation. Under the influence of Heidegger and following the same turn taken by Heidegger in the latter's shift away from Husserl, Gadamer moves from the question of interpretation at an ontic level, that is, from a more narrow, technical level, to an ontological level, that is, an examination of the ground upon which any interpretation must take place. Such a ground consists of the existentials that crucially and fundamentally establish a structure through which interpretation can emerge.

Then we turn to the Frankfurtians, and we are in that context interested in examining the attributes of a critical stance toward the question of interpretation. Adorno provides us with a position that is characteristic of the first school of interpretation at Frankfurt. It is characteristically called by him "negative" (in contrast with the style of interpretation of Hegel, among others), and is concerned with debunking the ostensively given interpretations of texts and examining their underlying layers of meaning, which are crossed with tensions and conflict, unresolved, and which must be brought to bear against the apparent smoothness of the unmediated facade.

Habermas, a representative of the second generation of Frankfurtians, revives our interest in transcendentalism and language, with an interest in the formal structures of communication, grounded on universals, that hypothetically serve as a basis for any interpretative problematic. In so doing, and in reaction to Gadamer, Habermas places the question of interpretation within a narrow aspect of a much larger critical enterprise.

As a possible conclusion to these analyses, we offer the idea that interpretative programs are diversified according to the specific location that they have in a metatheory of knowledge. Although that might well be the case, we are not prepared at this point to offer a synthetic approach that would in an unambiguous, theoretical sense pull together all of these contributions. It seems that this is not possible at this time, and appealing at least to Adorno, it seems that it would be not only premature, but also uncritical to attempt to close these approaches into a homogeneous system that would, by definition, negate the viability of interpretation as a creative process in human life.

The title of this work is somewhat telling, in that it refers to a dimension of sociology that has in many ways been repressed in the profession. And, as Adorno would say, such repression signifies a regression, a retreat from understanding and interpretation, which were crucial to the founders of the discipline of sociology, to a thoroughly instrumental and administrative rationality. Our intent herein is to stake out a critical position, from which the relevance to contemporary sociological research these theories of interpretation or hermeneutics (which terms are used nearly synonymously) can be adumbrated.

This work has long roots in our own projects of immersing ourselves in the life-world. Some of the more specific terrain that we have covered goes back to discussions of Gadamer's *Truth and Method* held by the Notre Dame theory circle, members of which included Jerry Wallulis (South Carolina), Jeffrey Crane (Hawaii), and Ray MacLain (Fredonia). In addition, one of the authors attended seminars and lectures presented by Gadamer in Heidelberg and Adorno in Frankfurt. He has also had more limited contact with Betti and Habermas. In all of these contacts and contexts, the central issue involved the question of how it is possible to have a sociology without interpretation. The primary thrust of our efforts is to clarify the meanings implicit in the life-world, in social behavior, and in human action.

It is true that since hermeneutics has been central to continental social thought, the authors included in this investigation are representatives of the European, and especially of the German, tradition. A case could be made for interpretive positions developed by American theorists, but such a study would give rise to additional tensions and questions of intellectual relations, which issues would constitute a different project. Accordingly, in a number of places we have used sources of Continental origin, sometimes still untranslated into English; we hope that our own translations will give the reader a sense of the ongoing discussions.

At this point we wish to thank a number of institutions and organizations that have made it possible for the authors to follow their intellectual muses. Direct contact with scholars in Germany, France, and Italy and access to libraries and archives in Paris, Berlin, Rome, and Perugia have been supported during summers and sabbaticals by the University of Notre Dame, for which we are extremely grateful. Colleagues such as Fred Dallmayr, Joseph Buttigieg, Steve Watson, Gerald Bruns, Eugene Halton, and Andrew Weigert have been gracious with their assistance and steady in their willingness to challenge our assumptions. The level of encouragement and support we have received from Purdue University North Central, especially from Howard Jablon and LeeAnn Wall, has been extraordinary. We also would like to thank the large number of students with whom we have interacted as we taught Sociological Theory on both the undergraduate and graduate levels. Many of the ideas expressed herein were first developed during class discussions, and we thank our students for their patience and insights. In addition, we would like to thank our editor at the State University of New York Press, Megeen Mulholland, for her timely professionalism, and our indexer, Carol Roberts, whose breadth of expertise and extraordinary eye for detail have saved us many hours of labor and much embarrassment.

Finally, in a world of interpretation, we would be remiss if we did not thank our families, with whom we have shared an ongoing hermeneutic project in a very real day-to-day adventure.

INTRODUCTION:
SOCIOLOGY AND INTERPRETATION

In order to determine the profile within which the interpretive project attempts to reach "knowledge," it is helpful to contrast that profile with two others that have wide currency in contemporary social theory, namely the naturalistic and the critical. These three modes of investigation constitute a general model of integrated scientific activity. Such a model was first advanced by Törnebohm (1968–69) and was also adopted by Radnitzky (1973) for his analysis of contemporary schools of metascience. Generally, this model of scientific activity assumes an identifiable form (Figure 1).

Central to the model is the Ego, often working in isolation, or, as is the case with those branches of science called the "hard sciences," supported by a staff of associates. These people, whether the lone investigator or the research staff, participate in a defined community of investigators, the members of which are related by a common research program. In turn, these investigators are influenced by other dimensions of the scientific enterprise, particularly the knowledge domain in which they operate. This knowledge domain provides themes for their investigation and also constrains the research to acceptable topics. Each research community is engaged in the formulation of a project for investigation, which is defined by both the knowledge domain and the domain of research strategies.

Every project, to be acceptable to the larger scientific community, has an ostensive or potential application within the reality sphere of the life-world of the community. As this application is delineated, results are identified and evaluated, and if found satisfactory, the same application is appropriated by generalized users of scientific knowledge, and by specific clients, for whom the project has a particular use. This model features a recursive movement, in that specific clients and generalized users of the science can themselves influence the selection of themes and the overall formulation of the project. Thus, a number of factors, directly influenced by the characteristics and self-interests of the research community, the characteristics and self-interests of the generalized users, and the characteristics and self-interests of the clients, act in concert to define the ways used by the scientific community to formulate and disseminate results of scientific research.

Three types, or modes, of scientific orientation are adumbrated by this model of activity. They are the metascientific domains of the:

1. naturalistic scientific project
2. critical scientific project
3. interpretive scientific project

Each mode has a distinctive research strategy and orientation, and each operates as the model proposes. Naturalistic science is characterized by "objectifying" techniques, the heuristic conversion of objects of study into objects of nature (such as in Durkheim's earliest statement of sociological methodology — "treat social facts as though they are things"). Critical science identifies social situations as political structures open to potential alteration toward the goal of overcoming phenomena identified (by scientist, generalized user, or client) as problematic. This was the approach taken by Marx and his followers. The third mode, interpretive science, addresses phenomena that are found to bear problematic meanings, toward the goal of investigating the possible meaning

FIGURE 1

Scientific Activity

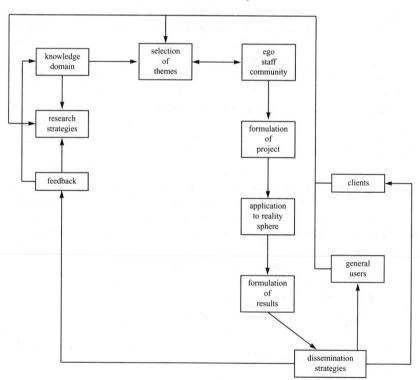

constellations so as to provide the grounds for meaningful action (to use Weber's phrase). Before beginning an exploration of the dimensions of the interpretive mode, it would be useful to sharpen the distinctions between that mode and the other two, in terms of the elements defined by Radnitzky.

Naturalistic Science

The general aim, and central theme, of this approach is improving human adaptation to an existing environment, whether natural or social. Thus, naturalistic science is grounded in, and proceeds according to, "instrumental reason," to use a phrase popularized by the critical theorists. Instrumental reason, as a human capacity, is utilized to manipulate things and processes for human advantage.

This mode of science consists of a central set of figures — Ego, staff, and investigative community. In this case, Ego is usually a specialist, with particular training in a specific discipline. This specialization is invariably characterized by separation. That is, the Ego, or naturalistic scientist, is separated from his or her society-at-large, at the very least in terms of the particular contexts and substantive matters that fall within his or her area of specialization. One's ways of looking at the world, the defining of approaches to the subject matter, and the use of definitions derived from investigation — all are different for the natural scientist than for the nonspecialist. The social context of this Ego is generally populated by peers who share a similar knowledge domain. In turn, the knowledge domain is identified as that of scientifically tested results from the particular area of inquiry, and especially that which has been processed by Ego's community of associates. Furthermore, in this mode of science, knowledge is believed to be both crescive and supported by general laws and causal explanations. Because such investigations deal with the search for laws, research strategies are constructed at an abstract level and are grounded in logic. Finally, the technology used to gather and analyze data is consistently of the quantitative type.

The process of naturalistic science is fairly well known. The dynamic by which this mode of science proceeds involves the formulation of a research project from the activities of the research community. Hence, the criteria for the operation of the project are internal to the discipline, are time specific, and follow historical precedents. Those efforts that are accepted by the community of investigators are applied to the reality sphere in such a way as to call for the construction of well-defined experiments, or by calling for the emulation of mathematical/logical procedures.

As the scientific work continues, and results are obtained, those results are formulated and reported according to established rules of communication. Each mode of science includes the delineation of appropriate means of communicating findings, and the naturalistic style of communication emphasizes the methodological approach and procedures used to obtain the results. Consequently, criticism of naturalistic science often focuses on perceived methodological weaknesses. One of the primary claims of this mode of science is that the results of a particular project are understood within the community of like specialists, and not necessarily by those scientists operating across disciplinary boundaries.

Generally, the dissemination of the results of naturalistic science involves scholarly conferences and specialized journals, which methods of communication afford the scientist with a quick and efficient turnover of material, thus ensuring that the work of critical evaluation and further research occurs in the shortest possible period of time. Positive research results tend to bring about an integration of like-minded specialists into a collegial community. Negative results, on the other hand, lead the community of specialists to focus on the procedures followed by the errant investigation, which in turn leads to calls for the research process to be subjected to clearer controls and better-defined sanctions.

As a consequence of the requirements of specialization, in terms of the clarification of procedures, the delineation of community boundaries, and the control of information, generalized users of scientific knowledge must make use of mediators, who translate the results of naturalistic science to the non-specialized audience. There thus emerges a differentiation between "pure" and "applied" science within the naturalistic realm. The knowledge of pure science is restricted to the narrow community of specialists, and its translation into knowledge appropriate to the general users is effected by cadres of "applied" scientists.

Clients of naturalistic science, on the other hand, are identifiable on the basis of specific characteristics. Because contemporary naturalistic science is highly diversified, very complex, and requires large amounts of capital and other resources for its operation, the clients of such science tend to be governments and branches of government, foundations, and large industrial concerns. The results of activity sponsored by these clients may be disseminated to generalized users, but the clients generally have more say in the formulation of the project itself.

Critical Science

The goal of critical science is the attainment of enlightened knowledge that will give the individual, as well as the community-at-large, alternative ways of transcending existing social and personal problems. That is, the critical model involves the identification of problematic situations or behaviors and the elucidation of strategies by which to overcome or change the problematic condition. This is a model that is clearly political, since it is a political process (called "conservative" or even "reactionary") that operates to erect blockages, or at least to minimize along lines of established interests the processes of social transformation.

When conducting the work of critical science, the Ego usually operates without a staff, and her or his community becomes that of like-minded peers — "fellow-travelers," so to speak. For the most part, members of this community of critical scientists deal with or belong to the "oppressed" or disenfranchised portion of the general community. Those members of the community defined as "oppressors" most often are defenders of the status quo, whether by virtue of their positions in the authority structure or by virtue of their system of beliefs, and hence must be led to change through the evidence and prompting of the critical scientists. Often, advocates of the critical perspective understand there to be a dialectical relationship (usually, though not always, in the Marxist sense) between the critical scientist and the sociocultural collectivity under study (and its subunits).

The knowledge domain of the critical sciences encompasses the processes of change (on the level of the sociocultural structures) and of inhibitions to change. The critical social scientist investigates situations that are problematic for (even if not recognized as such) members of a segment of society and the blockages to structural transformations that would cure or modify those problems. This mode of study has been followed by Marx (on the dynamics of sociopolitical and economic formations); by Freud (on the self and human psyche); and by Nietzsche (on the dominance of the ethical and the knowledge of groups in social formations).

In this mode of science, the formulation of a research project rests upon the Ego's analysis of blockages to appropriate or desired transformations of the social situation. The critical social scientist assumes, *a priori,* that change, rather than stability, is what characterizes human societies, since societies are *living* totalities. Moreover, the critical scientist accepts that life itself is characterized by change, i.e., "growth," rather than stability, i.e., "crystallization," which is a feature of "death" or "nothingness."

For the most part, the application of the critical model of science proceeds as a critique of ideology; in other words, in certain situations, members of the oppressed class, or their sympathizers, envision blocks to the closing of the gap between social ideals and social reality. Therefore, one of the key concerns of this mode becomes the analysis of distortions of perception and knowledge, at both the individual and collective levels. One example of such an analysis would be the investigation of knowledge distortions in Fascism; another might involve the ideological hegemony of naturalistic medicine.

The formulation of results of critical analyses generally follows a dialectical process, in which the scientist communicates results to her or his peers and receives their comments. Peer review involves argument about matters of substance, rather than about matters of method, as found in the naturalistic model. The results of critical investigations are reported in monographs, aphorisms, essays, and/or pamphlets, and these are most often disseminated via independent channels of communication, rather than by means of the scientific conference or journal. In this manner, the critical scientist avoids the blockages to communication she or he may encounter in channels controlled by oppositional special interests, including those interests that represent the establishment under critical review.

The critical scientist intends the results of research to be used by the society as a whole, especially since the aim of critical research is the enlightenment of all. The audience, in fact, tends to be smaller, as the critical scientist presumes that the consumer is a mature individual with an educated grounding. Indeed, because critical science tends to critique current structures and systems of authority, members of the ideological elite avoid or dismiss such results, and as a consequence the actual audience for critical science becomes limited to other critical humanists, specialists holding similar interests, and oppressed minorities and their sympathizers.

Interpretive Science

The goal of interpretive science is to reach intersubjective understanding of symbol systems and their derivations (such as a specific text). In addition, hermeneutic science seeks to reach a meaningful translation of traditions from different times and/or different places so as to illuminate our own system of meanings. The Ego involved in the interpretive process is grounded immediately in the life-process. That is, each member of a society is engaged in the interpretive process, although without structure or historical consciousness. The interpretive scientist is not different than other members of her or his society, except that the scientist seeks to explicate systems of meaning with greater than normal rigor, especially when meaning becomes problematic or inchoate. Interpretive scientists do not view themselves as dependent on a staff or community of like specialists, but rather in a relationship with other Egos and communities here and now or separated by time and/or space.

The knowledge domain of interpretive science involves the clarification of meaning, particularly when the flow of communication is interrupted. Accordingly, research strategies are directed to the examination of meaning systems. "Reader" and "writer" thus become primary characters in the unit of theoretical analysis. As a consequence of this dialogical/interactive focus, language emerges as the central medium for investigation.

Compared with the naturalistic and critical modes of science, the interpretive mode admits of more types of research projects. These types include: the consideration of a problematic text, which may require various technologies (i.e., palaeography, grammar, etymology, etc.) in order to translate the text into a meaning system familiar to other members of society; reproductive interpretation, such as in the reproductive performance of a piece of music or a play; and pragmatic interpretation, as is found in the application of a general law to a specific case.

Users of interpretive science include all subjects who face questions regarding problems in the understanding of texts or meaning systems. More specifically, the clients of interpretive science include persons concerned with specific tasks of hermeneutics, such as theologians, critics involved in the interpretation of ancient texts, or members of the legal profession. The spectrum of potential clients for interpretive science is larger than those of the other modes of investigation, because scientists following those modes may also need clarification of texts and because any member of society is potentially concerned with the illumination of meaning. The application of interpretive knowledge to the reality sphere may therefore be diverse, complex, and lengthy.

In general, consideration of the three modes of scientific research leads to the realization that they consist of different orientations to the world and are directed toward the attainment of different kinds of knowledge. Thus, the enterprises are grounded in different intentions, and their practitioners subscribe to different motivations. Nevertheless, they are all concerned with the discovery of solutions to fundamental and perennial human problems: adaptation, enlightenment, and the understanding of self, others, and society. These models can be sharply contrasted only at an analytical level, since in practice they may overlap, even if the practitioners eschew such integration.

The task of this book will be to construct a historical portrait of the interpretive mode of social science. This task cannot escape occasional discussion of the naturalistic and the critical enterprises. However, the focus will be the development of interpretive social science from the later decades of the nineteenth century to the present. As with any work of historical analysis, many important thinkers are omitted; the intent is to explore the signal persons and concepts that have informed today's interpretive sociology.

A final issue must be noted: in this volume we have chosen to direct our attention to specific contributions and contributors to European social thought, not only because the bulk of interpretive theory has its genesis there, but also because questions of interpretation have been crucial to Continental thinking since at least the time of Martin Luther. In the United States, with a new country to populate and explore, immigrants to incorporate, and potential to develop, questions of interpretation took a back seat to the more pragmatic issues at hand. This is not to say that such questions were not considered — early sociologists were indeed concerned with issues of "understanding," such as the interpretive position regarding religion and cultural assimilation developed by the Chicago School. More recent sociological theorists have been engaged in a "turn to language," not only as an academic issue but also as a practical one. By reviewing the historical development of interpretive sociology, we hope to explore the original roots of this nascent theoretical "conversation."

I

THE ORIGINS OF INTERPRETIVE SOCIOLOGY

Although the science of hermeneutics, especially as applied to Biblical exegesis, has a long and productive history, the first sociological use of the hermeneutic perspective is found in the work of Max Weber. Therefore, a discussion of Weber's sociology and its context will begin our exploration of a variety of theoretical projects that have used hermeneutics to enhance sociological understanding.

1

Max Weber and Interpretive Sociology

Max Weber was born into a wealthy family from Western Germany, whose fortune and tradition were in the field of textile manufacturing. Weber's father was a prominent jurist, active in municipal and national affairs. Weber spent most of his youth in his parents' household, which was a meeting place for influential liberal politicians and professors from the University of Berlin. Thus, Weber developed intellectual interests from early in life.

After concluding his secondary education (the *gymnasium),* Weber attended the University of Heidelberg as a law student. In 1883 he went to Strasbourg for a year of military training and returned to Strasbourg for brief periods in 1885, 1887, and 1888. He studied law at the universities of Göttingen and Berlin from 1884 to 1885 and took his examinations in law in 1886. He continued to study in Berlin and received his law degree from Göttingen. From 1886 to 1890 Weber pursued graduate studies in law at the University of Berlin, carrying on independent work in the field of legal history *(A Contribution to the History of Business Organizations,* 1889). There, his interests concerned the various legal principles through which costs, risks, and profits of an enterprise were to be born by several individuals.

Soon, Weber began to undertake the training required for appointment to the bench, which included the study of political problems of agrarian society. This led him to study legal institutions and to qualify as an instructor of law at the University of Berlin. In 1891 he presented his second work, *Roman Agrarian History and Its Significance for Public and Private Law,* which dealt with sociopolitical and economic developments in Roman society. In 1892 he carried on extensive investigations of rural labor in the German provinces east of the Elbe River, which were published as *Peasant Relations in Far Eastern Germany* (Vol. 4 of the *Schriften des Vereins für Sozial-Politics).*

In 1893, Weber married Marianne Schnitger and finally left the house of his parents. The following year he became a full professor of economics at Freiburg University, delivering his inaugural address on "The National State and Economic Policy" in 1895. One year later he accepted a position in economics with the University of Heidelberg.

From 1897 to 1900 Weber was stricken by illness brought on by exhaustion and anxiety and was forced to reduce, and finally to suspend, his academic work. During this time he enjoyed traveling, especially to Italy, and he spent some time in Rome. By 1901 Weber was recovered enough to return to academic work, but setbacks occurred with unfortunate frequency. In 1903 he became associate editor of the *Archives for Social Science and Social Welfare,* renewing his contacts with the intellectual community.

Weber's only visit to the United States occurred in 1904, when he accepted an invitation to participate in a congress of arts and letters held in St. Louis. In that year he also published the first results of his more recent scholarly activities — an essay on methodology, a discussion of agrarian policies in Eastern Germany, and *The Protestant Ethic and the Spirit of Capitalism.* However, he remained unable to resume all his academic duties, and only through an arrangement with the University of Heidelberg and the German Ministry of Education did he receive adequate financial support. In 1907 a private inheritance enabled him to give up the association with Heidelberg and live as a private scholar, a freedom that led him to commence an intensive scientific activity.

Weber served during World War I for a time as the director of army hospitals in Heidelberg. In 1918 he became a consultant to the German Armistice Commission at Versailles and to a commission charged with the task of writing the draft of the Weimar Constitution. During the summer of 1918 he taught a course at the University of Vienna and, in 1919, feeling well enough to resume his academic career, he accepted a position at the University of Munich. Weber died in June, 1920, at the age of 56, with most of his work unfinished or unpublished.

The Historical Context of Weber's Position

Max Weber's sociological theory and methodology find their historical presuppositions and referential relevance in the discussion and polemics that, beginning with the middle of the 1800s, impregnated German culture with the task of reaching a precise accounting of the sociohistorical sciences and of the validity of their investigative procedures. Such controversy led to a little-understood and gradual crisis of the programmatic orientation that the historical school had promoted in order to ground concrete research on the presuppositions of romantic ideals. The research program of the historical school intended to give each discipline of human science a solid foundation of evolutionary, legitimizing history. The possibility of attaining this goal was questioned by several intellectuals, as were the procedures developed to establish historical validity. Few disciplines were spared controversy. Political economy, sociology, law, and psychology were each characterized by lengthy debates that lasted nearly a half-century and that resulted in the formation of the human sciences on their own merits, and not as the fulfilment of a historical process. These debates, most of which focused on methodological issues, served to clarify the nature and parameters of the disciplines, as well as the appropriateness of different research methodologies. In the end, the historical school was not totally refuted, but was subjected to corrections and transformations through which the social sciences were constructed in a new configuration.

In 1883 Menger raised a strong critique of economic historicism, and his was one of the first and most thorough revocations of the historical school. Menger's dissent was adopted by Roscher and then by Hildebrandt (and others). This criticism was directed toward the tendency found in classical economics to base theoretical conclusions on the fiction of *Homo Oeconomicus,* a figure that was always identical in his atemporal structure and that served as the self-reflective mirror for the satisfaction of his economic needs. Menger and the others opposed a historical economy devoted to adapting laws of economic development, laws based on the positing of organic connections linking economic phenomena to other kinds of social phenomena. In their criticism, the new economists appealed to a conceptual scheme contrary to the Romantic notion of inexorable progress, namely the idea that economic structures and practices form an integral part of the life of a people as a manifestation of their particular, epoch-specific "Spirit." In *Research on the Method of the Social Sciences and of Political Economy,* Menger attacked the reigning methodology of the historical schools and advocated the appropriation of hypothetico-deductive methods. On the one hand, then, the legacy of the historical school was being altered by Schmoller and his followers, through their demand that economic phenomena be properly historically researched, i.e., without recourse to stereotypes. On the other hand, the science of economics, invigorated with analytical models, became autonomous from historiography. Economics thus moved towards what came to be known as positivism, and asserted an independence from the other sociohistorical disciplines.

The methodological controversy in economics illuminated analogous problems being raised in other social disciplines. In addition, the problem of the interrelationships of the social disciplines gradually became widely addressed, and it was in this debate that Max Weber assumed an important role. In the late nineteenth century, sociology was a discipline just beginning to achieve its own autonomy and scientific respect. The historical school blocked the possibility of an independent sociological enterprise by asserting as the ground of each social science the storiographical systematization of their individual materials. Thus the work of sociology became secondary to understanding historical processes.

For those who objected to the narrow view of historiography, one alternative was to follow the methods of French or British positivism; however, this was a view that German sociologists did not find palatable. Instead, they focused on the question of the relation of sociology to storiography and to the other social sciences. Two solutions were forthcoming, the first somewhat more consistent with the historical school, as represented by Karl Marx, and the second emerging through a critique of the philosophical implications of positivist methodology. In the end, the reduction of sociology to a storiographical basis, as earlier intended, could no longer be maintained. Instead, sociologists needed to identify the specificity of sociology and its categories.

Ferdinand Tönnies, while still linked to Romantic ideals, approached an independent position for sociology in *Community and Society (Gemeinschaft und Gesellschaft,* 1887). This work established a distinction that would remain operational in the development of subsequent German sociology, including that of Weber. To the positivist presupposition of a necessary order of social laws that the sociologist must determine, and to the Comtean analogy between sociology and physics, German sociology responded with a focus on typical forms of social relations as they characterize different social epochs.

In their separation from storiography, then, sociologists developed two research orientations. First and most immediately, sociologists gave up the pretense of sociology's being the science of society as a totality, and posited instead a more specific function of sociology within the constellation of social sciences. The questions of the differences in character between sociology and other social disciplines, and the question of the connection between sociology and historical research were among the issues addressed by Georg Simmel in *Sociology* (1910). Other sociologists soon entered the dialogue, which led to various elaborations of *formal* sociology, the analysis of the forms of social relations as they exist independent of historical contexts. Other sociologists, such as Oppenheimer and Alfred Weber, moved in a different direction, concentrating on the examination of cultural phenomena.

Practitioners of the sociohistorical disciplines found themselves confronted with methodological controversy and were forced to deal with substantive questions of orientation. Thus by the time Max Weber became coeditor of the *Archiv für soziale Gesetzgebung und Statistik* in 1903, historiography was already under lethal attack. Max Weber and his contemporaries realized that the polemics concerning appropriate social scientific methodology, which included matters of political and ideological significance, demanded a specific delineation of social scientific procedure in contradistinction to that found in the natural sciences. The debates internal to the domains of economics, sociology, and political science were linked by a problem of a more general order — the nature of the *geisteswissenschaften.* Progress had already been made in the field of economics, especially by Menger. Similarly, the ongoing debate within sociology against the Comtean equation of physics and social science had provoked statements of an antipositivist character. What was required was progressive liberation from the historical school, yet with a concession to the need for some historical orientation within the social sciences. Only by constructing a heterogeneous sociology, incorporating both historical influences and static, nonpositivist analyses, could German sociologists legitimately posit the attainment of objectively valid knowledge.

Two systems of sociology emerged in answer to this challenge. On the one hand, Wilhelm Dilthey suggested that the social sciences involve the study of *spirit*. Such sciences differ from those oriented to natural phenomena by virtue of differentiations in the field of study and in the diversity of methods employed. For Dilthey, the domain of nature is distant from, and alien to, the domain of human affairs. The starting point for social science will thus be human experience *(erlebnis)*. In his *Einleitung in die Geisteswissenschaften (Lectures on the Sciences of Spirit)*, written in 1883, Dilthey proposes that the human being's immediate, lived experience of the world constitutes the fundamental relationship to be studied by the social sciences. This relationship concerns the historical objectification of erleben and the human "understanding" that attains such an objectification in the light of its own origins. Dilthey is proposing a science of Spirit, and thus the sociologist must translate the structural forms of life into the abstract notions of value, meaning, and scope. This is necessary in order to identify and illuminate the manifestations of "Spirit" that appear as a result of human agency in a particular historical setting. The procedure used by Dilthey to examine these manifestations is "understanding," which we may consider analogous to the more familiar technique of "introspection."

Through his emphasis on the subjective, Dilthey established a clear distinction between his perspective and that of the sciences of nature. Natural sciences work with categories of causation and attempt, via the verification of causal relationships, to construct systems of laws. The world studied by the natural sciences is always foreign to the human being. It is a world with which the person has a constant and ongoing relationship, but it is a world that is always recognized as "other" to the observer and that can be grasped only through "natural" categories. Dilthey's analysis of the historical school did not lead him to reject objectification outright, however. He sought to establish a connection between human science and objective storiography through the focus on understanding. The target of understanding, and the subject matter of the human sciences, always involves objectifications of human mind (or "Spirit"), in which category Dilthey includes both objective texts and human behaviors in their historical contexts. The goal of analysis of such objectifications, however, is the disclosure of the subjective meanings with which they are imbued, by both the mind of the author of the behavior and the value-context within which the author exists. Methodologically, then, the difference between the *Geisteswissenschaften* and the natural sciences rests within the antithesis of explanation and understanding and within the antithesis of causality and meaning.

The methodological solution arrived at by Windelband and Rickert is quite different than that proposed by Dilthey. Windelband and Rickert addressed the problem at the level of logic, an approach tracing its roots back to neo-Kantianism. Their critique of Dilthey rejected the subjective orientation as resting on a metaphysical, and hence irrational, foundation. In *Geschichte und Naturwissenschaft (History and Natural Science)*, published in 1894, Windelband suggested that the human sciences and the natural sciences could be differentiated on the basis of their particular cognitive scope. On the one hand, the sciences of nature are nomothetic (oriented toward the construction of a system of general laws); on the other hand, the social sciences are ideographic (oriented toward the determination of the individuality of certain phenomena). From this perspective, Dilthey's attempt to construct a position between the sciences of "Spirit" and the natural sciences loses its importance. That is, any phenomenon, whether natural or spiritual, can be investigated by considering it a particular case of a norm or by considering it in its individual and non-repetitive character. Because the phenomenon is to be considered by either one method or the other, the connection between the two perspectives sought by Dilthey thus falls as soon as it is proposed.

Rickert, in *Die Grenzen der Naturwissenschaftlichen Begrifssbildung* (1896–1902), further developed the contrast established by Windelband and sought to propose an *objective* mediation between nomothetic and ideographic methods, in contrast to the subjectivist perspective of Dilthey. For Rickert, nature is to be referred to in the general, by inclusive and universal propositions. History, on the other hand, is to be considered with reference to the individual occurrence of the phenomenon. Thus the historical object or event is viewed in its particular form as a "relation of value" that makes possible the isolation and characterization of the historical object's individual context and character. The historical world, then, most often emerges as an organized multiplicity of individual events, as a totality, and within a developmental process. Rickert suggests that the theoretical grounding of our understanding of historical events involves an empirical reality constituted by values and relations of values — or "culture." The realm of historical knowledge is that of culture, and the values embedded in the historical object or event are cultural values. Consequently, the proper sciences for the study of historical phenomena are those that nomothetically investigate the relationships of values that make up the meaning of the historical object. Rickert realized, however, that values are not thoroughly objective, and in 1921 he accepted the notion of "understanding," defined as the comprehension of meaning, as the aim of the science of culture. Rickert proposes, then, that the logical distinction between the natural sciences and the historical sciences be changed into a distinction between fields of research, identified and justified on the basis of the presence or absence of a "relationship of value."

Weber's Interpretive Sociology

In general, from about 1883 until the early years of the new century, the antithesis between the natural and social sciences remained at the center of the methodological controversy, and on the resolution of that controversy rested the validity of the sociohistorical sciences. The polemics that emerged led to an ongoing and exhaustive debate involving attempts to prove or refute one thesis or the other or to devise some form of reconciliation. Dilthey indicated that the validity of the sciences of "spirit" could be established in the circular relationship of experience, expression, and understanding. These sciences find their guarantee (even if limited and conditioned) in the identity of the cognitive subject and its world. The investigator and the field of research are the same. The human being can understand his world, the sociohistorical world, because he is a part of it, and can therefore grasp it from the inside. Dilthey's fundamental thesis, which was supported by a number of sociologists of the day, including Georg Simmel, constituted one dimension of the critique of the sciences of man. For Rickert and his followers, however, the validity of the sciences of culture is contained in the philosophy of values and draws its strength from the thesis of the character of absoluteness that must be attributed to such values.

Max Weber developed his sociohistorical methodology within this environment of confrontation. His interests seem to have been twofold: First, he attempted to devise a precise methodology for conducting sociological research. Second, he sought a method of reconciling objective sociohistorical research with political interests. A fairly broad and diverse set of problems emerged during his research, and Weber intended to devise a way of dealing with them all. While studying the history of commercial law during the Middle Ages and the history of Roman agrarian law, Weber had to confront the problem of the relationship between economic institutions and their corresponding juridical concepts. One of the issues Weber addressed in this area was the question of the difference between historical research and juridical analysis. His analysis of the socioeconomic breakdown of ancient civilization then led him to investigate the significance of economic factors in the course of history. However, his participation in the editing of the *Verein für Sozialpolitik* and his research into the conditions of farmers in the eastern part of Germany also led him to a consideration of the nature of sociological field research and the relationship of field research to the political movements that change human living conditions. Another set of issues, and one that is more purely sociological in character, emerged as a consequence of Weber's analysis of the influences of industrialized labor on human social arrangements and behavior. In each of these cases, Weber's investigative work was linked to the question of method and to the logical formation that would most accurately obtain meaningful results.

Weber's methodology was thus developed during the process of concrete research, in contradistinction to some of the earlier sociologists, and responded to the question of how to adumbrate the functions of empirical analyses in the domains of sociohistorical and political action. The first statement of this methodology may be found in an essay written during the final decade of the nineteenth century, *Roscher und Knies und der logischen Probleme der historischen Nationalökonomie*. In this work, Weber analyses, and disputes, the presuppositions of the historical school of economics, which argument requires that he take a position regarding the inheritance of Romanticism. Simultaneously, he clarifies the methodological conflict defined by the positions of Dilthey and Rickert.

Weber begins by accepting Menger's critique of Romantic historicism. Indeed, economic historicism is viewed not as an authentic historiographical procedure, but rather as a form of research caught up in evolutionary presuppositions and prejudiced by Romantic categories. The positivist answer to this flaw is to admonish the researcher to investigate history accurately by carefully and objectively analyzing the individual economic structure and the process that leads from one structure to another. Rejecting the notion that there can be a "spirit of the people" that would serve as a cause of sociological phenomena, and also rejecting the transposition of biological concepts into the sociological sphere (as in "organic interpretation"), Weber proposes a wider frame of analysis than did Roscher and Knies, a frame of analysis that joins objective knowledge with hermeneutic understanding. Weber therefore refused to accept the metaphysical presuppositions of the historical school, namely that history develops in a universal sequence susceptible to nomothetic acquisition.

History, for Weber, is a form of knowledge that may *possibly* be confirmed as valid, but the autonomy of that knowledge is not guaranteed by either a specific psychological reality or a specific empirical reality. Neither the phenomenon studied nor the methods used can themselves constitute the logical structure of research; nor can they, in themselves, certify the objectivity of that research. In order to devise a method that would ratify the validity of knowledge, Weber rebuts positivism in favor of the position of Dilthey.

Weber's methodology is not wholly appropriated from Dilthey, however. Weber refuted the notion of historical subjectivism implicit in Dilthey's method. Moreover, Weber rejected Dilthey's methodological reliance on intuitionism. For Weber, the sociohistorical sciences are not different because they take Spirit as their object rather than nature, nor are they different because they proceed through the internal understanding of meaning, rather than through causal explanation. What distinguishes sociohistorical knowledge from natural science is its particular logical structure, which consists of an orientation toward individualization. This focus on individualization, as noted earlier, is an essential component of Rickert's position, and Weber adopts this argument from Rickert in order to reach a reconciliation of the conflict between positivism and interpretation. For Weber, then, not the object of investigation, but rather the scope of the investigation and the method of its conceptual elaboration are the key issues. Dilthey's method of descriptive psychology is unsatisfactory. Instead, the sociohistorical sciences are distinguished by the mode in which research leads to empirical verification and results are translated into a specific form of causal explanation.

The combining of Dilthey's and Rickert's perspectives means that Weber advocates a modified form of interpretive methodology. The sociohistorical sciences are to use a form of interpretation adequate to their object of study, and such a position is legitimate if the intent of the procedure is not immediate "understanding," as an act of intuition, but rather the formulation of interpretive hypotheses open to empirical verification and causal explanation. Thus understanding no longer excludes causal explanation, but coincides or is compatible with a specific form of explanation. The sociohistorical sciences thus are disciplines which use a process of interpretation to establish causal relations regarding individual phenomena. The interpretation of meaning, then, coincides with the determination of the conditions of the event.

As a consequence of these investigations, Weber developed a new research strategy, a strategy that was faced with an old and serious question — the question of objectivity. In order to guarantee objectivity, Weber had to come to terms with two conditions. First, his methodology had to avoid any presupposition of value-assignment to the phenomenon under investigation. Second, the methodology had to admit of verification of social scientific assertions through causal explanation. The analysis of these two conditions, which needed to be met for his method to warrant acceptance, was conducted in two essays: the first, *Die "Objektivitat" sozialwissenschaftlicher und sozialpolitischer Erkenntnis,* written in 1904, and the second, *Kritische Studien auf Gebiet der kulturwissenschaftlichen Logik,* from 1906.

Weber addressed the first condition, that of value-free research, by utilizing Rickert's differentiation between "judgments of value" and "relations of value." The conservative, "organic" conception of society found in the old historical school was not as much a method of analysis as it was a means of supporting political and ideological valuations of social phenomena. Overcoming such presuppositions meant a liberation from the political implications of historiography. This necessity corresponded with practical questions raised by the changes in the German socioeconomic structure and Germany's emergent position as an international power.

In Weber's view, the human sciences can consider the questions of sociopolitical life and can contribute to the solutions of problems raised by ideological orientation, but the investigation itself must remain objective. Thus the sociohistorical sciences cannot formulate judgments of value, and their results must not become the basis for a political orientation. Such orientations are located not at the level of the ideal validity of values, but at the level of *de facto* existence. Accordingly, it is not possible to say that particular values are or are not valid politically; it is not possible to prescribe one action rather than another. What *is* possible is the investigation of the influence and consequences of values in the historical process. Scientific research is independent of value positing; it establishes that which is, rather than suggesting that which should be. Thus there exists a discontinuity between value judgments and scientific research.

The foregoing deals with value judgments, not value relations, and Weber carefully made this distinction. That is, the sociohistorical sciences do not include practical valuation as a matter of method. Sociohistorical research does, however, involve a theoretical relation to the values that delimit the object of analysis from the empirical context within which the phenomenon occurs. "Value relation" is thus not an assignment of value made by the scientist, but a discovery of the choices made by the actors under investigation. By making this distinction, it is possible to establish a sphere of research in which the investigation proceeds in an objective manner and that leads to the construction of causal explanation.

Weberian methodology thus begins with Rickert's analysis of historical knowledge. "Value relations" make possible the determination of the historical object, constituted by its "cultural meaning." Such meaning is always individualized, and the meaning of a particular phenomenon is conditioned by relations with other phenomena. Weber modified Rickert's approach by redefining the relationship between the historical object and values. For Rickert, this relationship constitutes the foundation for the unconditioned validity of historical knowledge. The values ruling the emergence of the historical phenomenon are universal and necessary. Weber argued that the relationship of empirical data to values is not necessary and that the data involve criteria that are not universal, but rather are the result of situational choices. The relations of values discovered by the researcher thus influence the direction taken by the research and the viewpoint that delimits the field of inquiry. Each sociohistorical science, then, does not deal with a predetermined realm of phenomena but is constituted by the particular viewpoints identifiable in the phenomenon under investigation. The internal relations among the sociohistorical sciences are determined by the problem at issue, and not by a systematic delineation of scientific interest. Furthermore, culture itself no longer is presented as a determined field of research grounded on necessary values. Culture becomes an autonomous domain of investigation that varies with the historical development of each social scientific discipline.

It would seem that Weber advocates a position of extreme relativity, one that views social phenomena as unique manifestations of value relations. If this were the case, it would be impossible to establish causal relations. Weber recognized this and proposed that causal explanation in the social sciences is possible and that it is of a different character than that sought by the natural sciences. The question is: how can we arrive at a causal explanation that is at the same time a meaningful understanding of the historical object? Such a causal explanation demands a selection of empirical data and a disclosure of relations among empirical elements of the phenomenon. While the totality of relations available for investigation can potentially yield a conceptually inexhaustible set of causal relations, the research into causal explanations is necessarily selective and follows the specific viewpoint that orients the investigation. Thus, *explanation is restricted to a finite series of elements, determined at each step on the basis of a theoretical viewpoint, and which proceeds along a particular direction of relations.* "Direction" here refers to the theoretical acceptability of possible causal elements to the general model guiding the research. This direction is abstracted from other possible research strategies. Thus, the cause of an event is imputed to that event through the process of sociohistorical research. This methodology, however, faces the problem of empirical verification of the imputed cause. Because a selection of relations has occurred, how is it possible that these, and not some other set of relations, led to the phenomenon?

Weber says that the authenticity of the causal explanation can be demonstrated through the imaginative construction of a hypothetical series of relations, which is abstracted from the empirical series of relations. Then, the researcher systematically compares the two. This strategy thereby leads to the development of a hypothetical explanation, more or less commensurate with the real one, and therefore the resulting causal explanation is more or less relevant to the phenomenon. The imputation of the cause of the event is thus indirect and involves judgments of "objective possibility." These judgments, moreover, are distributed along a continuum of adequacy from "adequate causation" to "accidental causation." When the hypothetical construct is not explanatory, the researcher must acknowledge that the elements excluded from the explanation are pertinent to "adequate causation." When the hypothetical series parallels the real, empirical process, the researcher must conclude that the elements excluded from the explanation are linked to the phenomenon by "accidental causation," and, indeed, their presence in the event is more or less indifferent.

The ongoing comparison between hypothetical and real series of relations makes it possible to establish at each step of the investigation the causal importance of a particular element to the occurrence of the phenomenon. The "causes" thus revealed are not *all* the causes of the event in question, but rather compose the conditions acceptable to a certain line of research, according to the assumptions of a particular viewpoint. It becomes clear that by delineating such qualifications, Weber gives up any insistence on the classical model of causal explanation and proposes in its place an explanatory methodology that yields theoretically possible causal sequences, rather than nomothetic absolutes. For Weber, the sociohistorical sciences do not establish the determinant factors of a phenomenon; rather, they individualize a certain group of conditions that, among other possible groups of conditions, make the phenomenon possible. To the necessary relationship of cause and effect, then, is added a conditional relationship of meaning, and the manner in which this is accomplished will be considered a little later.

Although the social scientific scholar investigates a domain that is at least partly subjective in character, and although she operates in a limited research field, the results of research are objectively validated by virtue of the logical structure of the explanatory procedure. The guarantee of objectivity rests on the correct application of methodological procedures. At this point, then, Rickert's position seems decisive and incontrovertible. Weber, however, views the domain of the social sciences differently. For Rickert, historical science was constituted by a system of disciplines (the sciences of culture) that were linked by nonmodifiable relationships, with each domain assigned a specific realm of study. Weber views such rigidity as problematic, since the sociohistorical scientist works from within a viewpoint that may change as new problems or new situations emerge. Thus new disciplines can arise, and the boundaries between disciplines can shift or disappear. What is common to the social sciences is Weber's methodology, the orientation toward the explanation of events through the investigation of the individual constellation of empirical elements, and the use of procedures that make the causal-meaningful explanation of events possible.

The Meaning of the Ideal Type

We are at this point presented with a difficult problem. How can it be possible to construct sociological generalizations from the causal-meaningful explanation of an event? In other words, what is the status of nomological knowledge in Weber's scheme? In order to prevent the results of social science from being completely relative and provincial, Weber responded to these questions with the theory of the ideal type. Whereas natural science aims at a system of general laws to explain a particular multiplicity of phenomena, and to obtain increasingly general levels of explanation, sociohistorical science uses uniformity in the formulation of general statements to aim at the explanation of an individual phenomenon. Thus nomological knowledge pertains to both kinds of science, but it functions differently in each. What for the natural sphere is the end of research is for the social scientist an interim moment of the investigation.

The explanation of the individual instance thus presupposes nomological knowledge, the knowledge of typical uniformities of human behavior that can be empirically verified. This knowledge of uniformities, a general conception of behavior, is constituted through a procedure of abstraction that isolates some factors from the multiplicity of empirical data and coordinates them into a coherent, noncontradictory framework. The result of this process of abstraction is always an ideal type. On the one hand, the ideal type is different from reality and cannot replace it, and on the other hand, the ideal type must provide the instrumental device by which to explain the individual instance of the phenomenon.

The ideal type provides two guidelines for sociohistorical research. First, the ideal type establishes a criterion against which to refer empirical data collected during the research. Second, the ideal type provides a conceptual frame by which to orient the research project. In a sense, the rules followed by the scientist during the process of explanation themselves assume an ideal-typical character. The discipline of economics especially, and, in an analogous manner, all of the other social sciences, entail such ideal-typical rules of investigation. While all of the sociohistorical sciences pursue the explanation of the individual case, the path toward such explanation proceeds through the general, through nomological knowledge. In this way, historiographical investigation and the abstract social disciplines, such as economics or sociology, are linked by the same procedures — the elaboration of ideal types. And the objectivity of social scientific knowledge is guaranteed by the nomological grounding of the ideal type.

Thus for Weber, the problem of securing the objectivity of the social sciences finds its solution in the examination of the logical structure *internal* to the sociohistorical disciplines (i.e., the rules of explanation). Weber's epistemology becomes a methodology and is configured as a style of analysis that he believes will enable the sociohistorical scientist to work most effectively. As a product of his own research into specific historical phenomena, Weber's methodology derives its vitality from his efforts to solve problems that faced the nascent social scientific disciplines. In other words, Weber's methodology emerged from his research projects, and his research projects emerged from his methodology. Perhaps Weber's work in the sociology of religion best demonstrates this relationship between sociohistorical research and methodology. His explanatory scheme is demonstrated in *The Protestant Ethic and the Spirit of Capitalism* (1904–5), in *The Protestant Sects and the Spirit of Capitalism* (1906), in *The Ethics of the World Religions* (1915–19), and with special clarity in the section on the sociology of religion in *Economy and Society,* published posthumously in 1922.

With the conception of the ideal type, Weber mediates, or establishes a middle ground, between the earlier historiography and social scientific disciplines, between positivism and interpretation. Certain issues remained: how thorough an understanding of the phenomenon results from the use of ideal-typical methodology? Or, to ask the same question in another way, what are the limitations of the ideal type as a heuristic tool? Answers to these questions will suggest the strength of the mediation between historiography and social science. For Weber, sociology becomes the forge in which this linkage is created, and the works on the sociology of religion, as well as the essay *On Some Categories of "Understanding" Sociology* (1913), clarify the utility of the ideal type.

The ideal type captures the "uniformities of human achievement" in terms of their embodied meaning. The autonomy of the sociological discipline is ensured by this focus on uniformities of behavior accessible to the observer's understanding. These "uniformities" are not "laws" as sought by positivist sociology; instead, they are empirical constellations of phenomena that are expressed in the ideal type. And the "understanding" that characterizes the sociological approach brings to light the uniformities of the phenomena under investigation as well as the concepts that determine the meaning of the phenomena. This is the beginning of a description of Weber's *Verstehen* sociology.

The *Verstehen* approach posits its own research realm, which begins with a particular orientation to the phenomenon. An "orientation" here refers to any kind of human action that takes a position regarding an object as its term of reference. In such a situation, the object becomes identified with human action as it is simultaneously objectively conditioned. The issue here is not human action as such, but rather human action as it is thoroughly *social*. In other words, the action towards the object at issue for the sociologist is that which refers and relates to the action of other persons. What thus characterizes sociology is the regard for the orientation of other individuals, and the consequent possibility of understanding action because of that regard. Therefore, the "meaning" of an orientation is constituted by the subjective intentions of the actor toward the object of action and the coincidence or opposition of that meaning with those of other actors. The possibility of sociological understanding consists of the determination of the goals of action and their underlying behavioral directions.

To establish the aims of an orientation, however, to establish the ways in which the orientation emerges and is maintained (e.g., its conditions of possibility), represents the assumption of a position regarding those conditions of possibility in a determined social relation. *Verstehen* sociology thus has the task of elaborating the kinds of social action that can be found to recur in the behavior of individuals in terms of their orientations to social phenomena. The elaboration of these orientations is the ideal type, and the key to such analysis is the immediate interpretive intelligibility of the rational orientation toward goals maintained by the social individual on a recurrent basis. Moreover, this form of ideal-typical methodology can formulate other explanations of behaviors that consist of orientations to social objects, but that reflect lesser degrees of rationality.

Indeed, ideal-typical explanation treats behavior that can be distributed along a scale of decreasing intelligibility. Weber, in *On Some Categories of "Understanding" Sociology,* constructs a typology of meaningful actions divided into "rational-instrumental," "value-oriented," "affective," and "traditional" types. Rational-instrumental action is that undertaken by virtue of its logical connection with a desired goal. Value-oriented action is that undertaken on the basis of a value or moral judgment, regardless of its instrumentality. Affective action is that which is consistent with the affective state, or the desired affective state, of the actor. Traditional action is undertaken as a consequence of the dictates of the customs of the group. Later, in *Economy and Society,* Weber typologized action into "action in community" and "action in society," a division reminiscent of Tönnies' distinction, and which reestablishes a relationship between Weber and the tradition of German sociology. *Economy and Society* in fact emerges out of a systematic study of the relations of orientations and the corresponding (and resultant) systems of social relations among individuals, on the one hand, and the description of types of economic organization, on the other. Much of Weber's discussion forms an answer to Simmel's analyses of forms of social relations, in which Weber attempts to overcome certain presuppositions regarding the way of life of individuals. For Weber, the analysis of individual orientations and actions moves quickly to the analysis of relational cases, which are established on the basis of reciprocal orientations. That is, the social action undertaken by the individual occurs within a constellation of orientations pertinent to other persons, and all of these orientations condition each other. The explanation of social action, then, requires the construction of the ideal type.

Earlier, it was mentioned that one of Weber's typifications of action involved a value orientation. The question of value, which was central to the positions of Windelband and Rickert, became quite important for Weber during the political situation that led to World War I. Weber consistently made a distinction between objective social research and judgments of value. With the breakdown of German culture during the war, Weber renewed his efforts to separate the two. In the essay *Der Sinn der "Wertfreiheit" der soziologischen und ökonomischen Wissenschaften* (1917), Weber addressed the question of the difference between political valuations and empirical grounding of sociohistorical science. While his arguments tended to restate assertions he had made as early as 1904, a problem of grave consequence did emerge. Always for Weber it was true that sociohistorical research cannot formulate judgments of value or provide justification for such judgments, but is that to suggest that the sociohistorical sciences must remain mute when it comes to questions concerning values? Is a critique of values possible? Weber confirms that the sociohistorical sciences cannot say anything regarding the normative validity of values, but they can indeed establish the empirical existence of values and can throw light on the conditions and consequences of their realization.

From the moment that a person acts on the basis of a value-orientation, which always implies a certain "cost," there is an engagement of determined means and determined consequences. Thus, a technical critique of value-orientations can establish the coherence of the means/goals relationship and the relations of these means and goals with other social phenomena. Thereby the critique of values can be obtained on an empirical level, through the identification of means and the typification of conditions for the realization of values selected as goals. The social scientist cannot say whether a value is valid or not, but she can demonstrate that determined means are or are not suitable for the attainment of given values. Above all, the social scientist can demonstrate how means toward a given value threaten or block the exercise of others, and the various conditions that each require to be expressed.

Weber thus reaffirms the multiplicity of value-orientations and the relations, including those characterized by tension, that exist among them. That the social scientist may encounter a multiplicity of phenomena has already been acknowledged in Weber's discussion of the diversity of viewpoints from which social scientific inquiry could proceed and the links between the viewpoint of the scientist and ideological and cultural orientations. Human action implies the taking of a position towards values, and such a position is based on the acceptance of certain values and the refusal of others. Social research is also human action and thus involves a selection of values and of viewpoint. These value spheres do not offer unconditional validity, for either the person involved in social action, or the social scientist involved in research. The subject must decide every time, in each situation, which values to call his own, and which to refuse, in order to act historically. Values are no longer, as they were for Rickert, absolute normative criteria, indifferent to the human effort of realization of goals. Values subsist in their possibility of orienting human action by virtue of a selection recognized by the actor as normative, and thereby in their possibility of orienting action. The ontological existence of values is eliminated, and what remains is their normative transcendence based on the irreducibility of *de facto* existence. Thus can Weber write, in 1919, about the meaning of science and of politics as *vocation (Wissenschaft als Beruf and Politik als Beruf)*.

By enunciating and exploring the philosophical implications of methodology, Weber was able to carry out an analysis of the historical situation of humans in relation to values. From these examinations was derived the coherence of new interpretive categories, in their nonprejudiced use and explanatory rigor. These interpretive categories and the conceptions that lead to them constitute a significant modification of German historicism and a decisive change in the process of the development of the German sociohistorical sciences. Because he was able to mediate between historiography and Dilthey's descriptive psychology through the use of the ideal type, Weber ushered interpretive sociology into a new and promising domain.

II

SUCCESSORS AND FELLOW TRAVELERS

During the first four decades of the twentieth century, Weber's lineage carried hermeneutics in new directions, with varying levels of success and insight. Three social theorists developed interpretive sociological positions that were superior in their thoroughness and influence. Alfred Schutz sought to mediate phenomenology and Bergsonian life-philosophy in a hermeneutics of the life-world. Karl Mannheim took a different tack and constructed an interpretive sociology of knowledge. Finally, Max Scheler extended his phenomenological roots into an interpretive and subjectivist ethics. It is to these three seminal thinkers that we now turn.

2

Alfred Schutz

Alfred Schutz was born in Vienna in 1899, and he attended the University of Vienna, from which he received a degree in law. Instead of taking up a career as a lawyer *per se,* he entered the field of banking, in which he worked for many years. Banking provided him with economic rewards, but it did not satisfy his intellectual needs, and Schutz eventually pursued his interest in phenomenology and the possibility of reformulating sociology on a phenomenological basis. To that end, he spent time in academic environments and participated in a number of academic events. His interest in sociology was particularly focused on Max Weber's interpretive sociology, and most especially with Weber's theory of ideal types and the ways in which ideal types can be constructed or applied to varieties of social action. Schutz, however, was critical of Weber's attempt to construct a synthesis between interpretation and explanation.

For Schutz, the crucial flaw in Weber's program involved the question of meaning. For Weber, meaning emerged as a consequence of the sociohistorical interaction of the analyst with the phenomenon; thus, meaning is imputed by the analyst. Schutz felt that meaning should be grounded upon the phenomenon itself. Within that framework, he turned to the work of Edmund Husserl, who placed the construction of meaning at the center of his philosophy. In his studies, Schutz was also influenced by the life-philosophy of Henri Bergson. These approaches enabled Schutz to confront Weber's formulations at a foundational level and to reconstruct Weber's interpretive sociology into a phenomenological sociology. The results of these investigations were collected in *The Phenomenology of the Social World* (1932, translated into English in 1967).

At the outbreak of World War II, Schutz moved first to Paris and then to the United States, where he continued his career in banking and also where he began teaching phenomenological sociology, at the New School for Social Research in New York City. This academy had originated as an institution in which the displaced members of the Frankfurt School could continue their investigations into what came to be known as critical theory. In 1956 Schutz gave up banking to concentrate entirely on teaching and writing. His phenomenological sociology, which was rooted in the Continental and German Idealist traditions, was quite alien to the intellectual context of American sociology, which made him a marginal intellectual in American circles, or, to put it more positively, made him an *avant garde* sociologist during his lifetime. Eventually, changes in the tenor of American sociology, combined with the thoroughness and intensity of his theoretical explorations, made Schutz a key figure in modern sociology, particularly after his death in 1959.

Alfred Schutz's Sociology

The phenomenological sociology designed by Alfred Schutz is a major attempt to uncover meaning at the level of the subject, especially the subject in the modality of everyday life. Since relations with others are perspectival, not only physically, but also culturally and biographically, there are by definition multiple realities to any context of social life. Somehow, for life to go on, some way of working out these multiple realities, of comprehending and moving through them, must be established by the actor. Indeed, even the most hesitant of actors must construct at least superficial strategies for dealing with the complexity of social existence. Therefore, Schutz embarked on a phenomenological analysis of the social world, concentrating on the preconstructions of meaning brought to any social encounter by the actors (this is the notion of "pre-predicative meaning structures").

As one might suspect, the fundamental question here involves the phenomenon of shared meanings, as those meanings are created and transferred during the course of everyday life, activity that Husserl described as occurring within the "natural attitude":

. . . in the natural attitude of everyday existence, one accepts the existence of other men as taken for granted. The human bodies that I find in my surrounding world are for me obviously endowed with consciousness; that is, in principal they are similar to mine. Further, it is obvious to me that the things of the external world are fundamentally the same for others and for me. And, in relations with my fellow-men, that I can communicate with them, and finally that a structured social and cultural world is historically already given to me and my fellow-men. We want now to examine these aspects of the natural attitude in greater detail, beginning with the prior givenness of fellow-men. The *fundamental axioms* of the social, natural attitude are, first, the existence of intelligent (endowed with consciousness) fellow-men and second, the experienceability (in principle similar to mine) by fellow-men of the objects in the life-world (Schutz and Luckmann 1973, 59).

This perspective marks the theoretical shift from Schutz' earlier dependence on the life-philosophy of Bergson to the more radical phenomenology of Husserl.

As a consequence of this shift, Schutz comes up against the question that vexed Husserl again and again — the problem of intersubjectivity.

Because Husserl's attempt to recognize and overcome the linkage between knowledge and interests takes the form of a reduction that brackets one's interests in order to unveil the constitutional aspects of reality, and thence to ground philosophy (and correlatively, science) in transcendental experience, regardless of its adequacy, a rather serious problem arises. The problem is solipsism, and whether or not transcendental idealism can account for inter-subjectivity and thus become a legitimate foundation of an absolutely grounded knowledge. Such a ground would overcome the problems of the linkage between knowledge and interests, and would permit true science. However, if such a foundation is not possible, then transcendental phenomenology must remain trapped within the sphere of the solitary Ego. Husserl himself posits the question:

When I, meditating I, reduce myself to my absolute transcendental ego by phenomenological epoché do I not become *soluspsipse;* and do I not remain that, as long as I carry on a consistent self-explication under the name phenomenology? Should not a phenomenology that proposed to solve the problems of Objective being, and to present itself actually as philosophy, be branded therefore as transcendental solipsism? (Husserl 1970, 89)

Thus Husserl must present a fifth Cartesian meditation.

Basically, the issue concerns how phenomenology answers the question of solipsism regarding our experience of the other. As a *transcendental* philosophy, the problem of the existence of the external world (and hence of the foundation of the sciences) is a crucial part of its program. The method of phenomenology (called "epoché," "reduction," or "bracketing") moves the investigation to the analysis of the analyst's own consciousness, in its processes and structures. But this means that in the confines of consciousness, the other appears as an object of consciousness, rather than as the other that is naturally and really out there. Thus the program requires a movement from transcendental analysis of consciousness to one of the world and of how it is possible to explain the other. Such a move has far-reaching consequences since the world itself, as a meaningful complex, includes the "there" of the others and of everything else — objects, culture, history, aesthetics, emotions, ethics. Thus the issue of solipsism becomes central to the project of *any* phenomenology.

This transition from the individual to the social means that the problem of the other *and* the problem of shared meanings becomes: How are these at all possible in spite of the impossibility that experience can ever be completely shared? How, in such a situation, in the everyday life that we all go through, can anyone ever claim that they share meanings? In other words (reflecting the issue with which we began this section): how is it possible that human beings are able to go through their lives at all, every day? A resolution of these questions must be constructed in the same way that the natural attitude is constructed. What, however, does this statement mean?

An answer to solipsism cannot be constructed in any active, subject-oriented way, as one might generally imagine it. I, for instance, do not construct my friends (and vice versa). We go through encounters and experiences "trying out" our meanings. Schutz begins with a new communal vocabulary, one in which Weber's "ideal types" are not carried as applicable paradigms, but rather one in which ideal types are evolved through the process of interactive communication. These types apply to the basic processes of human interaction, and not the more complex ones (like growing up, making it through school, developing healthy relations with parents/family/friends, growing old, and enjoying life in all its aspects). Those experiences involve not ideal types, but rather complex structures of the life-world (such as is described in Schutz' sensitive "Making Music Together"). This conception of complex structures not only makes a point, but also erects a kind of living statement that Weber was never able to discern.

The basic principle of a phenomenological position is that anything which has a sense of existence receives this sense from the process of constitutive synthesis at the level of transcendental experience. Since in our normal conscious experience the other does exist as an other, and as part of an objective world experienced by myself and all others, we must start with an examination of how the other comes to *be* for us, of how the objective world and the other are constituted. Because the other and the objective world are both in question, it is necessary to perform a reduction beyond that taken by Husserl. This is a reduction that takes us beyond the transcendental experiencing of the world and puts into parentheses all aspects of intentionality relating to others' subjectivity. Thus a reduction beyond the epoché of the objective world of the earlier meditations must be performed, further bracketing any results of the constitutional processes of intentionality that relate to other subjectivity, a reduction to the sphere of peculiar ownness.

In this sphere of peculiar ownness as a special sense, I alone remain, with no other, nothing associated with others or anything experienceable by everyone. It is an essential structure, part of the whole of all experience, but uniquely where my transcendental Ego resides. The sphere of peculiar ownness is the Ego as monad. As such, it includes my every intentionality but with the limitation that the constitutional effect of the other is bracketed. In this sphere is constituted I, myself, my very ownness.

With the first reduction, the *epoché,* we gained the world as phenomenon, as presented, as intended, and as undergoing a process of verification and constitution. This second unique epoché goes further and lets us reach the realm of experience that is my own. Everything alien must be purged, all cultural predicates, all characteristics of the surrounding world as meant. We are left with a founding stratum. We are left only with ourselves. We have only our own body and our psyche. We have our own "nature," but my "nature" is different from the one that includes the sense "our nature." And we have our own "worldly" experiences, but these likewise are different because they are peculiar to a special "world," that of my primordial ownness. At this point the obvious question becomes — how can we possibly proceed? In this sphere, any intending of anything alien is problematic, for is not any synthesis in this sphere peculiarly my own? How is it possible from this position for my Ego to form in itself intentionalities with a sense of existence, whereby it completely transcends itself? Is this not a contradiction? Husserl does not stop reaching for this most fundamental level, but in the end he must concede that he has arrived at a solipsistic position. Schutz, because he is concerned with the social world, rather than a *tout court* foundational philosophy for all knowledge whatsoever, makes a turn toward the context on which the social world exists, and furthers his research through the examination of the foundations of the social world.

The Social World of Shared Meanings

The resolution of the problem of shared meanings in the social world, Schutz argues, is to be found in the constitution of the natural attitude, which is as fundamental a structure of social life as space and time are for the natural world. Why this is so can be clarified by recalling the character of the natural attitude. The distinguishing feature of the natural attitude is the epoché that suspends doubt in the reality of the world. This reality is, by virtue of the epoché, simply taken for granted. Such taken-for-grantedness is a requirement for any activity in the world, and thus for the activity of sharing meanings. In addition, the natural attitude is constituted in terms of certain intentional activities of consciousness. In this context, the problem of shared meanings is a matter of how the taken-for-grantedness of shared meanings is constituted. Or, in other words, one asks: what particular intentional activities and modifications of these activities (i.e., pre-predicative meaning structures) are involved in the constitution of the possibility of shared meanings? Questions of this type require a turn from the epoché of the natural attitude to the phenomenological epoché, since it is only under the latter that the constitution of the natural attitude can become a subject of investigation.

Following Husserl, Schutz and Luckmann (1973, 7–8) identify two elementary intentionalities, or "idealizations," that are "essential aspects of thinking within the natural attitude." They are essential inasmuch as, being elementary, they underlie all pre-predicative meaning structures of the social world. In other words, all pre-predicative meaning structures are modifications of the more elementary intentionalities. This foundational character is indicated by the fact that the two intentionalities so decisive here were formulated by Husserl originally in his investigation of the logical structure of mathematics. The first intentional activity is the "and so forth" idealization. By virtue of this idealization, the world is intended as essentially continuous; there is a "constancy of the world's structure," and this constancy underlies the possibility of everyday common sense activity. The second intentional activity is the "I can always do it again" idealization, which refers to the constitution of activity and its consequences as essentially repeatable. The two idealizations are furthermore correlative:

> So long as the structure of the world can be taken as constant, as long as my previous experience is valid, my ability to operate upon the world in this or that manner remains in principle preserved (Schutz and Luckmann 1973, 7).

So the natural attitude is grounded upon these two idealizations of consciousness. As such, these are the "conditions necessary for the possibility of experience . . . [and] . . . general or essential features of the given, not . . . concrete, personalized units of meaning" (Natanson 1973, 35). What is in need of further investigation is the question of how these idealizations relate to the problem of shared meaning.

The resolution to this question is based on two further idealizations, which can be viewed as modifications of those noted above. Both pairs of idealizations operate on a pre-predicative level, but the pair currently at issue can be considered to be the pre-predicative meaning structures of the phenomenon of shared meaning. That is, these two idealizations underlie and give rise to the whole phenomenon of shared meaning. They are described by Schutz and Luckmann as follows:

> First, the idealization of the *interchangeability of standpoints*. If I were there, where he is now, I would experience things in the same perspective, distance, and reach as he does. And if he were here where I am now, he would experience things from the same perspective as I. Second, the idealization of the *congruence of relevance* systems. He and I learn to accept as given that the variances in apprehension and explication which result from differences between my and his biographical situations are irrelevant for my and his, our, practical goals. Thus, I and he, we, can act and understand each other as if we had experienced in an identical way, and explicated the Objects and their properties lying actually or potentially in our reach. And (this is added to and combined with the idealizations of the "and so forth" and that of the "I can do it again"), we learn to accept as given that we can in principle proceed in this manner, that is, we learn that not only is the world that we have experienced in common socialized, but also that the world I have still to experience is in prin-

ciple socializable. . . . together [these idealizations] form the *general thesis of the reciprocity of perspectives.* This thesis is for its part the foundation for the social formation and linguistic fixation of objects of thought. To prevent one from mistaking these Objects of thought as results of a *contract social* it must be emphasized that they are already encountered in language by every individual born into a historical situation. The fact that the individuals can acquire the life-world's linguistic (that is, social) formation as the basis of their worldview, rests on the general thesis of reciprocal perspectives (Schutz and Luckmann 1973, 60).

The significance of the reciprocity of perspectives to the problem of shared meanings can now be put concisely. The possibility of sharing meanings depends on the setting aside of necessary differences in experience, which is accomplished by the two idealizations of which the general thesis of reciprocity is comprised. Common-sense experience is, then, pre-predicatively structured in such a way that the other is constituted not only as one with whom an identity of meanings is unattainable, but also as one with whom meanings can nevertheless be shared for all practical purposes. Such structuring is necessary as a condition for the existence of everyday activity. Thus, sharing meanings, which is taken for granted in the natural attitude, is accounted for in the phenomenological attitude by showing how this particular aspect of the natural attitude is constituted in terms of the intentional activity of consciousness.

The reciprocity of perspectives is a constitutive feature of the natural attitude; it is one pre-predicative meaning structure of the social world, namely the one that underlies and makes possible the particular phenomenon of shared meanings. It is analyzable into more elementary intentional activities; and it is, itself, modified into other meanings that are constitutive of the natural attitude. In this last regard, it has a specifiable place within the overall pre-predicative structure of the social world.

There is, in other words, a formal structure to the phenomenon of shared meanings, and the elements of this structure are a particular set of pre-predicative meaning structures. These forms are not empty abstractions, but rather are forms that are manifest in the texture of everyday reality and that gain their full meaning only within the context of their own constitution and modification. To generalize this point, one may say that any social phenomenon has a formal structure, which can be analyzed in terms of the concepts and procedures associated with the notion of pre-predicative meaning structures.

The general thesis of reciprocity also has important methodological implications. Schutz' approach, and the phenomenological approach in general, secures the methodologically crucial advantage of proposing a plausible theoretical framework for positing, identifying, and analyzing a realm of meanings that are not context bound. Since they do not arise out of any particular process of interaction, they can serve as the basis for generalizing across interactional contexts. The reciprocity of perspectives, for instance, is not a shared meaning which arises out of the process of interaction, but is rather a pre-predicative meaning that is necessary for the existence of any particular process of constructing and sharing meanings.

A more general grasp of the methodological importance of pre-predicative meaning structures can be gained by returning briefly to Weber's view of the procedure of *Verstehen*. The difficulty with the procedure of *Verstehen* (as discussed earlier) parallels the problem just noted. Even if through this method the subjective meaning of actors can be adequately known, the question remains as to how it is possible to proceed from these subjective meanings to an objective, that is, a non-context-bound account of them. It is exactly to this problem and its consequences that the argument of the *Phenomenology of the Social World* is addressed. It is implicit in the discussion of shared meanings but quite explicit elsewhere in Schutz's writings (especially 1962, 48–66) that *Verstehen* is a procedure that actors themselves employ as a basis for engaging in everyday activity. Actors systematically interpret the subjective meanings of other actors. As a result of the natural attitude, subjective meanings are objectified and typified in everyday life; and because of this typifying activity, a basis is established for the use of the same kind of activity by sociologists. The analysis of this typifying activity in everyday life depends upon the results of the phenomenological reduction, which reveals how such typifications are constituted. That is, the analysis depends upon the identification of the pre-predicative structures of the life-world.

This discussion of the nature and sociological relevance of the pre-predicative meaning structures that underlie the phenomenon of shared meanings can be extended to provide a general perspective on the work of Schutz. A major part of Schutz's writings can be understood as an attempt to catalogue and analyze the constitution of the pre-predicative meaning structures of the phenomenon entitled the "social world." The overall import of this attempt is that it establishes a theoretical foundation for a systematic interpretation of the subjective meanings of actors in terms of their own systematic interpretive activity. Schutz's lifelong project was a phenomenology of the natural attitude. The character of such a project should be clear from the foregoing: the natural attitude is the foundation of the life-world, the taken-for-granted world of everyday, common sense experience. The everyday world is taken for granted to be a typified world: the natural attitude is a typifying activity (Schutz 1962).

It is because the life-world is intended, or meant, as a typified world that it can be taken for granted in the first place. A phenomenology of the natural attitude is an analysis of the typifying activity of consciousness. Its aim is to arrive at the features of the natural attitude that are constitutive of the common-sense world; in other words, its aim is to identify the formal structure of typification. As Schutz notes: "The individual's common-sense knowledge of the world is a system of constructs of its typicality" (1962, 7). A phenomenology of the social world, then, will result in the identification and description of this system of constructs of its typicality.

The system of constructs proposed by Schutz has been well-analyzed and discussed by Gurwitsch (1966), Natanson (1970), and Zaner (1970), among others. The temporal and spatial structure of the social world; the world within reach; the world of contemporaries, consociates, predecessors, and successors; the reciprocity of perspectives; because and in-order-to motives, the social stock of knowledge; the social distribution of knowledge, and so on — these and other elements of Schutz's conceptual apparatus comprise the system of constructs of the world's typicality. They are the constitutive features of the social world as it is conceived in the natural attitude.

Because they are constitutive, these features are therefore defined as the pre-predicative meaning structures of the natural attitude and can be understood as the pre-predicative structures of the social world. Any social world is always experienced pre-predicatively in terms of these meaning structures, which, in turn, are the basis for any predications that are made in the natural attitude by members of any particular social world. In other words, these pre-predicative meanings are "given" to the social world. Any sociohistorically circumscribed world will be endowed with these meanings, which are conditions for the possibility both of there being a social world and of the sociohistorically unique meanings that are predicated on phenomena in each social world. To put the same matter one final way — all actors interpret their social world in terms of these pre-predicative meanings, which then serve as the basis for their further interpretation of the socially unique meanings that are constructed in any particular context.

The methodological process through which Schutz arrives at a description of the system of constructs of the world's typicality (specifically in his mature period, because earlier he was influenced by Bergson) follows the broad outlines of the program of Husserl's phenomenology. In his writings, and especially in the *Phenomenology of the Social World,* Schutz proceeds by examining the constitution and modification of the pre-predicative structures of the social world. Beginning with the undifferentiated stream of consciousness, he analyzes the constitution out of elementary intentional acts of the basic category of meaning and the modifications of this basic category in the various structures of the social world. The conceptual framework that is the outcome of this general movement between constitution and modification, between elementary structures and higher level pre-predicative structures, is the framework in terms of which actors construct the social world. Its categories are the interpretive categories in terms of which actors pre-predicatively experience their world. Similarly, each of them pertains to the way in which actors construct their own and each other's subjective experience.

In order to understand the dimensions of Schutz's constitutive categories, we must address the relationship between his work and that of Husserl. A major issue at stake was Husserl's move toward the transcendental Ego. Schutz's concern with and eventual repudiation of the capacity of the transcendental Ego to account for intersubjectivity is a topic he carefully explicated. What is not fully examined, however, is the nature and extent of the consequences of this challenge to one of Husserl's most fundamental tenets. The central problem is the question of history (taken up by Husserl only in his last major work — *The Crisis of European Sciences and Transcendental Phenomenology* — but still not fully explicated in its consequences for transcendental phenomenology and its impact regarding previous works). In Schutz's last work, we find significant formulations regarding this question.

Schutz (and Luckmann, 1973) struggled with the relationship between the realm of pre-predicative meanings and the domain of sociohistorically relative meanings, a relationship that was brought to light in the *Crisis*. It is clear in this work that pre-predicative meaning structures retain the status and function that had already been described. The authors write, for example:

In every situation the ontological structure of the world is imposed on me. The situation is absolutely *limited;* knowledge of this is a basic element of the stock of knowledge. The structure of the subjective experience of the life-world is also imposed on me: the arrangement into provinces of finite meaning-structure with their own experiential style, and further the spatial, temporal, and social structures of every experience. The situation is consequently unalterably prestructured: knowledge of this kind is a basic element of the stock of knowledge. In this sense, the situation is limited from the very beginning; it is articulated and predetermined (Schutz and Luckmann 1973, 114).

The contrast between the influences of pre-predicative structures and sociohistorical structures is illustrated in the following passage:

This province of the practicable meets its absolute limitation in the unmodifiable ontological structure of the life-world, especially in its temporal structure. This province is also relatively limited by the technologically practical (also somewhat indirectly by the theoretical, scientific) state of knowledge of the society into which I was born, and by my own previous experiences. The province of the practicable is thus also limited immediately through my historical and biographical situation (Schutz and Luckmann 1973, 50).

But what does it mean to say that ontological structures absolutely limit and historical structures relatively limit? A particularly helpful statement on this matter is found toward the end of *Structures of the Life-World:*

Knowledge concerning the social distribution of knowledge is a component of the social stock of knowledge. It is thus for its part socially distributed. And, since the social distribution of knowledge changes historically, the knowledge concerning it also changes correspondingly. For this reason the subjective correlates of the social distribution of knowledge assume various historically conditioned forms. Therefore, we cannot be satisfied with the description of the basic characteristics of the subjective correlates of the social distribution of knowledge. Indeed, in every society the individual will grasp typical differences between specialists and laymen. And in every society this will be a moment of the orientation to the social world in general. The current historical expression of the social distribution of knowledge determines the forms and the content of being a specialist and of being a layman, and their significance for orientation in the social world. With historical change in the structural bases for the social distribution of knowledge, the basic characteristics of the subjective correlates to the latter express themselves in various ways. It hardly need be emphasized that an investigation of the historical multiplicity of these expressions would exceed the scope of the present work. This is rather one of the tasks of the *empirical sociology* of knowledge (Schutz and Luckmann 1973, 324, emphasis added).

Thus it appears that the relative sociohistorical limitations are nothing more than instances of the absolute limitations: pre-predicative meaning structures "assume various historically conditioned forms." They "express themselves in various ways." Therefore, contrary to Husserl, who leaves room for the view that the historical dimension has an independent status, Schutz and Luckmann see the variety of sociohistorical contexts more as various workings-out of the formal structures of the social world (a theoretical position close to that of French structuralism). Thus, Schutz and Luckmann resolve Husserl's ambiguity on the concrete and abstract senses of the life-world in favor of the abstract.

The Possibility of a Science of Society

Until now, we have considered Schutz's contributions from the perspective of their relevance to the interpretation of actors' meanings. This subject is crucial, since the phenomenological conception of social reality is that human meanings are the basis of all social reality. But the interpretation of actors' meanings is not the final task of a phenomenological sociology, since the questions of whether these meanings can or must be handled within a scientific framework remains to be considered. It might be argued that a thoroughgoing analysis of meanings on both the pre-predicative and sociohistorical levels is sufficient in itself and that to approach these meanings scientifically is impossible, inappropriate, or simply incidental once the interpretive task has been completed. Such arguments, though, run contrary to the phenomenological understanding of the nature and importance of the scientific enterprise. From the phenomenological point of view, science is not to be dismissed or depreciated but is to be reinterpreted in terms of its own meaning and the meaning of its findings. Husserl's effort, one may recall, was to develop phenomenology precisely as a means of providing a secure foundation for all knowledge and specifically scientific knowledge. It is the foundational character of the life-world that makes this reinterpretation necessary.

The epoché of science pertains to all scientific activity. With respect to this epoché, no distinction is made between the natural and the social sciences. Yet it is clear that such a distinction is essential, for in its absence the way is left open for two perennial arguments as to the nature of social scientific activity — arguments that are both, Schutz notes, false (Schutz 1962, 48ff). On the one hand, it might be argued that the *methods* of the natural sciences are appropriate for the study of social reality, and that if social science is to be scientific, it can be so only on the basis of these methods. On the other hand, the argument can be made that the methods of the social sciences are totally different from those of the natural sciences and that social science rests exclusively on the method of *Verstehen*. This position leads to the various forms of the "nomothetic vs. ideographic" and "explanation vs. understanding" debates that figured prominently in the previous chapter. Neither position is acceptable, however, and for essentially the same reasons. Both involve fundamental misconceptions about the nature of social reality and the nature of science. The general features of the misconstrual of science, which both arguments presuppose, refer to their inability to discern the relationship of science to the life-world. As a result, science is presumed to deal with a mathematically idealized reality, and thus the origins of science within the life-world itself are ignored.

The parties to both arguments also misunderstand social reality to the extent that they identify the method of *Verstehen* as a social scientific procedure that is dependent upon the subjective state of the observer (Schutz 1962, 52, 56). In fact, the primary referent of the term is actually the actor's own form or style of experiencing the life-world.

Despite these misunderstandings, and due to the fact that science is a matter of a specific epoché, the natural and the social sciences share some common ground. Much of this commonality concerns concrete methodological procedures. What is shared is that "the principles of controlled inferences and verification by fellow scientists and the theoretical ideals of unity, simplicity, universality, and precision prevail" (Schutz 1962, 49). This includes the notion that statements must be made in propositional form and that theories will involve "determinate relations between a set of variables in terms of which a fairly extensive class of empirically ascertainable regularities can be explained" (Schutz 1962, 49). Nevertheless, the distinction between social and natural science must be made, and the question remains concerning the basis on which such a distinction might rest.

The answer, according to Schutz, is that certain methodological problems are peculiar to social science as a result of the nature of its subject matter. As Schutz observes:

It is up to the natural scientist and to him alone to define, in accordance with the procedural rules of his science, his observational field, and to determine the facts, data, and events within it which are relevant for his problem or scientific purpose at hand. Neither are those facts and events pre-selected, nor is the observational field pre-interpreted. The world of nature, as explored by the natural scientist, does not "mean" anything to molecules, atoms, and electrons. But the observational field of the social scientist — social reality — has a specific meaning and relevance structure for the human beings living, acting, and thinking within it. By a series of common-sense constructs they have pre-selected and pre-interpreted this world which they experience as the reality of their daily lives. It is these thought objects of theirs which determine their behavior by motivating it. The thought objects constructed by the social scientist, in order to grasp this social reality, have to be founded upon the thought objects constructed by the common-sense thinking of men, living their daily life within their social world. Thus, the constructs of the social sciences are, so to speak, constructs of the second degree, that is, constructs of the constructs made by the actors on the social scene, whose behavior the social scientist has to observe and to explain in accordance with the procedural rules of his science (Schutz 1962, 58–59).

It is thus the preinterpretation of the social world by actors within that world that accounts for the unique but still scientific tasks of sociology. Even if this solves the problems of showing the basis of the difference between natural and social science, it nevertheless raises the still more central and difficult problem of how actors' meanings can be known in such a way that objective knowledge can be built upon them. This problem is the central issue of Schutz's *The Phenomenology of the Social World* that suggests: "The problem of every social science can therefore be summarized in the question: How are sciences of subjective meaning-context possible?" (Schutz 1967, 223). On the basis of our previous discussion, the question can be rephrased as: how is idealized or objective knowledge of actors' subjective meaning possible?

The general outline of an answer to these questions has already been formulated; what remains is to recall this formulation and to take it out of the context of the interpretation of actors' meanings and set it in the context of the scientific structures that are now under discussion. It was pointed out earlier that actors themselves understand their social world in typified terms. These typified terms are pre-predicative meaning structures. As a whole, these typifications are features of the universal natural attitude that is the object of a phenomenology of the social world. The claim of such phenomenology is that the knowledge of the features at which it arrives is rigorous and replicable. The typical constructs of everyday life experience are to a greater or lesser degree, depending on the aspect of social reality in question, objectifications and idealizations. Because everyday knowledge is objective knowledge, and because it can be rigorously described by means of the phenomenological reduction, a foundation is present for subsequent scientific idealization and objectification of this same everyday knowledge.

The same point can be made in terms of the concept of *Verstehen*. By now it is clear that *Verstehen* is, primarily, a procedure employed by actors in their everyday life. Actors conduct their affairs in the common-sense world by themselves interpreting the subjective meanings of others. It is the scandal of philosophy, Schutz remarks, that the question of how *Verstehen,* in this sense of the term, is possible, that has not been satisfactorily resolved. The phenomenological resolution, as noted above, is that the categories of *Verstehen* are the pre-predicative structures, the constitutive features of the natural attitude, which are the object of a phenomenology of the social world. Again the conclusion pointed to is that the very "common sense" of the social world is due to the fact that the actors objectify and idealize meanings. This objectifying and idealizing activity is a condition for the possibility of there being a social world, and also of there being a science of it.

The idealizing activity of actors resolves the problem of how objective second-order constructs of subjective meaning contexts are possible, but it leaves open the issue of how the social scientist might use them. This issue brings up the problem of the relationship between sociality and science. If science is understood as a finite province of meaning, then the scientific self is a solitary self, and thus it must be explained "how this solitary theorizing self can find access to the world of working and make it an object of its theoretical contemplation" (Schutz 1962, 240). Of course, for the scientist *qua* actor this problem does not arise, since he is, or in principle could become, a member of the life-world in question. The interpretation of plausibility structures was seen to be based on exactly such membership. In the epoché of science, however, this membership is bracketed. Schutz presents the issue as follows:

Since the social sciences *qua* social sciences never actually encounter real people but deal only in personal ideal types, it can hardly be their function to understand the subjective meaning of human action in the sense that one person understands another's meaning when he is directly interacting with him. However, we saw that the nature of subjective meaning itself changes with the transition from direct to indirect social experience. In the process of ideal-typical construction, subjective meaning contexts that can be directly experienced are successively replaced by a series of objective meaning-contexts. These are constructed gradually, each one upon its predecessor, and they interpenetrate one another in Chinese-box fashion, so that it is difficult to say where one leaves off and the other begins. However, it is precisely this process of construction which makes it possible for the social scientist, or indeed for any observer, to understand what the actor means; for it is this process alone which gives a dimension of objectivity to his meaning. Of course, this process of constitution can only be disclosed to the interpreter by means of his own typifying method. What he will thus come to know is only a conceptual model, not a real person (Schutz 1967, 241–42).

The typifying methods and conceptual models of interest here are scientific ones. The central feature of any scientific model is that it is an idealization which is of a different *order* than the idealization of the actor, even though it is based on the actor's idealization. Scientific structures are based on, but are irreducible to, the formal structures of these meanings. Such irreducibility is an aspect of the definition of any province of meaning. This means that the models of the social scientist are never "peopled with human beings in their full humanity, but with puppets, with types . . ." (Schutz 1962, 255).

Schutz further clarifies what he has in mind by such a statement:

How does the social scientist proceed? He observes certain facts and events within social reality, which refer to human action, and he constructs typical behavior or course-of-action patterns from what he has observed. Thereupon he co-ordinates to these typical course-of-action patterns models of an ideal actor or actors, whom he imagines to be gifted with consciousness. Yet it is a consciousness restricted so as to contain nothing but the elements relevant to the performing of the course-of-action patterns observed. He thus ascribes to this fictitious consciousness a set of typical notions, purposes, goals, which are assumed to be invariant in the specious consciousness of the imaginary actor-model. This homunculus or puppet is supposed to be interrelated in interaction patterns to other homunculi or puppets constructed in a similar way. Among these homunculi with which the social scientist populates his model of the social world of everyday life, sets of motives, goals, roles — in general, systems of relevances — are distributed in such a way as the scientific problems under scrutiny require (Schutz 1962, 63–64).

The most important element of this description of social scientific activity, for our purposes, is the notion that what is relevant to the model is dictated by the scientific problem. It is the relevance system of science, not the relevance system of actors, which determines the context of the scientific model, since this is, so to speak, the only relevance system that science has. It is this fact that makes it necessary to speak in terms of homunculi and puppets. Once such a model has been proposed:

> As the next step, the circumstances within which such a model operates may be varied, that is, the situation which the homunculi have to meet may be imagined as changed, but not the set of motives and relevances assumed to be the sole content of their consciousness. I may, for example, construct a model of a producer acting under conditions of unregulated competition, and another of a producer acting under cartel restrictions, and then compare the output of the same commodity of the same firm in the two models. In this way, it is possible to predict how such a puppet or system of puppets might behave under certain conditions and to discover certain determinate relations between a set of variables, in terms of which . . . empirically ascertainable regularities . . . can be explained (Schutz 1962, 64–65).

The models set up by the social scientist, even though they are based on the first-order constructs of actors, are not simply reflections of everyday life. They always remain, instead, reflections of the relevance system of science. In this regard, it makes sense to refer to them as "sociological structures" in order to emphasize the fact that they are structures that have their meaning only within the context of the finite province of meaning of science. Sociological structures are substitutes for the structures of the everyday life-world that are employed for scientific purposes. The answer, then, to the question of how the solitary theorizing self can find access to the social world is that access is always indirect. The methods of social science are artificial devices designed to establish "indirect communication" between the finite province of science and the paramount finite province of everyday life (Schutz 1962, 255).

Indirect communication is characteristic of the relationship between two finite provinces of meaning, since no formula for translating between one province and another is possible; and this fact poses a difficulty for any attempt to describe the everyday world in scientific terms. The source of this difficulty is that:

> Language — any language — pertains as communication . . . to the intersubjective world of working, and, therefore, obstinately resists serving as a vehicle for meanings which transcend its own presuppositions (Schutz 1962, 233).

Every finite province of meaning must, therefore, rely on an indirect language, and scientific terminology is one such language. Sociological structures are the terms of the language by means of which indirect communication between sociology and the everyday world can be established. These structures are the terms of a language of objectivity. Sociology provides an idealized language for the objective examination and description of everyday life. The relationship between the objective scientific description and understanding of the sociologist and the everyday description and understanding of the member always, however, remains indirect.

This necessary indirectness raises further serious questions about the relationship between the life-world and the social scientific understanding of it. The central question is this: how can assurance be obtained that sociological structures in fact accurately represent the first-order constructs of actors? If the connection between first- and second-order constructs is in fact an appropriate connection, then the relationship between science and sociality seems established.

The proper activity of science, phenomenologically understood, is, according to both Husserl and Schutz, idealization; that is, the production of objective knowledge. In the case of social science, then, science will consist of objective knowledge of subjective meanings. What is meant by objective knowledge is that it is not experienceable directly; and this, it can be argued, is exactly the contribution of science to the everyday life-world. Science provides a perspective on events that expose features of those events that cannot be experienced directly. This is easily seen in the case of natural sciences which expose, for example, the chemical composition of materials, their atomic structures, etc.; and it seems that the transition to social phenomena can be made directly. Social science may show, for instance, that certain objective relationships exist between religious values and economic values, as one finds in Weber's analysis of the Protestant ethic. Of course, such a relationship may be intuited by the everyday actor on the basis of a single case; but this is a different matter, since this knowledge is characterized in everyday life exactly by the fact that it is not accepted as objective, but rather as prejudiced, stereotypic, or as possibly correct but unconfirmed. Here, the usual rules of logical inference come into play. Is the relationship between values and economic behavior spurious? Is it reversible? Does it pertain only to a single or a few sociohistorical instances? If so, under what conditions does it come to apply in one society and not in another?

All of these questions call for a perspective that goes to a greater or lesser extent beyond what is accessible to experience. It is important to emphasize that all questions about the meaning of this relationship have been suspended for the moment; the assumption is being made that this meaning is known, i.e., that second-order constructs are properly formulated. Given this assumption, the conclusion as to the import of the epoché of science is simply that it provides a perspective which is objective, or in other words, inaccessible to immediate experience. In this regard, the relationship between science and the paramount reality of everyday life is different from the relationship between this paramount reality and other finite provinces of meaning *only* with respect to the character of the perspective that is provided. Fantasy or art or any other finite province of meaning consists in a different cognitive style from that of everyday life. They provide, therefore, a different perspective on everyday reality, one that, however, will not be objective. Viewed in this manner, it makes no more sense to dismiss the possibility of a science of social reality than it would to dismiss an artistic expression of this same reality.

Social science necessarily deals with two types of constructs, everyday and scientific; and the procedures of verification that are peculiar to it arise out of the need to establish the relationship between these two. In addition to the problem of developing methods for dealing objectively with subjective meaning contexts, the main problem of the social sciences is to achieve assurance "that the thought objects of the social sciences . . . remain consistent with the thought objects of common sense, formed by men in everyday life in order to come to terms with social reality" (Schutz 1962, 43).

According to Schutz, three requirements must be met for sociological structures to be considered satisfactory with respect to these two problems. These requirements are set out in the form of three postulates. Given our previous discussion, the first two postulates can be handled rather easily. First, sociological structures must satisfy the postulate of logical consistency:

> The system of typical constructs designed by the scientist has to be established with the highest degree of clarity and distinctness of the conceptual framework implied and must be fully compatible with the principles of formal logic. Fulfillment of this postulate warrants the objective validity of the thought objects constructed by the social scientist, and their strictly logical character is one of the most important features by which scientific thought objects are distinguished from the thought objects constructed by common-sense thinking in daily life which they have to supersede (Schutz 1962, 43).

The postulate of logical consistency is rooted in the notion of science as a finite province of meaning. Each finite province of meaning is characterized by a "logic" peculiar to it, and in the case of science, this is the formal logic that governs all sciences. In order to provide idealized and objectified knowledge, which is the proper, and indeed the only activity of science, the formal rules of logic must be adhered to, since it is in these rules that scientific activity resides.

Second, sociological structures must satisfy the postulate of subjective interpretation:

> In order to explain human actions the scientist has to ask what model of an individual mind can be constructed and what typical contents must be attributed to it in order to explain the observed facts as the result of the

activity of such a mind in an understandable relation. The compliance with this postulate warrants the possibility of referring all kinds of human action or their result to the subjective meaning such action or result of an action had for the actor (Schutz 1962, 43).

The basis for the postulate of subjective interpretation is the phenomenological understanding of the nature of social reality and, ultimately, the nature of human consciousness. The relationship between the subject and the object of consciousness is inherently intentional, and the fundamental mode of intentionality is grasped in the notion of the natural attitude. The everyday life-world, which is constituted in terms of the pre-predicative meaning structures that are the features of the natural attitude, is presupposed by all other thought and activity. Because of the foundational character of the life-world, i.e., because everyday life is the paramount finite province of meaning, it is the ultimate ground of all scientific activity.

As indicated, this fact has particular implications for the social sciences, since it is the everyday life-world that is the object of their inquiry. Because of this, and because science itself involves a particular modification of the cognitive style of everyday life, the postulate of subjective interpretation is necessary in order to warrant the possibility of a connection between the first-order constructs of everyday life and the second-order constructs of the sociologist. Schutz provides a helpful elaboration of the issue:

> On the one hand, it has been shown that the constructs on the first level, the common-sense constructs, refer to subjective elements, namely the *Verstehen* of the actor's action from his, the actor's, point of view. Consequently, if the social sciences aim indeed at explaining social reality, then the scientific constructs on the second level, too, must include a reference to the subjective meaning an action has for the actor. . . . The postulate of subjective interpretation has to be understood in the sense that all scientific explanations of the social world *can,* and for certain purposes *must,* refer to the subjective meaning of the actions of human beings from which social reality originates (Schutz 1962, 62).

The postulate of subjective interpretation can be said, on the basis of terminology developed earlier, to presuppose both an analysis of pre-predicative meaning structures and an analysis of plausibility structures. These two kinds of analyses are required to establish the claim that the subjective meanings of actors are known, and thus that the sociological structures in fact refer to them.

The third postulate, the postulate of adequacy, is a quite different matter. It is this postulate that has clearly generated the most sociological interest. Despite this interest, very little critical evaluation of the notion of adequacy has been generated. Even more noteworthy is the fact that Schutz himself provides virtually no elaboration of the postulate or discussion of its import or of what would be involved in fulfilling it. Whereas the basis and import of the first two postulates are readily apparent, it is not even clear, at first, why the postulate of adequacy is required.

Schutz's statement of the postulate of adequacy is quite straightforward:

> Each term in a scientific model of human action must be constructed in such a way that a human act performed within the life-world by an individual actor in the way indicated by the typical construct would be understandable for the actor himself as well as for his fellow-men in terms of common-sense interpretation of everyday life. Compliance with this postulate warrants the consistency of the constructs of the social scientist with the constructs of common-sense experience of the social reality (Schutz 1962, 44).

The problem here involves the fact that we do not know *how* to meet this postulate, since that which is "understandable" to the actor may not be understandable to "fellow-men." In addition, there is no clear identification as to what constitutes the "common-sense" experience of reality. If such an interpretation is not at all "common," then why do we need the postulate?

Schutz's emphasis throughout his research project is clearly on the phenomenological foundation of the interpretation of actors' meanings and on the capacity of a social science built upon a phenomenological foundation to remain scientific. The knowledge domain within which Schutz operated followed from the tradition of interpretive social science and maintained a consistent dialectical-critical relation to the work of Weber. That sociologist, indeed, was the first influence on the problematic developed by Schutz. Other influences included the methodological conflict present in German sociology at the time, the life-philosophy of Bergson, Husserl's developing phenomenology (with its call to "the things themselves"), the critique of Kant and psychologism, and the key concept of a "life-world." These influences led Schutz to evolve a research program involved with "pre-scientific" and hence a-prioristic phenomena.

This focus directly influenced the themes that he would consider important — the immediate, day-to-day questions that underlie human interaction and the real processes of that interaction. At the time, Schutz' program was consistent with the intellectual concerns of German sociology, but when he moved to the United States, his work became marginalized, since the American academic community was characterized by a very different perspective. This marginalization is clear in the correspondence between Schutz and Talcott Parsons, then the dominant figure in American sociology. Their misunderstanding of each other seems to have been fairly complete.

One of the reasons that phenomenological sociology was considered an alien perspective by American sociologists may be that Schutz' insights, however fundamental, nonetheless require a kind of classical education that had practically disappeared by the 1930s and that perhaps never existed in American schools. To study Schutz demands an involvement, a dedication, and a background not commonly found among American undergraduates. His phenomenological approach is certainly not directed at a mass society searching for quick and easy answers. In a time characterized by polls and professional sociometrists, Schutz' sociology seems elitist and opaque, and so it loses much of its critical edge. Fortunately, his insights and enthusiasm continue to guide sociological work on the Continent and in Japan, where phenomenology has been a productive approach. Some American sociologists, most notably George Psathas, and members of the small, but thriving, Society for Phenomenology and the Human Sciences, continue to work in the knowledge domain adumbrated by Schutz.

3

Karl Mannheim

Karl Mannheim was born in 1893 and grew up in Budapest. At the time, intellectual life in Budapest was similar to that in Germany, in that the primary focus of intellectual debate involved methodological disputes among the sciences. The "Social-Scientific Society" of Budapest, under the leadership of Oscar Jaszi, disseminated a number of texts and proposals for social reforms and political action that would improve the Hungarian way of life. During the same time frame, Georg Lukacs called for cultural renewal through humanistic studies, in opposition to the then dominant positivism.

Before he was twenty, Mannheim had cultivated strong ties to Lukacs and his associates, and he joined the discussions at many of their public meetings. Toward the end of World War I, Mannheim moved to Heidelberg, where he found an intellectual community divided in much the same way as that of Budapest. The intellectual groups that appealed to him included the literary anti-positivist movement headed by Stefan George and the community of cultural sociologists represented by Alfred Weber (Max Weber's brother).

For Mannheim, traditional culture lagged behind the cataclysmic changes taking place at the time, and he called for an intellectual renewal in which history took a central role. In 1917 Mannheim gave a lecture on "Soul and Culture," which emphasized the role of aesthetic criticism and formal analysis of structures as the best, although still inadequate, means of understanding social events. In 1925 Mannheim became *privatdozent* at Heidelberg, and he received an appointment as professor of sociology and economics at the University of Frankfurt in 1929.

With the rise of National Socialism in Germany, Mannheim found his position tenuous, and eventually he was dismissed from Frankfurt. He moved to England, where he first joined the London School of Economics as a lecturer in sociology and then moved to the Institute of Education at the University of London. His first major work was *Ideology and Utopia* (1936), in which he proposed to bring together political and scientific vocations into a politics of science based on an intellectual community free from local and class commitments. His contributions include not only works in the development of a sociology of knowledge, but also important contributions directed to the process of sociopolitical reconstruction following World War II. His work emphasized the role of education and planning in the context of a free and democratic society. Mannheim died in England in 1947 and remains one of the most important contributors to the sociology of knowledge. One of his most crucial books, *Structures of Thinking,* appeared relatively recently (1982), even though it had been written between 1922 and 1924.

Mannheim's Concept of the Sociological Enterprise

Mannheim conceives sociology as including three distinctive realms: systematic or general sociology, comparative sociology, and structural sociology. The first deals with the conditions, factors, and effects of social life that tend to be repetitive in the most varied cultural and historical situations. Thus, the goal is to discover the basic elements of social phenomena and the fundamental concepts through which they may be universally described.

Comparative sociology takes into consideration the conditions, factors, and effects that determine how social phenomena vary in the history of different societies. Thereby, it supplements the abstract analysis of systematic sociology by offering an empirical system of reference within which discoveries can be validated or invalidated. Moreover, the research of causes and tendencies falls essentially within this realm of analysis.

Finally, since sociology is not only concerned with the identification and abstraction of general social factors, but also with specific problems, it is the goal of structural sociology to research the basic elements of society and their different historical manifestations. Working with data that is localized in space and time, structural sociology is not equated with either history or social history. Its task is not to answer the questions concerning the causes of historical phenomena, but rather to discover schemas that will show how basic social factors or groups of factors are interrelated and produce certain sociohistorical effects. Moreover, this realm of sociology is further subdivided into static structural sociology, in which social factors are considered in equilibrium, and dynamic structural sociology, in which social factors are viewed through the effects of the tensions of conflict they produce. Thus, structural sociology aims at the analysis of all structural social phenomena that may be defined by the sociologist in relation to phases, developmental stages, and durations of global social systems (i.e., caste, feudal, and capitalist systems).

Mannheim's topography of the sociological enterprise can be considered the first specifically sociological attempt to delimit the realm of sociology. Nevertheless, it shows inconsistencies. The most important problem concerns the manner in which each subdivision is defined. Mannheim divided sociology on the basis of its objects of study. He did not consider the differences that might involve gradations of method, from abstract and axiomatic analyses to those resulting from empirical, inductive study. This approach had been taken before, particularly by Ferdinand Tönnies, but it reflects a relative misunderstanding of present possibilities of sociological analysis. Since the 1920s specialists dealing with the problems of systematic sociology have been working with purely inductive techniques, discarding comparison as a necessary criterion for the empirical verification of concepts or results (see also the work of F. Znaniecki for a similar argument). Moreover, the systematic sociologist eventually finds it necessary to call upon a comparative perspective in order to justify the validity of the systematic approach. While Mannheim's typology of sociological work may be susceptible to critique, his more important work involved the sociology of knowledge, and it is in this realm that an interpretive sociology can be found.

The Sociology of Knowledge

Mannheim's sociology of knowledge is found in its most complete form in *Ideology and Utopia*. There are further writings, particularly those on the sociology of the mind, that represent not only an extension and elaboration of the theses of *Ideology and Utopia*, but also a set of descriptions of the sociality of mind. Mannheim's sociology of knowledge sought to outline a method for the study of ideas as functions of social involvements. This position has the initial requirement of excluding the possibility of an autonomous evolution of ideas. Mannheim maintains this position in his study of German intellectual conceptions.

For Mannheim, society exists not only in acts of sociation and the coalescence of humans into structured groups, but also in the meanings that likewise join or divide persons. As there exists no sociation without particular understanding, so there are no shared meanings unless they are derived from and defined by given social situations. The dichotomy of the two realms of analysis, namely Simmel's science of forms of sociation and the sociology of ideas, does not bespeak two separate entities in the real world, although the necessities of academic specialization may make their thematic isolation temporarily expedient. There is no harm in such abstraction so long as it is treated as an artifice. Ultimately, however, the duality of the ideational versus the social realm of things must resolve itself into a single view of the original subject of human reality from which the two aspects of sociology were originally abstracted.

Schemes of specialization that isolate certain aspects of reality for the purpose of topical analysis must, at their very inception, bear some sort of design of the ultimate synthesis that reestablishes and articulates the context of the original subject. Specialization must not lead to blindness in the understanding of phenomena that straddle various areas. There must be, and indeed there is, a growing sensitivity to those configurations of reality that the segmental view conceals.

We must learn to see discrete facts in their interrelationships and to fit segmental vistas into a concrete perspective. The question points to the problem of the sociology of the mind as the counterpart of the sociology of society. Inasmuch as society is the common frame of interaction, ideation, and communication, the sociology of mind is the study of the mental functions in the context of action. It is from this approach that we must expect one of the possible answers to the needed synthesis. The sociology of mind, indeed, is conceived as an integrated view of social action and of mental processes, and not as a new philosophy of history.

Synthesis may be expected to grow from observations made with a view to integration. To argue that the business of integration must be adjourned until all the pertinent facts are assembled in the respective subfields is to misjudge the nature of the synthetic procedure. Moreover, integration does not begin with the completed accumulation of facts, but rather with each elementary act of observation. Integration is not a mere final adjunct to the fact-gathering routine; it embraces the whole process, beginning with the research design's test for relevance and proceeding to the condensation of the pertinent material assembled regardless of departmental pedigree. While the vertical division of labor relieves the specialist of a full account of his subject, the alternative method of specialization (horizontal) converges on given topics from a multitude of directions in which pertinent relationships may be located. The aim is a condensed account of those relationships that are relevant to the generalizing approach to a chosen subject. This call from Mannheim maintains quite a bit of similarity to the intentions of other sociologists (like Georges Gurvitch) who call for an integrative view of social phenomena at all levels of social reality.

It was from earlier studies (by Max Weber, Dilthey, Sumner, W. I. Thomas, and others) and *Ideology and Utopia* that the thesis of the existential involvement of knowledge emerged. This thesis holds that the relationship between particular conceptions of reality and given modes of involvement in reality is capable of scientific articulation. A discussion of the sociology of the mind, nevertheless, requires a preliminary consideration of the appropriate uses of the concepts of history, society, and mind. Mannheim presents his review of these notions in the context of German sociology and philosophy.

German humanistic learning partly lost and partly never really possessed an essential view of things that Americans and Europeans elsewhere were able to capture — the realization of the social character of one's thought and action, the familiarity with social history, and most importantly, the capacity to see action and thought, trivial or sublime, in their proper perspectives. One cannot gain a true historical perspective without an awareness of the social set of historical events. In many ways the situation itself imposes constraints both on social and on ideational processes. This practical notion was not grasped by German humanist intellectuals, who tended to cling to the older notion of evolutionary consistency.

The thesis of the immanent evolution of ideas is predicated upon the assumption of a self-contained intellect that evolves by and from itself through pre-ordained sequences. Such a conception in German intellectual circles involved a number of elements:

1. The ideal was mainly supported by members of the teaching professions — philologists, historians, and philosophers. The context in which they lived itself provided the grist for such views. While people who daily face the rough and tumble of life employ thought as a tool for coping with situations that arise, academics invoke thinking as a medium in which to reconstruct and visualize accomplished facts. While the mental functions of the practitioner both originate and terminate with his problems, the cogitative processes of the scholar are sparked and nourished by the thoughts of others. Scholars form an enclave that provides the conditions of isolation for the continued support of these conceptions. Nevertheless, with the breakdown of such social strata, we may study the concomitant shift in their mentality. Action exposes illusion more quickly than contemplation. Thus, the position of the scholar entails a potential source of bias, the tendency to idealize its subject. The antidote for such bias will be found neither in a refined methodology nor in a more copious use of source material. The corrective must come from the consistent effort to understand thought in its situational context.

2. The illusion of the immanent flow of ideas receives an additional support from the manner in which the humanist encounters his source material. The works of the past appear to the scholar as pictures in a gallery — an array of discrete entities. The temptation to construe this array in an organic and continuous pattern of growth is irresistible to those who confine their interest to the historical records of creative expression. What is ignored in this imagery are its intervening connections in which humans act and react as social beings. Thus, the idealistic delusion is rooted in the conceptualization of the two-dimensional scheme in which the elements (ideas, cultural works) are presented. Expressions of thought and perception are in themselves mere fragments of reality, and their complete chronology is, by the same token, not history, although there is no harm in such construction as long as it is used as a classificatory device; it is their reification that is the ultimate hazard.

3. In Germany the third element deals with the religious origin of the concept of "Geist." It was Luther, in particular, who transmuted the religious conception of the spirit into secular philosophy. Earlier, the medieval Church enunciated the antagonism of the spirit and the flesh, but the void between the realm of the spirit and that of human life became absolute only in Luther's radical dualism. The oversublimation of spirit and related concepts found in German sociology is attributable to the continuing influence of that dualism.

4. There is still another root found in German religious teaching, namely the doctrine of "spiritual freedom," an idea also elaborated by Luther. A secular version of this doctrine became the cardinal thesis of German idealism. Luther's freedom (from temptation) came to mean indetermination; his conception of spirituality (one's communion with God through faith) developed into the doctrine of self-evolving, sovereign intellect. On the negative side, his moral conception of bondage evolved into the philosophical thesis of determination in the physical realm. "Thought, or knowledge, possess themselves in absolute freedom . . . freedom as such is the ultimate basis of all consciousness." (Fichte, *Bestimmung des Gelebeten,* 1794) Understandably, this dualistic conception has effectively inhibited the rise of any milieu theory or deterministic and sociological approaches to intellectual topics. Such "externalism" cannot gain a rationale from a philosophy that is predicated upon the absolute freedom and indeterminacy of the mind. This introverted conception of freedom became the keystone of the immanence theory and one of the main academic barriers to a sociological approach to history, thought, and politics.

The tacit abandonment of the immanence theory fostered by the social sciences in the early decades of this century undoubtedly widened the scope of these studies. Still, they had not advanced the cardinal questions: Whose mentality is recorded in these products? What is their social identity? What action situations and what tacit choices furnish the perspectives in which artists perceive and represent some aspects of reality? If cultural works reflect points of view, beliefs, affirmations, and so on, who are the protagonists and who are the antagonists? Whose orientation is reflected in the changes of style? Such questions do not arise within the fragmentary view of cultural products. The conceptual vacuum between them will be only concealed, and not bridged, by such traditional constructs as "the spirit of the time." Only society as a structural variable has a history, and only in this social continuum can cultural products be properly understood as a historical entity.

A second fallacy, which, much like the immanence doctrine, has encumbered German reflections on history, is expressed by the polarized conception of the *ideal* and the *material* realms of things. How was it possible to doubt the social character of the mind and to ignore the mental involvements of social behavior? To cogitate and conceive of abstract intellect without concrete persons who act in given social situations is as absurd as to assume the opposite, a society without such functions as communication, ideation, and evaluation. It is in this strained dichotomy that the term "material" was devised as the opposite of a disembodied spirit.

The materialism espoused by the left-Hegelians injected into the political literature of the middle of the century the question of the makers of history. Who makes history, the outstanding individual or the masses? The question is really fallacious since these two categories cannot exist as polarizations continuously in time. While the "great men of history" do not transcend the social realm of phenomena, no sociologist can reasonably doubt or ignore their existence. However, when events are viewed in retrospect or from a distance, the temptation grows stronger to attribute the known results of an unrecorded chain of actions to a known person who formed the last link; in other words, to ascribe the unknown to the known. It therefore makes little sense to attribute ideas only to great individuals and to reserve the epithet of "material" for the masses. Whatever the merit of the materialist thesis, the insistence on the primacy of the economic infrastructure over the ideological superstructure does not posit the primacy of matter over ideas, but the primacy of one type of social interaction (the economic) over the others. Both species of action involve ideation and communication, as well as biological needs and a material apparatus.

The materialist interpretation of history referred to above, and that figured prominently in *fin-de-siecle* sociology may mean one or all of several things:

1. It may claim that the functions of society that meet the basic, biological wants of persons have a greater urgency and are less amenable to postponement and sublimation than are those that meet the so-called secondary needs.
2. It may claim that economic activities have a more limited scope of variability than other activities, and therefore the latter are to be subjected to the "strain of consistency" with the former.
3. It may claim that economic activities have an absolute continuity, and in that sense they form the primary basis of social integration.

These propositions can be intelligibly discussed without recourse to the unrewarding antinomy of mind and matter.

The entire complex of social functions constitutes a structure because their relationships show a recurrent pattern which is characteristic of a given society (or group). It is only through the articulation of these permanent functions that the continuity of life becomes manifest and the discrete events may be understood as elements in the historical continuum. What makes an account of change continuous, then, is not a "complete" record of events, even if this were possible, but the narration of events in the particular context of continuing functions.

The reluctance to face social reality as the matrix of change also explains the overworked dichotomy of nature and history, which leads to the conflict between the natural and the social sciences. What is dialectical is not history, but rather particular social situations that reveal inconsistencies or contradictions in the social structure. The seat of contradictions is not the mind, or the foreordained rhythm of history, but concrete social situations that give rise to conflicting aspirations and, hence to antagonistic interpretations of reality. The persistent evasion of the analysis of real life once again proves to be the source of mystification.

Knowledge of a subject that cannot be encompassed in one act evidently requires a series of acts chosen not at random, but according to a scheme that fits the structure of the field. The problem is one of strategy. It is a question of selecting vantage points of consecutive observations so that they will bear on one another and ultimately disclose the design of the field. Now, all analyses take their departure from random encounters, that is, from some immediately apparent aspect of the subject. Subsequent considerations derived from additional exposures to the subject, however, modify the interpretations of what was first perceived. Its new meaning is no longer based on direct, *ad hoc* experience, but is "mediated" by subsequent phases of the analysis. Thus, the inquiry progresses from the direct and immediately given view of the field to its derivative aspect, or, to use Hegel's classic term, to "mediate knowledge."

Sociology is a field of scientific inquiry inasmuch as the structure of its subject does not become apparent in the random context of day-to-day encounters. The complex, therefore, is grasped in a series of interrelated acts. At certain stages the data of immediate experience assume new, derivative, meanings as they become redefined in each newly discovered universe of discourse. Each induction and generalization pertains to a corresponding set of assumed or perceived circumstances that imply a universe which is subjected to revision and expansion. The consecutive revisions and extensions of the scientific universe of generalizations also bear a resemblance to Hegel's dialectic. Three features in particular suggest the analogy: the qualified affirmation of the previous hypothesis, the abandonment of its sphere of generalization, and the establishment of a wider sphere of accountable relationships. The aspect of Hegel's dialectic that is missing here is the speculative identity of subject and object, which forms the cornerstone of his panlogistic system.

The basic deficiency of the positivistic reaction to speculation is its failure to provide for a method of inquiry into fields that are not accessible to direct approach. It is the failure to transcend the immediate and fragmentary scope of observation into the realm of objective structures that still hamstrings the social sciences of our time.

Thinking in mediate terms is by no means the same as departing from the realm of verifiable experience into the rarefied air of speculation but is rather an advance from the fortuitous and subjective view to objective analysis, from isolated fragments to the whole, and from raw observations to the grasp of structures. It is in these progressions that we substitute defined situations and relationships for the labels that we used to attach to haphazardly encountered phenomena. The interactive process encompasses a variety of aspects of culture, and it necessarily involves the mind. Indeed, one cannot separate the social from the mental domain of behavior. It is senseless to pose questions such as whether the mind is socially determined, as though the mind and society each possess a substance of their own. The sociology of the mind is not an inquiry into the social causation of intellectual processes, but rather a study of the social character of those expressions whose currency does not reveal, or adequately disclose, their action context. The sociology of mind seeks to uncover and articulate those acts of sociation that are inherent in, but not revealed by, the communication of ideas. The blindness to the action context of ideas gains support from the fact that ideas remain communicable and seemingly understandable long after the social situation that they helped to define or control has ended. Actually, ideas take on new meaning when their social function changes, and it is this relationship of meaning and function that the sociology of the mind elaborates. This approach does not seek to relate two discrete sets of objects, the social and the mental, to one another; it merely helps to visualize their often concealed identity. It is also misleading to speak of the social determination of the individual, as though the person and his society confronted one another as discrete entities.

Besides the analysis of the relationships between the person and the arenas in which he or she acts, it is also necessary to discuss (a) the complementary social situations and (b) the social circulation of perceptions. The first concerns a shared situation that elicits inverse perceptions between partners in such a way that ideation (feelings, valuations, ideas, etc.) often develops in response to a contrary disposition of a partner. Such dispositions, when viewed apart from their complementary functions, will not help to predict future behaviors that occur in a different situation or functional structure. Thus, complementary ideational and behavioral traits may be confined to only one social situation. Again, what is needed in this context to find a pattern of continuity in the actor's behavior is a mediate approach that takes into account the partnerships in which compensatory habits and perceptions are formed.

The emphasis here on the social and functional aspects of personality should not be interpreted as an implicit denial of the individual realm of existence. Nor does our insistence on the sociological perspective mean that the individual is less real than his relationships. The individual is, in almost any culture, a member of a variety of groupings. It is this multiple involvement that ordinarily prevents the preponderance of a single attribute.

Similar processes occur within groups. A social stratum takes on a new structure when it encounters a new situation and evolves a new way of life. The new ideals that are born in this encounter give added impetus and direction to the initial reorientation. The sociological view of this change may appear to ignore the role of the individual or to reduce the individual to a mere shadow of social functions. This assumption is unwarranted since any institutional accommodation evolves out of the needs and the elements of a solution that is inherent in a situation. The concrete analysis of the individual does not minimize the scope and value of liberty, although this is only outlined by the needs of the group to whose challenge the individual responds. Thus, there is freedom within the range of given alternatives and available means; all other conceptions are purely philosophical or metaphysical. Two conclusions follow from this: (a) immediate perceptions are in themselves incomplete and often accessory phenomena that do not explain themselves and (b) the referential character of perceptions significantly depends on their function and social world.

This discussion should have demonstrated that the ultimate reality (or existence on the level of ontology) attaches only to the individual, and only he constitutes the ultimate unit of social action. And yet social action cannot be understood without its group context. We can resolve the seemingly insoluble controversy between the nominalists and the universalists if we concede to the former that the individual is the seat of reality and the reality of the group is derivative, and if we at the same time insist that the individual can be understood more satisfactorily through analysis of the group (i.e., the group is the unit of mediation in sociological analysis). To recognize that the individual is the focus of reality is not the same as to construe the self as an isolated entity. To understand the behavior of the individual, one has to know the constellations in which he acts.

For Mannheim, the method necessary for this type of analysis is one of discovering the action situations, the group structures, and the choices that, in one way or another, are involved in meaningful utterances. The sociology of the mind has a universal application to thought in history inasmuch as social situations are tacit components of all mental acts, no matter what academic discipline or socially established divisions have custodial care of them.

The Conduct of Interpretive Sociology

Mannheim suggests that interpretive sociology consists of three steps:

1. Recorded expressions of thought, sentiment, or taste are scrutinized for their inherent or intended meaning. All inquiries into their intrinsic validity or verity are delayed until the third step.
2. The whole gamut of social relationships in which these utterances are conceived and made is traced and established. Particular attention is given to the choices and other preferences that are implicitly manifested by the actions of the participants in the given situation.
3. The content analysis of the utterances is resumed in the restored context of the original situation of interaction, and their complete situational meaning is reconstructed.

The first level of sociological inquiry is that of *general sociology*. This is the level of abstraction in which behavior is conceptualized; its subjects are

the acts of sociation conceived in relative isolation from their historical incidence. General sociology construes, rather than describes its subjects, and it
proceeds typologically from elementary to complex phenomena. Elementary
phenomena are those acts that enter into all or many relationships. Complex
phenomena are those that present combinations of elementary acts. This was
the level in which Simmel projected his "formal" sociology, and it also includes
other projects, such as those of Park and Burgess.

The next level of analysis, in order of concretion, is the historical. Its aim
is the constructive grasp of the singularity of historical structures. What is proposed is an understanding of the broad structural changes that become manifest on the various levels of social interaction. Its character is to visualize unique
events not as events but as components of singular structures in the process of
change.

Mannheim makes a number of methodological assumptions concerning
these levels of analysis:

1. General sociology constitutes a legitimate frame of reference. Its categories, by virtue of their general scope, take precedence over the categories
   of historical description. On this level the singular phenomena of history
   are construed as particular combinations of suprahistorical tendencies as
   they are observed on the level of general sociology.
2. Single causes become compounded and integrated into collective processes.
3. Such a composite of causative impulses must be understood as a structure
   whose dynamics are not fully described by the actions that compose it.
   Causal relationships make up, but do not account for, the dynamics of complete structures.
4. The dynamics of change may at times take an antithetic course and invert
   a given trend. This is the meaning of the observation that some historical
   changes are dialectical. Mannheim here uses the term "dialectical" in its
   narrow sense, reflecting a dialectics of polarization. Georges Gurvitch, for
   instance, held a much broader conception of the term, of which polarization was but a subcategory. Change through opposites, however, is by no
   means a universal feature of history, but is only one of its possible courses.
   The apodictic generalization that history necessarily and invariably proceeds through structural inversion is a part of the Marxist view, and not
   Mannheim's.

In summary, then, we note that sociology may be developed in its three
dimensions, namely as general, comparative, and structural sociologies. Meaning and symbolic acts may be studied within each dimension.

For Mannheim, meanings attain their first social significance through their
dissociation from the original act. As soon as a meaning emerges from the subjective perception that brings it to light, it relinquishes its previous singularity

and becomes a common focus. We are concerned here with the difference between thinking and thought, or the act of doing and the deed. Deed, or an accomplished action, is to be considered here as the realization of a collective conception, in the manner in which the maker of an effigy gives expression to a common image. An objectified meaning is a product of sociation. We objectify not only thought, but also emotions, moods, and whatever filters "out" of the closed circuit of singular experiences. The impetus to objectify meanings is eminently social, and no consciousness can evolve in an unsocialized individual. Meaning, therefore, is a sociological term and is inseparable from some phase of sociation. It is not our concern with identical objects that brings us into a social nexus, but the identical meanings that we jointly attribute to objects; we encounter one another not in things but through their significations. We conceive meanings, however, not only in communicative acts, but also in solitary moments. We perform an act of sociation already in an isolated moment of contemplation. Thus, cognition and communication are inseparable functions.

The original seat of meaning is, presumably, the cooperative situation. The identical manipulation of identical things opens up certain common avenues of approach (for more on this, see Edmund Husserl's *The Crisis of European Sciences and Transcendental Phenomenology,* especially the discussion of the "life-world"). A log may be potentially a canoe, a spear, a raft, fuel, and so on, depending on the needs of those who intend to use it. It is the joint actions of persons in given or potential situations that fix the common or variable view of a thing (this underlies the question of "things" in the art of Dadaism, for instance). Once a common approach to a thing takes hold, it needs only a symbol to attain an objective import. The common appellative is therefore not an abstraction, and not a derivative of individual significations, but the primary form in which each individual comes to attach meaning to the object. Simple social situations provide for unity of meanings, whereas complex situations entail a greater variety of views. The common frame of reference disappears only when two or more groups or cultures exist side by side, each having its own approach to things, and the individual is in a position to choose among them. Furthermore, we are still groping within the solipsistic realm of appearances so long as we do not look beyond the objectivity of significations. At that level, we are still dealing with nothing but individual meanings, and we are not cognizant of their relationships. We cannot reconstruct social changes from the mosaic of individual utterances, and we cannot account for an event of the past or the present without having a name for its milieu. What Hegel's "Geist" implies — beyond the discernment of objective meanings referred to — is the collective framework of history, which we have to know to understand its continuity. It is such a framework that structures the role of the person and in which his actions and expressions take on a new sense. It transcends those meanings that the individual "intends" when he cogitates or conveys an experience.

As soon as we speak of structured behavior or thought, we are moving onto this second level of objective significations; we seek to grasp the meaning of many possible meanings by attempting to reconstruct the context of individual action and perception. This tends to assume that social processes are always structured, which may be a problematic assumption. Georges Gurvitch notes that only global societies are always structured and that units and segments of societies may be equally or less well formed. A social segment may be structured, structurable, or unstructured; or, it may be in the midst of a process of structuration or de-structuration.

However, it is not necessary to conceive and use structured situations in the analysis. For instance, the malpractice of presenting the structure of things as their essence (in other words, that the character of social phenomena comes from their structure) is responsible for the expository approach to the historical analysis of thought, as opposed to the explanatory approach. One conceives change as a goal-directed process through which a preexisting scheme comes to its inexorable realization; we narrow our focus down to the basic design that seems to map out the place of each event as it occurs in a predetermined sequence. What is attempted thereby resembles the performance of a person who pours over a jigsaw puzzle. He seeks correspondences between the basic design and the single pieces as he fits them together. His procedure is expository in the same way that we try to understand the meaning of a single sentence in the context of a whole speech. It is assumed thereby that history has a preordained design. Once this assumption is made, the problem is how to unravel the intrinsic plan that unfolds itself, and it becomes superfluous to wonder about the causal relationships of single events. The flaws in such an approach are palpable.

Nevertheless, we need not discard the expository method entirely, since we may still retain the structured meaning of historical change. The fact that the positivistic type of historical research is inconsistent with a broad teleological interpretation does not mean that we must perforce restrict our approach to the fragmentary and microscopic view of events. We need not apply the teleological hypotheses to history to realize the structured character of change. As soon as we try to outline a phase of history as a concrete set of alternatives, we envisage history as a totality, as a configuration. We cannot gain such a perspective without the expository intent of fitting fragments into a larger pattern. But this is not the same as the Hegelian method of tracing (by deduction) a phase of history back to its universal design. We are not looking for the telic meaning of events, but for their structural setting.

Of course, the structural approach does not prevent one from the conduct of causal analysis. Nevertheless, that must be combined with a functional approach to achieve a wholistic view. The causal perspective makes it clear to us why an actor performs his role, but it is the functional scheme that shows us how he may perform successfully and what his scope of action is. The sum total of causal motivations does not explain the complete structure; in fact, not all actions for which inducements exist are necessary for the functioning of a given system (Mannheim is thinking here about "function" in the classical formulation given by Malinowski). Not only does almost everybody do a good many things that are irrelevant to the operation of the system, but there are social enclaves, such as isolated communities, which are bypassed by certain changes, so that their scheme of life is not the "blueprint" of other segments of society. Thus, it is necessary to distinguish between structurally relevant and irrelevant actions and motivations.

In the end, these two aspects, the causal and the functional, are interrelated. The functional design of a performance outlines the scope within which the play of causative agents is relevant to the structure of the system. The performer need not be aware of the functional meaning of his actions, and he is rarely motivated by it. Max Weber's oversimplified conception of the "meaning" of action — as an intended or unconscious aim — prevented him from realizing the objective or functional meaning of behavior. And, the structural interpretation of behavior does not obviate the causal. The equilibrium of a system depends for each of its functions on the free play of trial and error. The motivations that underlie this free play are for all practical purposes fortuitous, and yet their incidence is essential for the maintenance of the equilibrium.

The Sociology of Mind as a Social Psychology

On the basis of the preceding theoretical analysis, it is now possible to sketch the sociology of the mind as an area of inquiry. The primary aim of the sociology of the mind is the study of mental processes and their significations in their social context. The subject of this investigation is envisaged on three levels:

1. The axiomatic view — the development of a social ontology of the mind with a view to its social character. Analysis of the basic constants of sociation that condition continuity, tradition, discontinuity, and the dynamics of thought. The problems of continuity may be approached under the following aspects:
    A. Amorphous and discontinuous sociations as the basis of discontinuity, and the lapse of tradition in the stream of mental processes.
    B. Continuous contacts in space and time as the basis of current and historical traditions. The phenomena of continuity, interruption, regression, single and multilineal traditions. Also, the succession of generations, stereotyping, and innovations.
    C. The contingency of dynamics. The relationship between group closure and the incidence of compact periods of thought. The significance of the initial situation.

2. Comparative typology — the attempt to elaborate the concrete variations of elementary social processes and to identify their corresponding variations in the realm of thought.
3. The sociology of individualization, which is divided into two components:
   A. The genesis of structures, which includes (a) the study of the relationship of social motivations to thought structures, (b) the study of the significance of social groupings for the genesis of standpoints, and (c) the study of the relevance of structured situations to the formation of concepts.
   B. The dynamic of structures, which involves the study of social change and its significance for the concrete dynamics of thought.

The integration of different styles of thought into a "real" and "total" conception (in the sense, for instance, advanced by Hegel and Marx) will not evolve a superimposition or reelaboration of ideas, but will rather be intentionally presupposed in the structure of knowledge itself. In fact, such a way of perceiving and analyzing problems is not entirely new; moreover, it results from precise conditions of social existence in which the global unity of a system depends upon the efficient interrelationships of parts and subsystems and, thus, from a minimization of disruptive tendencies. One might add to these reasons the obvious observation that such a possibility of thinking in contextual terms is the foundation of scientific and particularly of sociological knowledge (Mannheim explored this in the preface he wrote for Viola Klein's *The Feminine Character.)* In this sense, it appears reasonable to understand interdisciplinary cooperation as leading to a "new science of behavior" (cf. Linton, 1945). Mannheim believed this attempt to be possible because the integration of perspectives will occur not at the level of results or content of thought, but rather in its foundation, or, in other words, in the grasp of the problem itself. Such a condition will make possible, no doubt, a more efficient control of situations of existence inasmuch as it offers, or even guarantees, a more certain knowledge about them. This approach will emphasize the topical problems of our society, thus favoring deliberate intervention into their conditions and consequences.

The Role of the Intelligentsia

We can now examine the ways in which these ideas are related to the social functions of the intellectual stratum. The intellectual will operate as an active element of the "synthesis of perspectives" on two interrelated levels: that of ideas and that of actions. The intellectuals, according to Mannheim's analysis in "The Problem of the Intelligentsia" *(Essays in the Sociology of Culture),* are not a class nor do they constitute a coherent party nor are they capable of coherent group action, because they have few common interests. Nevertheless, these characteristics do not make the intelligentsia a rootless stratum. It is more appropriate to understand them as an aggregate with a peculiar position since this aggregate is placed among the social classes rather than above them. That does not prevent members of the intellectual segment from giving support to certain class interests. Nor does the concept deny the intelligentsia their peculiar characteristics, especially that of being able to face the same problem from several different viewpoints. While this diversity of viewpoints brings about a widening of observation, it does not provide that the intellectual will be able to arrive at a more exact or decisive formulation than other people. Indeed, the presence of a multiplicity of viewpoints results in a greater loss of confidence and increased scepticism regarding the validity of the results. This problem was felt deeply by Mannheim, and he tried to deal with it by suggesting solutions that were not too simplistic, but that were perhaps overly optimistic.

In any case, Mannheim believed that the intellectuals are the only segment of society able to reach a "synthesis of perspectives" regarding issues in their life world so as to act rationally in the flux of social life. Two questions result from this assertion:

1. To what degree will the synthesis of perspectives become effective as a means to overcome a present crisis?
2. Does Mannheim's argument transcend sociology itself, in that propositions of the problem of rational intervention in social situations — i.e., planning — are oriented by arguments more appropriately assigned to social philosophy rather than a discipline of science?

As it turns out, both questions are correlated, and we are able to address them in the same general explanation.

It is true that since the synthesis was a project indicated by objective diagnosis of the situation, there will be also, at least potentially, a possibility for its objective solution. There is a positing of empirical adequacy between the definition of the situation and the proposed solution, since the latter expresses the real elements of the first. However, if a proposition of such a nature seems to be objective, the same does not hold with its supporting arguments. That is, in Mannheim's argument, there is a coexistence of real, positive elements side-by-side with volitional, extratheoretical elements, which, although not made explicit in the general formulations, may be clearly inferred from them. So, which would be the elements of reality, and which are the elements that are intentional and nonexplicit?

The sociological analysis of the composition and social roles of the intellectual segment of society is simultaneously objective, suggestive, and rigorous. Those who have studied the position of the intelligentsia in society realize the difficulty of accurate results because there are no theoretical explanations that are fully satisfactory and because there has not been a rigorous systematization of the little data that has thus far been collected. As a result, the sociology of the intelligentsia sketched by Mannheim is of undeniable value and opens up new possibilities for fruitful research. The specification of the intentional content of Mannheim's formulation leads us to the analysis of the ideological aspect of planning as a mode of rational intervention. Such an aspect may be seen in all of Mannheim's works and is particularly evident through the conviction that the synthesis of perspectives favors the tendency toward the transformation of the present. As Mannheim proposes, a synthesis of perspectives aimed at social change does not lead to any ideological compromise, but involves instead the definition of a position of action supported by knowledge of a political nature. If we examine such a proposition, we can see that it is characteristically radical inasmuch as such a proposition would include a tendency toward regulating intervention. The scientific perspective that would study these phenomena, however, resists ideological immersion and hence seeks to exercise a neutralizing influence. But neutralization is not possible, since any such attempt contains ideological connotations, inasmuch as it includes intentional, volitional, and nonexplicit elements. Moreover, we can grant that the neutralization of impulses toward action compromises the action itself, and this means that an adequate scheme for integrating action with knowledge has not yet been found. Perhaps analytic success requires a different type of society, one similar to that characterized by undistorted communication, as described by Jürgen Habermas.

These questions of planning become crucial to the development of Mannheim's thought since a substantial part of his work was aimed at devising a solution to the ideological difficulty (see especially his *Freedom and Planning*). While this is not the place to elaborate the criteria he devised in that connection, we can nonetheless indicate that these criteria do not seem to be consistent enough to support his optimism. This observation is further justified in light of the realization that today there still remains a relatively strong conviction that we have more intellectual resources for objective and critical knowledge of a situation than we have defined motivations to act with coherence and rationality. This position is argued even more strongly in the writings of the postmodernists (e.g., Lyotard's *The Postmodern Condition)*. Certainly, Mannheim believed that these motives could be created or redefined, and the probability of such renewal is possibly an imperative for the survival of our culture and democratic ideals. Nevertheless, we think that it is still premature to posit any definitive evaluation of the intended results.

To return to the theme of the above discussion, we can now state that it was probably these observations that led Mannheim to dedicate his attention fully to the theoretical elaboration of democratic planning. In this regard, the sociology of knowledge came to fulfill an important function in his program, since it made possible the delineation of a "comprehensive method of interpretation" *(Ideology and Utopia)*. This method consists of the objective diagnosis of the situation emphasizing democratic planning as an innovative social process, characteristic of the present conditions of existence. Thus, democratic planning is susceptible to analysis as a social process and as a social technique because it expresses the complementary structural and functional aspects of the global social system.

It is certain that in the theoretical perspective of the sociology of knowledge, these two aspects are not included in an explicit and systematic form. However:

1. In the analysis of the process of rationalization and secularization of culture, the problem of rational intervention in the nonrationalized spheres of social life is already present.
2. The same question continues to attract Mannheim's attention when he develops the theory of the intelligentsia attempting to objectify in terms of rational action the effective control of social life.
3. Although the solutions proposed by Mannheim are debatable, there is no doubt that the theoretical development of an interpretive sociology of knowledge enabled him to place in a highly suggestive perspective the problem of the process of planning in the sociohistorical context of the present (for an alternative position, see Paulo Friere's *The Pedagogy of the Oppressed*).

It remains for us to comment briefly on a final problem raised by Mannheim, that of the relationship between a sociology of knowledge and democratic planning, which is one of the crucial applications of that sociology. This relationship is seen as not irreversible but dynamic. If it were true that the analysis of thought included a palpable intention toward control, it is no less true that the theory of democratic planning led Mannheim to the delineation of the field of problems for his sociology of knowledge. In this regard, Mannheim states that:

> It is, of course, true that in the social sciences, as elsewhere, the ultimate criterion of truth or falsity is to be found in the investigation of the object, and the sociology of knowledge is no substitute for this. But the examination of the object is not an isolated act; it takes place in a context which is coloured by values and collective-unconscious, volitional impulses. In the social sciences it is this intellectual interest, oriented in a matrix of collective activity, which provides not only the general questions, but the concrete hypotheses for research and the thought-models for the ordering of experience" (Mannheim 1936, 5).

He goes on to note that in the process of democratization, the thinking of the lower classes gains validity and begins to clash with the thinking of the dominent. This conflict of thought processes leads to a fundamental question for planning: "May it not be found, when one has examined all the possibilities of human thought, that there are numerous alternative paths which can be followed?" (Mannheim 1936, 9). The reference to a present turned toward the future and the nearly exclusive view of the specific problems of the present limit and define the realm of investigation of a sociology of knowledge, making it possible to refer a dimension of life and social reality to the theory of democratic planning. Ultimately, this will lead to the ideal of social reconstruction to which Mannheim dedicated his last efforts.

Mannheim's career was unfortunately truncated. In his earlier work, that he completed while still in Germany, he pursued issues brought to light through the insights of Marx, and on that groundwork Mannheim wrote his most influential work, *Ideology and Utopia.* Initially, this work was widely criticized, most often because of the problematic idea of the "free-floating intelligentsia." Mannheim's concept, however, was eventually appropriated and acquitted in the work of Alvin Gouldner and more recently in Jean Francois Lyotard's essays on postmodernity.

When he migrated to England, Mannheim reconstructed his research program with an emphasis on facing the problems of post–World War II society; namely, the problems involved in putting things together again. As a liberal, he turned to the domain of education as a field of answers, a remaking of sociology not as an intellectual, but rather as a political domain . . . as an applied field.

Looking back, such a rupture of his project into two different domains was not particularly effective. Mannheim's initial, theoretical studies were criticized at the time and were only much later retrieved by theorists who seldom acknowledged Mannheim's seminal influence. His second project, as might be expected when dealing with practical and immediate concerns, was subject to transcendence by changing times and changing social interests and eventually was infrequently acknowledged, except in occasional academic references. Today, in a period characterized by a division of sociology into a helter-skelter array of agendas, both foci of Mannheim are beginning to capture the attention of academics, and new works about his theoretical position are appearing in Germany and Holland. In addition, some social commentators are also giving Mannheim's applied (and Anglican) sociology a certain reconsideration, such as is found in Florestan Fernandes' *Democracy and Planning,* from Brazil.

4

Max Scheler

Max Scheler was born in 1874 and studied philosophy at the University of Jena under the direction of Rudolph Eucken and Otto Liebmann, both of whom were developing important reactions to the pervasive standpoints of naturalism and positivism. In his thesis, entitled *The Transcendental and the Psychological Methods* (1900), Scheler attempted to show the weaknesses of Kantian transcendentalism and psychologism. After teaching at Jena for a few years, during which time he encountered the phenomenology of Edmund Husserl, both through a meeting with Husserl and an exposure to *Logical Investigations,* Scheler received an appointment to the University of Munich. There, he met and worked with a number of phenomenologists who were beginning to employ Husserl's method in a variety of domains. Scheler soon became a master of the new method and emerged as a leader of the phenomenological movement.

Scheler's reputation as a phenomenologist was established with his book *Sympathy* (1913), and was enhanced by the publication of his major work, *Formalism in Ethics and Nonformal Ethics of Values* (volumes of which appeared in 1913 and 1916). In these works, and in the series of essays written from 1912 to 1914, published as a volume titled *The Overturn of Values* in 1919, Scheler explored his interest in political and social issues. This interest was only increased by the force of events that led to World War I, and Scheler wrote a passionate and very popular defense of the German participation in the war, called *The Genius of War* (1915). With the publication of *War and Reconstruction* in 1916, Scheler had turned to a less inflammatory and more philosophical concern with perennial values and their contemporary worth. In 1919 he was appointed to the University of Cologne, where he wrote on the philosophy of religion in *On the Eternal in Man* (1921) and on the sociology of "spirit" in *Sociology and the Science of the Conceptions of the World* (1922). In 1926 Scheler published a more systematic work, *The Forms of Knowledge and Society,* which constitutes the core of his sociology of knowledge, a field of sociology in which he was a seminal contributor. As a consequence of personal events, Scheler split with the Catholic Church, and since Cologne was a university steeped in Catholicism, his presence became politically embarrassing. He left Cologne in 1925 and spent several years traveling and lecturing,

because he was unable to find a position in a German university, having become *personna non grata* to the Ministry that would appoint him. Finally, in
1927, he received an invitation to join the University of Frankfurt. In that year
he published his final book, *Man's Place in Nature.* Scheler had been having
heart problems for some time, and on May 18, 1928, he suffered a fatal heart
attack.

As with Theodore Adorno, Alfred Schutz, and many other German intellectuals, the reputation and works of Max Scheler became victims of the Nazi
regime. Scheler was not associated with the Frankfurtians, but his works were
suppressed by the Nazis not only because of their moral tenor, but also because
Scheler's mother was Jewish. The fact that his father was Protestant and that
the younger Scheler converted to Catholicism as a youth did not matter. Scheler's
premature death in 1928, at the age of 54, meant that he was not witness to the
suppression of his writings. During the first two decades of the century, however, Scheler was considered one of the greatest and most subtle of philosophers. His contributions to the fields of sociology, philosophy, philosophical
anthropology, and ethics were extensive, original, and widely considered. Unfortunately, with the Second World War and its aftermath, and especially in
the frenzied academic world that followed the hostilities, Scheler's work remained unjustly forgotten.

This philosophical vacuum has been partially overcome through the publication in Germany of his complete works. Those works have by and large
been translated into English, and while exposure to Scheler's work has been of
limited scope in the English-speaking world, an increasing number of thinkers
are becoming aware of the richness of his ideas. A second reason for the slow
emergence of Scheler's project in the Anglo world rests with the dominance of
contrasting theoretical orientations, such as positivism, behaviorism, and analytical philosophy, to all of which Scheler is anathema. Similarly, many of
Scheler's important contributions, especially in the domain of ethics, have been
appropriated by others without sufficient credit. In such a situation, redress is
unfortunately slow. I. M. Bochenski, for one, has noted that Scheler was "endowed with an unusual personality . . . beyond doubt the most brilliant thinker
of his day" (Bochenski 1956, 140). Even as Scheler's works emerge from their
historical concealment, it remains true that among his contemporaries, Scheler
was unique, inasmuch as he brought together the German genius for metaphysics and the mastery of a wide range of empirical sciences. Such a feat is
rare.

The most notable characteristic of Scheler's personality, which also gives
us an important clue to the nature of his work, is that he was a man of passion,
charged with emotions, driven by compulsions, and torn by inner conflicts. In
a sense, he was more of a Wagnerian character, driven to new experiences and
knowledge, than a conformist to the current age. Such conflicts established and
nourished throughout his life a deep dialectic between the person and his sci-

ence; or in other words, between eroticism and rationality. This is the same ground from which Augustine and Pascal emerged, two thinkers to whom Scheler admitted significant debts.

In academia, there are not very many cases like Scheler's. In 1910 he resigned from the University of Munich, where he was a full professor, to become an independent writer. While his resignation was tainted with scandal, the incident can be viewed as symbolic of Scheler's life — movement between academic and worldly venues, subject to the drives of strong passions, brilliantly spontaneous, and seldom at peace. Scheler is thus a figure that stands in the stream of life, tempted equally by the pleasures of the lecture hall and the café. It would come as no surprise to learn that Scheler was a magnet for people; his conversational skill was well known. Because he was so much involved with life itself, his thoughts stemmed from and were reflective of the very real, nonrational *ordre du coeur* that drove him. He was something of an archetype, enveloped by passion and writing like a driven explorer in domains normally avoided by mainstream philosophers. Thus his work followed the contours of his soul, an exposure that to the observer features both appeal and threat. Far from being an academic of the "ivory tower" myth, Scheler was involved with his world, and his hermeneutics are those of the passions.

The Foundation of Scheler's Project

Commensurate with his gifts, Scheler was prolific in several philosophical and sociological fields. It would therefore help to understand his overall approach if one were to find a fulcrum about which Scheler spun his writings. Fortunately, Scheler himself gives us that very focus in a famous statement from the beginning of the Preface to one of his final published works, *Man's Place in Nature:*

The questions "What is man?" and "What is man's place in the nature of things?" have occupied me more deeply than any other philosophical questions since the first awakening of my philosophical consciousness (Scheler 1961, 3).

An investigation of Scheler's writings, therefore, will be aided by keeping this personal point of departure in mind. For Scheler, the centrality of these questions meant that any adequate metaphysics, and all sociology, must seek insight into three areas of inquiry:

. . . 1) in relation to a realm of values, both ethical and religious; 2) in relation to society, history and culture; 3) in relation to man's place in the universe of living things (Meyerhoff, in Scheler 1961, xii).

Although his last efforts addressed the third of these issues, Scheler did not approach them in any sort of chronological sequence, and he did not view them in a hierarchy of either importance or breadth. Rather, these domains of inquiry interpenetrate each other, and Scheler frequently considered all of them in the same general discussion. What our consideration of Scheler requires, then, is a work of exegetical interpretation, which can never do justice to the richness of his work, but can develop a systematic way of understanding Scheler's contributions.

Scheler's philosophy is structured according to conflicting problematics. On the one hand is the "life philosophy" of Bergson, Nietzsche, and Dilthey, which Scheler engages in the attempt to come to grips with the frustrating insecurities of human existence — the inability to communicate without hazard, the devaluation (or revaluation) of human existence in a world made mad by science, the struggle between the current of passion and the yolk of self-control.

On the other hand, Scheler explored with enthusiasm the new and radical approach advocated by phenomenology, which he was steered toward during a fortuitous meeting with Edmund Husserl in 1901. As a consequence of this meeting, and because of his affinity for the phenomenological method, Scheler became known as one of the primary adherents of the new philosophy. However, Scheler was much more than Husserl a "man of the world," and his phenomenology took on a much more "life-world" aspect than did Husserl's Cartesian approach. Scheler's strikingly different position, as well as his personal charisma, led to significant disputes with Husserl, which probably contributed to Scheler's governmental censure and his off-again, on-again banishment from academic positions (cf. Staude 1967 and Nota 1983 on this relationship).

Nevertheless, Scheler is a phenomenologist of the first order. A. Cuvillier, for instance, in his *Manuel de Sociologie,* states in the section on systematic sociology, that when one begins to consider phenomenology, it is Scheler that must be approached *first.* While Scheler may be considered more of a philosopher than a sociologist (which is quite an artificial distinction, considering, for example, the style of the Durkheimian school of sociology in France), Scheler nonetheless grounds his social thought on a doctrine of person and personal consciousness. Scheler admits, indeed, that sociological research is necessary for a phenomenological project of describing "essences" for two reasons. First, such a project will reveal basic data, a project resting with the individual. Second, such a project will make possible the differentiation of the "essences" from the collective "idolae" *(a la* Bacon) produced by the illusory logic of the social classes. Thus a "sociology of knowledge" is based on the idea that to each social unit there corresponds a particular kind of knowledge structure and that even the "natural attitude" (to use a phrase employed by both Husserl and Scheler), with its categories, forms of thinking, intuitions, objects of love, etc., is variable according to its historical epoch and social nexus. Thus phenomenology is capable of exploring, and is even *obliged* to explore, the three areas of inquiry noted above, namely, the realm of values, the realm of society and history, and the realm of philosophical anthropology. Indeed, it is *only* through the phenomenology of the life-world that authentic human understanding can be attained.

In the most prominent intellectual biography of Scheler, John Raphael Staude notes that Scheler

> agreed with Weber that *science* was unable to posit *Weltanschauungen,* but he insisted that *philosophy* had both the right and the power to fulfill this task. Through a metaphysics that could establish norms by which to evaluate *Weltanschauungen,* not only could the philosopher describe the various *Weltanschauungen* in terms of the interrelatedness of their ideal contents; he could also determine their objective value as knowledge, indicating both their errors and their insights (Staude 1967, 156).

For Scheler, science can only establish partial and tentative views of reality. Too many issues, phenomena, and areas of inquiry will always be concealed from scientific understanding. To suggest that eventually we will be able to comprehend love as a function of brain chemistry ignores the fact that what we mean by the term will be forever changing, forever enigmatic, and always a matter of valuing instead of analysis. For Scheler, ". . . metaphysics alone was the medium through which individuals, states, nations, religions, and even civilizations could understand one another" (Staude 1967, 32).

Comte's theory of the three stages of development is therefore incorrect. Religion, metaphysics, and science are simultaneous activities of the mind engaged in the interpretation of the life-world. Each is a separate program from the others, with separate logics, experiences, and results. The more important and fundamental question involves the character of the human mind that can develop all three styles of knowing the world, and how reality is perceived in such a way as to admit of such diverse modes of knowing. Thus, as noted earlier, Scheler begins — and ends — with a metaphysics of person.

From the outset, it must be noted that this position is not solipsistic. Unlike Husserl, who in the *Cartesian Meditations* was obliged to rely on the transcendental Ego to escape the problem of solipsism, Scheler avoids the issue from the beginning. The human being is primordially a member of a community, and it is the community that establishes the *a priori* modes of encounter with the world in which the person participates and may modify in his own unique way.

> . . . Scheler insisted that although different peoples saw reality differently, these different conceptions of reality could all be true. They were

simply viewing the same ultimate reality from a different *perspective*. Their perspectives were socially determined, but, to Scheler, this fact did not impair the truth value of their insights. The conditions of the genesis of thought did not detract from its validity (Staude 1967, 159).

There exists one reality. In the *Wissenformen,* Scheler states that "there are many different truths, but they all spring from the perception of the one ultimate realm of ideas and value orderings" (quoted in Staude 1967, 159). This notion of "value orderings" is crucial to any discussion of Scheler and will be considered later. At issue, however, is the relationship of the person to reality. We note that the different truths involve perception — and therefore any truth involves interpretation.

But what kind of "interpretation" would Scheler admit here? What we have at this point is a solitary though social individual perceiving reality from his own social vantage point, which still requires the transcendental Ego to engage others in authentic communication, and thus is susceptible to the charge of solipsism. Scheler displays his cleverness by shifting the interpretive standpoint of the individual away from an observational style to one of thoroughgoing pragmatism. (Scheler read the works of the American pragmatists carefully.) Herbert Spiegelberg describes the shift well:

Reality reveals itself by a peculiar phenomenon, that of resistance. But resistance to what? According to Scheler it is not the intellect which experiences it. It is rather our active, spontaneous, volitional life to which resistance is "pre-given," and with it reality itself. It is therefore not in perception proper that reality is experienced "in person," but in a preperceptive practical attitude. Hence reality is to Scheler relative to our practical interests, and in a sense a pragmatic affair (Spiegelberg 1971, 244–45).

Consciousness for the phenomenologist is always intentional. Yet intentionality proceeds from a ground of already established practices and pre-views. We engage our world from within a "pre-perceptive practical attitude." In other words, for Scheler, we *do,* and the one unique reality discloses itself to us in the process of our going about the business of living, as a resistance to "doing" that prohibits, inhibits, qualifies, or otherwise affects our practical intentions. Obviously, that "doing" can take place in the domains of religion, metaphysics, or science, and the orientation (and intention) toward doing is prior to the perception of the world that inhibits or qualifies the activity.

This notion of "resistance" is crucial to Scheler's metaphysics, for it is on this basis that he develops a conception of human life as essentially one of suffering and attempting to overcome that suffering. The world is not neutral toward our existence. Instead, our pragmatic attitude is forever being challenged, thwarted, or altered by the primordial infringement of reality. Our existence is therefore a matter of suffering the inhibitions that emerge during our projects and seeking those values that would alleviate our suffering. This necessarily involves the hierarchy of values discussed in the next section.

Is it the case, then, that there exists one reality, but each one of us just uses it differently? That would lead to a slippery relativism that might lead around to solipsism again. Yet that is nearly the case, as Scheler suggested in his statement about the existence of many truths, each of which is a perception of the one reality. Against this charge of anarchy, however, Scheler discloses that this reality is ordered, consistent, and eternal, and the intent of his metaphysics of the person is to describe our relationship to this reality in such a way as to disclose our place in it. For Scheler, the ordering principle that allows us to feel "at home," that captivates science and drives history, and that resists our practical activity as we engage the life-world is "value." This concept is Scheler's most fundamental contribution to philosophy and sociology but requires an extensive consideration of its character and the unique way in which Scheler formulates the notion and its consequences.

The Concept and Being of Value in Scheler's Philosophy

Each of the three areas of inquiry addressed by Scheler has the idea of value located at its center. In a sense, the genesis, existence, and discovery of values in each domain constitute the core of Scheler's efforts. Indeed, his root question, "Who am I?" calls not only for an analysis according to rational processes, but also an evaluation, and the latter is clearly the more important and more revealing. Our question thus involves Scheler's insights into the being and nature of values and the ways in which the person attends to or experiences values. This question is significant because Scheler's sociology of knowledge, anthropology, and understanding of history are founded on the ways in which human individuals and communities perceive and respond to values.

We can best begin with a statement from Scheler's most extensive work, the *Ethics:*

> . . . there is a type of experiencing whose "objects" are completely inaccessible to reason; reason is as blind to them as ears and hearing are blind to colors. It is a kind of experience that leads us to *genuinely* objective objects and the eternal order among them, i.e. to *values* and the order of ranks among them. And the order and laws contained in this experience are as exact and evident as those of logic and mathematics; that is, there are evident interconnections and oppositions among values and value-attitudes and among the acts of preferring, etc., which are built on them, and on the basis of these a genuine grounding of moral decisions and laws for such decisions is both possible and necessary (Scheler 1973a, 255).

As we engage the world from within the pre-perceptive practical attitude (a phrase reminiscent of Schutz' "pre-predicative meaning structures" — a comparison of the two notions would be interesting), the phenomena that brush up against our intentions, that offer resistance to our activities, are always imbued with value. Our encounter with them is always a *valuing,* and not the sterile meeting of a dispassionate observer with a disjoined thing, during the course of which meeting a value is assigned to the thing on the basis of its utility. Instead, Scheler suggests that the value is the *grounding* of the encounter, the authentic experiencing of the phenomenon, prior to any determination of the essence of the object. Indeed, the object is revealed in its "whatness" on the basis of its valuation.

This assertion requires that Scheler make a distinction between objects of desire (goals), goods, and values, with ". . . values being the good-making characteristics in a goal or good which by no means coincide with it" (Spiegelberg 1971, 252).

Because our primordial encounter with the life-world is practical, all phenomena are met and discovered on the basis of their value to our project. However, the value is not the object:

> Goodness was a quality of things, or more precisely, it was the *value* inherent in a thing. Scheler insisted that values could not be apprehended by the intellect. Instead, he posited a separate faculty in man for the perception of values. He called the nonrational faculty *value feeling (das Wertgefühl),* and he claimed that it was "rooted in the human heart" (Staude 1967, 15).

So the universe of "objective being" is primordially a *felt* universe, prior to any activity of analysis, or even identification, since the being of the object comes to light through our feeling of its value, a feeling that Scheler terms "preferring."

From within the pre-perceptive practical attitude, we "prefer" phenomena on the basis of their correspondence with our intentional activity at the time; and because the essential character of the world is resistance, it is to our benefit that we "prefer" values that grant us the highest level of success and peace. Even the positive scientist, prior to any operation of rationality, "prefers" certain phenomena to others at the outset of his investigations. There is, furthermore, a ranking of values that may — or may not — correspond to the ranking of our intentionalities. This ranking becomes a very important attribute of Scheler's universe, because the symmetry between the order of the universe of values and the order of the value-attitudes within our nonrational faculties determines our human success and happiness. In other words, as suggested earlier, we "prefer," or at least *ought* to prefer, values that occupy positions higher in the hierarchy:

In the *totality* of the realm of values there exists a singular order, an *"order of ranks"* that all values possess among themselves. It is because of this that a value is "higher" or "lower" than another one. This order lies in the *essence* of values themselves, as does the difference between "positive" and "negative" values. It does not belong simply to "values known" by us (Scheler 1973a, 86).

It is important to remember that Scheler's metaphysics is person centered. That is, the most successful comprehension of the universe will be obtained on the basis of the understanding of the character of the person, the position of the person in the universe, and the possible manners of experience with which the person encounters his or her world. Thus not only the things of experience bear value, but also "in contrast to these values there are two values that belong to the human person; (1) the value of the person 'himself,' and (2) the values of virtue" (Scheler 1973, 100).

In this argument Scheler, like Husserl and other phenomenologists, deals with adults, and presumes that a socialization process has taken place — a flawed presumption, perhaps, but one that admits of the possibility of a phenomenology of development. The person has developed in a social milieu and now exhibits a personality. That personality is to be valued both in its character as human *simpliciter* and as a bearer of values learned through his or her communal associations. It is this latter set of values, and their organization, which inform our pre-perceptive practical attitude, that Scheler is concerned with in the *Ethics*. Consistently, Scheler maintains a focus on the centrality of the person, and his ethical position was variously termed "ethical personalism," "emotional intuitionism," and "non-formal apriorism" (cf. Spiegelberg 1971, 232, and Scheler 1973a, xxii).

Whether our experience is of a thing or another person, that phenomenon is given as "value-able" to us, and its identity becomes disclosed on the basis of that practical valuation. "[Values] are given as the contents of immediate intuition in concrete cases of ethical experience, once we attend to the value characters in their pure 'whatness' regardless of their existence" (Spiegelberg 1971, 253). This is the case regardless of the manner in which the world is given by science or other "positive" modes of interpretation:

We expect an ethics first of all to furnish us with an explicit determination of "higher" and "lower" in the order of values, a determination that is itself based on the contents of the essences of values — insofar as their order is understood to be independent of all possible positive systems of goods and purposes (Scheler 1973a, 100).

The Ptolemaic worldview, the Copernican negation of that universe, the Biblical worldview, or the Koranic worldview — all these are "possible positive systems of goods and purposes," socially conditioned, communally established, and temporally valid. All are imbued with values, though the contents of those values may be preferred in a different order, depending on the person's milieu — a turtle, for instance, may be a totem or a pet, and "totem" bears a particular level of value, while "pet" bears another. However, for Scheler the most critical step for the philosopher to take is the realization that these values, in their *essences,* assume an absolute and ordered hierarchy — of which ethics is the study and the guide. As Scheler noted in the *Ethics,* ". . . the *'ordered ranks of values'* are themselves absolutely *invariable,* whereas the 'rules of preferring' are, in principle, variable throughout history (a variation which is very different from the apprehension of new values)" (Scheler 1973a, 88).

In positing this ordered universe, Scheler was for the most part issuing a commentary of Pascal's insight into *"le coeur a ses raisons."* In "Ordo Amoris," Scheler noted that ". . . there is an *ordre du coeur,* a *logique du coeur,* a *mathématique du coeur* as rigorous, as objective, as absolute, and as inviolable as the propositions and inferences of deductive logic" (Scheler 1973b, 117). Thus the universe is *not* objective, but it *is* totally ordered. The value-feeling *(das Wertgefühl)* by which we primordially engage the world encounters a natural, preordered hierarchy of values, and it is these that we "prefer" during the course of our life-project.

Now, it is possible for there to be order without hierarchy, and, we suppose, hierarchy without a high degree of order. For Scheler, however, the value-universe exhibits both: ". . . there is an order of preference or precedence among them [values]" (Spiegelberg 1971, 255). Scheler was not entirely clear as to the number of levels in the hierarchy of values. Spiegelberg and Meyerhoff suggest there are four levels, which the latter describes as: ". . . (1) values of sensible feeling (pleasant and unpleasant); (2) values of vital feeling (noble and vulgar); (3) spiritual values (beautiful and ugly, just and unjust); (4) religious values (holy and unholy)" (Meyerhoff, in Scheler 1961, xvii). Kenneth W. Stikkers, in his introduction to Scheler's *Problems of a Sociology of Knowledge,* identifies a fifth level, between levels 1 and 2 above. This level is that of ". . . the value sphere of utility, ranging from the useful to the useless and including the practical, the efficient, and the economical" (Stikkers, in Scheler 1980, 14). In either case, values are encountered in a hierarchy, and there exists, or can exist, a symmetry between the level of value and the level of human practical interest the value-bearing thing satisfies. It is not the case that our everyday operations are always carried out in harmony with this order of values; rather, Scheler suggests that our human *goal* is to bring our activities and interests into a harmony with the preestablished value hierarchy.

One may suspect that since there is an order of values in the natural universe, and since the human being participates in that universe, then there is also an order of values among humans and human affairs. Such is indeed the case.

The aforementioned "pre-perceptive practical attitude" consists of what Scheler called "vital drives," and we encounter and engage the world from within that orientation. Therefore, there must exist a hierarchy of vital drives; and furthermore, there must exist a hierarchy of persons themselves, according to the level of drives that are manifest in their daily activity. Staude notes that "values themselves could be arranged in an ascending hierarchy according to whether they satisfied man's animal or his spiritual needs. . . . Men themselves could also be arranged in a hierarchy of types" (Staude 1967, 32). The proposition that all men are created equal, then, while perhaps a useful statement for political purposes, is nonetheless false in the true nature of things.

Scheler's Personalism and the Philosophy of Love

At this point the person-centered character of Scheler's philosophy becomes clear in its detail and its consequences. Because we are dealing with a phenomenology, we must remember that the values exhibited by the things of the world are always values *for* someone, and that the intentional consciousness is always a *valuing* consciousness. Scheler's summarizing statement in the preface to the *Ethics* is unequivocating:

The most essential and important proposition that my present investigations would found and communicate as perfectly as possible is the proposition that the final meaning and value of the *whole* universe is ultimately to be measured exclusively against the pure being (and not the effectiveness) and the possible perfect being-good, the richest fullness and the most perfect development, and the purest beauty and inner harmony of *persons* in whom at times all forces of the world concentrate themselves and soar upwards (Scheler 1973a, xxiv).

This appears to be a resounding confirmation of the Aristotelian notion of man as the measure of all things. Such a conclusion seems to be strengthened later in the same book, when Scheler reinforces his position:

Only persons can (originally) be morally good or evil; everything else can be good or evil only *by reference to persons,* no matter how indirect this "reference" may be. All properties that vary (according to rules) with the *goodness of the person* are called virtues; those that vary with the person's being-evil are called vices. Acts of will and deed are also good or evil only insofar as acting persons are comprehended with them (Scheler 1973a, 85).

So far, our treatment of Scheler has disclosed the human-centered character of his metaphysics, namely, the focus on the individual, socialized human being as the source of the valuation of the phenomena of the universe. However, it is apparent that human beings are also members of the universe, and therefore one may ask how we fit into the scheme of things, especially in terms of values and valuations. Scheler recognizes that to identify human vital impulses as the source of values removes the person from the natural world and sets up a problematic dualism between the universe and the spirit — a reversion to Kantianism. Consequently, Scheler argues that all human beings are members of the ordered universe, that "within the world-order which is valid for all men, every particular form of the human is assigned some definite range of value-qualities" (Scheler 1973b, 111). As we indicated at the end of the previous section, persons themselves are arranged in a hierarchy of values, according to the worth of their intentional activity; and the gauge of this "worth" is the correspondence of the activity with the hierarchy of values noted above — the sensible, utilitarian, vital, spiritual, etc.

It would follow from this assertion that persons engage each other also on the basis of valuation, that our pre-perceptive attitude towards *others* also brings other persons into view on the grounds of their value to our projects. Scheler states: "Wherever he arrives, it is not the same men and the same things, but the same types of men and things (and these are in every case *types* of values), that attract or repulse him in accordance with certain constant rules of preference and rejection" (Scheler 1973b, 101). Our value-feelings, then, operate in the domain of the entire world, including its human component. Value-feelings, however, are limited in their operation. They open the phenomenon to us, and present it in an emerging objectivity, but they do not provide the "rules of preference and rejection." It is a function of some other quality of the human character that phenomena become *known* in their "whatness." As Meyerhoff notes: "Feelings make values accessible to us; love makes them known to us" (Meyerhoff, in Scheler 1961, xviii).

For Scheler, the springboard of knowledge is the passionate embrace of the world, or love. Indeed, his is a unique conception of love and its activity. While it is value-feeling that allows the world to come into view, it is love that enables the person to enter into a living relationship with that world.

> I find myself in an immeasurably vast world of sensible and spiritual objects which set my heart and passions in constant motion. I know that the objects I can recognize through perception and thought, as well as all that I will, choose, do, perform, and accomplish, depend on the play of this movement of my heart. It follows that any sort of rightness or falseness and perversity in my life and activity are determined by whether there is an objectively correct order of these stirrings of my love and hate, my inclination and disinclination, my many-sided interest in the things of this world. It depends further on whether I can impress this *ordo amoris* on my inner moral tenor (Scheler 1973b, 98).

It becomes apparent here that Scheler is establishing a philosophy of the person in complete contradistinction to rationalism and every form of psychologism (including that of Husserl). Indeed, for Scheler, "love is always what awakens both knowledge and volition . . . it is the mother of spirit and reason itself" (Scheler 1973b, 110). But just what is *love?* It is an emotional power, a desire to will into reality the being of the phenomenon that resists our practical intentionality. An old showtune suggests that "love makes the world go 'round," and Scheler seems to indicate that love not only makes it go 'round, but also *makes* it what it is. Scheler states:

> Man, before he is an *ens cogitans* or an *ens volens,* is an *ens amans.* The fullness, the gradation, the differentiation, and the power of his love circumscribe the fullness, the functional specificity, and the power of his possible spirit and of the possible *range* of contact with the universe (Scheler 1973b, 110–11).

Thus, the manner of the universe depends on my love for the values made accessible by my value-feeling. For Scheler, "the things and properties of which he can have knowledge do not define and delimit his value-world; his world of essential values circumscribes and defines the being he can know, raising it up out of the sea of being like an island" (Scheler 1973b, 111). This ordering of the universe includes an ordering of the persons discovered in it, inasmuch as each person bears a certain level of value. Yet there is something disturbing about this assertion, since the spectre of solipsism again emerges — for might it not be the case that each person engages in a unique ordering of the universe on the basis of a unique and incommensurate set of values *du coeur?*

This apparent contradiction is in fact a straw man. Scheler advocates a *logique du coeur* that is as firm and fixed as the logic of mathematics. This logic of love is inscribed on every human heart by virtue of being human, and such differences as might exist between our ordering of the universe and the authentic, objective ordering of the universe result from errors of love. Every object, every person, every concept occupies a place within an ordered universe:

> . . . we can imagine that the scale of what is worthy of love, both as it exists for everyone generally and, within this, as it exists for each single and social individual, is of such a kind that every object, when its contingency is stripped away and its essence is considered, occupies a completely determinate and *unique position* on this scale, a position to which a completely precise and nuanced movement of the spirit corresponds (Scheler 1973b, 124).

Now Scheler is ready to establish a sort of categorical imperative of love. Since every object, including every person and every spiritual being, occupies a unique position on the scale of *what is worthy of love,* the moral imperative of the person is that he or she bring his or her acts of love into correspondence with the order of worthiness of love. This correspondence yields personal and communal happiness, in that the individuals in the community will place more emphasis on those values more worthy of love, those values higher in rank, namely, those of spirit and religion. And these values are the more lasting, effective, and satisfying, not only ideally, but also practically.

It might be argued here that Scheler does not completely make his point, since values are continually evolving, especially in the domains of technology and science. Similarly, some values, namely, those of persons, may be altered through changes in personality or circumstance. Scheler accounts for both of these possible objections. First, it must be remembered that there is a difference between values and their *contents;* the content may change but the value is fixed, and the value-feeling engages the value, regardless of its emergent content. In addition, we note that love is not incapable of growth; Spiegelberg notes that love seeks to enhance, to develop values, through the activity of a love that is "a love which loves what is not yet lovable for the sake of what it might become" (Spiegelberg 1971, 261). Thus Scheler regards love as both actual and potential in its drive toward awareness of value.

Our daily activities also engage the universe negatively; that is, we may hate the object that comes to be in our value-intentionalities. Indeed, a world that not only witnesses, but also celebrates mass murder, excess, and celebrities run amok, seems a poor venue for the activity of loving. While that may seem to be the case, says Scheler, to suggest that a crazy world contradicts his scheme is inaccurate and superficial, for "loving can be characterized as correct or false only because a man's actual inclinations and acts of love can be in harmony with or oppose the rank-ordering of what is worthy of love" (Scheler 1973b, 111). Such problems as may occur in our society do so because the persons involved arrange their value-ceptions in an order that conflicts with the objective order manifest in the universe. Whether one is "looking for love in all the wrong places" or worshipping the banal, the solution is to bring one's personal *ordo amoris* into correspondence with the rank order of values expressed by the world. For Scheler, ". . . it always holds true that the act of hate, the antithesis of love, or the emotional negation of value and existence, is the result of some *incorrect* or *confused* love" (Scheler 1973b, 125).

Human perfection required a correspondence between the rank-ordering of values in the world and the practical interests, expressed in love, within the heart of the person. The lower values are the more powerful and alluring; the higher values are less powerful and more subtle. The lower values, however, yield less satisfaction and a more temporary pleasure; the higher values yield more deeply felt and enduring satisfaction. The ethical demand of the human is to approach the phenomena of the universe from within an attitude that appropriately loves the hierarchy of values — "appropriate" here refers to an ordering of the passionate impulses in an effective way. The resulting experience of the world is one of rich possibilities:

> This is the miracle of our world: through a *knowledge of essence* and knowledge of essential structure obtained from the forms of this actual, real world, we can know the constitution of every *possible* world, including even that reality which is shut off from our limited organization in life and hence transcendent to us (Scheler 1973b, 123).

And here is the foundation upon which Scheler can construct a phenomenological sociology of knowledge.

A Phenomenological Sociology of Knowledge

Like the universe in its infinite possibilities, and like the human individual, the community of persons also bears an *ordo amoris*. The community exhibits a value-feeling, an interpretive relation with the values of the life-world in such a way as to give rise to forms of knowledge, in an order corresponding to the rank order of communal values. Bershady comments that "Scheler showed how various feelings — community of feeling, fellow-feeling, vicarious feeling, emotional infection, emotional identification, suffering, *ressentiment,* love and hate — are structured by the values toward which they point" (Scheler 1993, 37). Consequently, the value-feelings of each social unit, from the smallest upward, and the activity of love of that community, give rise to particular structures of knowledge. And, as with the individual person, the moral dimensions of the community are related to the order of values and order of love exhibited by that community. Those communities that are, for Scheler, "humane" in character, are those that exhibit the greatest correspondence between their *ordo amoris* and the objective rank order of values in the life-world.

If we recall the ordering of values into the four or five levels mentioned above — the sensible, utilitarian, vital, spiritual, and religious — then we may suggest that communities exhibit trends toward the expression of a hierarchy of those values and that particular *kinds* of communities exhibit a prominence of one or another kind of value, such as religious orders. While there may obviously be subcultures that focus on one level of value, Scheler would argue more forcefully that the value-feeling of the entire community, which would include the regard in which it held its subcultures, also exhibits a hierarchy of value-feeling. Especially in his earlier works, Scheler advocated a conscious reordering of values in European civilization that would bring it more in accord with the natural rank order of values. Like Weber, he viewed European culture as overly concerned with the sensate, with the superficial appearances of mere rhetoric. Hence he sought a renewal of religious fervor (which he also longed for in his personal life) on the communal level.

In an argument reminiscent of Sorokin's description of the transitions of ideational and sensate cultures, Scheler warned that societies *(vice* community, *a la* Tönnies) whose values were perverted, that is, too directed toward the sensate and vital values and too little concerned with the higher values of spirituality and religion, would experience moral decay and deterioration. The community that promoted a socialization process that emphasized value-feelings commensurate with those of the life-world would flourish. It is therefore the obligation of the members of a given society to engage in such reflections as would enhance their love of life-world values (which is the goal of Scheler's ethical personalism noted above). Thereby the community as a whole progresses toward a situation characterized by mutually enhancing and nurturing relationships. In the end, Scheler's intent is to enrich human life, to invigorate a lethargic morality, to promote a movement toward a life characterized by the highest of possible values. Scheler's ideal is rather simple:

> Sharing a life in common, working and producing together, sharing beliefs and hopes, living for one another and respecting one another are themselves a part of the universal destiny of every finite spiritual being (Scheler 1973b, 104).

The *ordo amoris,* the disclosure of the appropriate structure of knowledge, the perfection of interpersonal relationships, the creation of a community that fulfills the human potential for loving and exciting relationships — all these are modes by which we may fulfill our universal destiny. Certainly this state of affairs would be ideal; Scheler's Catholic communalism, however, and his politics of emotion led him to advocate such a worthy, albeit unattainable condition of humanity.

III

Contemporary Trends

In this section, our analysis turns to four of the most important contemporary proponents of the interpretive style of social science. In addition, each has made significant contributions to theoretical sociology. Emilio Betti advocates a positivist mode of interpretive science. The interpretive theory of Hans-Georg Gadamer is more humanistic in its orientation. Finally, both Theodor W. Adorno and Jürgen Habermas represent critical theory, in its interpretive aspects. Adorno reflects the earlier form of critical theory, and Habermas presents the most recent synthesis of the critical approach. Although there is more to critical theory than interpretation, we shall consider only those works of Adorno and Habermas that relate to the interpretive project.

5

Positivist Interpretation: Emilio Betti

Emilio Betti was born at Camerino, Italy, in 1890 and earned Doctoral degrees in both law and philosophy. He was Professor of Civil Law, Roman Law, Civil Trial Law, International Law, Agrarian Law, and the History of Law at universities in Camerino, Maserata, Messina, Parma, Florence, and Milan. In 1917 he was appointed to the faculty of the University of Frankfurt in Germany. While teaching in Germany, he studied the interpretive theories of Wilhelm Dilthey, and those theories became central to his approach. It was also while in Germany that he published a number of articles that established his reputation as a rigorous thinker in the field of hermeneutics. In 1948, Betti returned to Italy, where he taught at the University of Rome. Originally, his title was Professor of Roman Law, but his interest in hermeneutics led him to create the Institute for Interpretive Theory, of which he became the first director.

The Possibility of an Objective Hermeneutics

Betti's work renews the project originally developed by Dilthey. That is, Betti seeks to consider hermeneutics, the theory of interpretation, as a foundation of the "sciences of the spirit." He accepts Dilthey's idea of the possibility of an objective, canonic mode of interpretation, and then, under the influence of Kant, Betti seeks to extend the fundamental categories of knowledge, which for Kant grounded only the natural sciences, to the "moral sciences" (considered generally as the humanities and the social sciences). In addition, Betti finds that Hegel provides a way to ascertain the validity of interpretation in certain of the passages of *The Phenomenology of Spirit* that concern the nature of consciousness.

Betti's focus in much of his work concerns two issues. First, he is interested in intuition and its operations. Second, he seeks to identify the manner in which the positive sciences, philosophy, sociology, psychology, jurisprudence, religion, art, criticism, history, and the performing arts are all linked to one another by the procedures of hermeneutics. For Betti, hermeneutics becomes the metalanguage of the "moral sciences," to which both epistemology and methodology are subsumed. Because his interests include the application of interpretation in the domain of the natural sciences, Betti remains within the confines of a general scientific project, with "science" here used in the classical sense. This position, then, will affect his search for an objective mode of interpretation. Betti therefore understands the hermeneutic process as a continuous movement of interpretation toward the capture of the object of analysis in its complex field of meanings.

The first problem Betti faces concerns the question of how to achieve an objective understanding. He begins with values and compares their status to that of objects. For Betti, objects are human constructs, objectifications of the human subjectivity that is intrinsic to all members of our species. The apprehension of objects belonging to the external world depends on a translation from their position without (in the world) to a position within (in human consciousness) through the categories of mind. Values, however, are found in consciousness, and not in the world, and thus do not have the same ontological status as objects.

These considerations lead Betti to take up the question of language. He analyzes the linguistic distinction between objectivity and actuality and constructs a parallel between that distinction and the notions of "langue" and "parole" in the work of Ferdinand de Saussure. "Parole" brings language into intersubjective reality. In the speech act, language is actualized and influenced by the specificities of the linguistic event. "Langue," though, suggests that language also exists objectively, independently of speech acts; it exists virtually in the mind of every speaker of the particular language.

The basis for this line of reasoning is the notion that linguistic elements can be brought out of unrealized existence by an act of consciousness. Thus, "langue" could be said to have an ideal objectivity. The degree of possible reflection that each speaker may dedicate to a speech act can be traced back to the idiosyncratic characteristics of the speaker. Regardless of such flexibility, however, we recognize that the linguistic system as such remains in existence. Furthermore, "langue" does not exist as an object of nature, but rather as an ideality. It appears that Betti has linked the Platonic Forms with a sort of Hegelian historical evolution in order to discuss the nature of language. Indeed, Betti translates the foregoing analysis of language into one concerning values.

Accordingly, Betti suggests that values also exist objectively in the status of an "ideal objectivity," a concept reminiscent of Scheler, except that for the latter, values are *real* and *ordered.* The natural objective base of values is portrayed through a strategy of triangulation: it exists for the self, for the other, and in a state of mediation (that is, in the object). For Betti, interpretation is a factor in each of these three domains. Ideally, objective values can become actualized as they emerge from a storehouse of values, in a manner similar to the activity of "langue." Therefore, an objective interpretation that leads to a full understanding is possible inasmuch as we can obtain ideally objective values for each of the three aspects, self, other, and mediation. It is the synchrony between the three that provides the validity of the resulting interpretation.

Values are formulations of social life; without them no understanding could exist in society. On the other hand, values could exist without society, since one of their attributes is that of being ideal (note that for Kant values exist not because they are logical, but rather because they are *necessary* for human life). Betti further conceives that at the limit, the value system is closed, a conception reminiscent of Hegel's notion of spirit knowing itself.

Each objectification of the human mind involves an actualization of the ideal level. In general this agrees with the idealist position according to which material elements are but a stepping stone to reach the ideal; the mind translates the material to the symbolic, through which materiality is minimized and ideality is maximized. However, Betti's position is not strictly idealist (as with Plato), because objective ideals are actualized in the self, the other, and through mediation.

The historical evolution of values is a function of the parameters of events, especially locations in time. Human beings living in different contexts face different problems. In such cases they retrieve different aspects from ideals and actualize those aspects. Indeed, if ideals did not exist, people would have to develop something *ex nihilo;* each solution would otherwise be discontinuous. Thus, there is no such thing as the discovery of new knowledge, but rather recollections of what is already there. Schematically, we can identify the two levels of values as follows:

ideal level:	no hierarchy, ahistorical	infinite systems of possible values
actualized level (human):	historical, hierarchical	specific values pertinent to situation

Because values exist objectively, we can reach an objective interpretation if we can locate the values inherent in the cultural object.

Interpretation is an occurrence that takes place in time and space, although the values that are present are retrieved from the ideal level. Historicality operates on the level of actualization, and variation is possible, since interpretation depends on the subject. Thus, subjects with broader or more diverse backgrounds may be able to reach a much richer interpretation than others. Events are also perspectival, again since they occur in time and space. Betti's concept here is similar to Edmund Husserl's formulation of the infinity of profiles of apprehension found in *Ideas: A General Introduction to Pure Phenomenology.*

As a result of the above considerations, and also as a consequence of his training in the field of law, Betti is now ready to establish his canons of objective interpretation. They are:

1. The autonomy of the subject. Meaningful forms must be regarded as autonomous and be understood within their own logic of development. This

includes their inner connections, rather than aspects of their external purposes that may seem relevant to the interpreter.

2. Coherence of meaning. There is a relationship of elements among themselves, and between those elements and their common whole, which allows for reciprocal illumination and elucidation of meaningful forms, in the relation of whole and parts, and vice versa.

3. Actuality and understanding. One must adapt and integrate understanding into one's own intellectual horizon, retracing the creative process in order to reconstruct it within oneself (this is also called "Verstehen" — a direct corollary with the project of Weber).

4. Correspondence of meaning. One must give one's full attention and have intellectual openness so as to avoid violence to the process of interpretation. One must put oneself into the process itself. Such a position implies an adequate background, and a rich variety of experience, particularly with respect to such things as freedom, education, equality, and the speech community.

With these canons, Betti aligns himself with the tradition of Schleiermacher and Dilthey. In his monumental *Teoria Generale della Interpretazione* (1955), the emphasis is on method, culminating with the foregoing canons of successful interpretation. The canons are directed at the specification of the character of the object of interpretation. Put simply, they involve the autonomy and immanence of the hermeneutic criteria and the totality and coherence of the hermeneutic task. Additionally, the canons are directed to the *subject* conducting the hermeneutic enterprise. In this regard they involve the actuality of understanding and the adequacy of understanding in the correspondence between meaning and the relationship of subject to object. His program also differentiates the entire spectrum of the hermeneutic enterprise by identifying the following areas in which hermeneutic activity takes place: (a) reproductive interpretation, such as translation and performance in theater and music, (b) normative interpretation, as found in law, theology, and psychology, and (c) phenomenology of interpretation, encompassing history and education.

To illustrate Betti's ideas, we can consider the case of reproductive interpretation, such as in musical performance, which shares the basic methodological postulates with all other types, including the canons. The specific understanding of what is musical interpretation remains difficult to determine as a result of an apparently unsurmountable dichotomy. As described by Richard Wagner, the ideal performer is one who is gifted with inventive talent, but also has a mental structure of duty that is congenially ready to assimilate the thinking of others — the composer and other previous interpreters. How might one mediate the antithesis between an inventive faculty, which is presupposed in the performer as artistic personality and the requirement of re-creating and re-expressing an idea and a creation of another, which is thus essentially alien?

The first requirement is grounded in the canon of actuality of understanding, which as operative for the cognitive function is also valid *a fortiori* for the transitive and reproductive functions of interpretation. The second requirement refers to the canon regarding the adequacy of understanding, which means correspondence with the object. This requirement also refers to the canon of hermeneutic autonomy and immanence. This places the interpreter, even in the context of reproduction, in the face of a challenge that seems closed and unsurmountable. That is, the interpreter seeks to link her expressive activity to a given object (i.e., the musical score) and make of it her obligatory inspiration.

It would be erroneous to attempt a resolution of this antinomy by opting for one of these demands over the other. Abiding by the first exclusively would lead to the creation of an entirely new work of art, one that is different than that given by the original creator. Abiding by the second will lead to a reproduction of the original work at a purely technical level, without lyricism or emotion. Moreover, different historical periods place different emphases not only on technical, but also on expressive requirements. Nietzsche, while contrasting the measured sobriety of ancient art with the passion of the art of his time, underlined precisely such differences and the need to accede to the demands of each epoch (Nietzsche 1986, 126).

Another possible resolution to the antinomy would be to consider artistic re-creation as equally interpretation and creation, qualifying the latter as itself interpretation. This would also be a mistake, because the work of art is always a configuration, according to its own logic and laws of artistic coherence. It is the configuration of a lyric content that lives in the personality of the artist and grows out of her experience. One should not simply identify the process of its genesis with that of its interpretation, which presupposes genesis. In the genetic process, the configuration of the work of art objectively obeys a "law of necessity," which is the law of its formation, which is autonomous and refers to its intrinsic coherence and logic (cf. Boeckh, *Kunstregel der Composition, Methodologie,* quoted in Betti 1955, 143).

The hermeneutic process follows a different method. The challenge here is to recognize through an intimate rapport, and through a congenial disposition, a means of operating within that law of necessity present in the structure of the work to be interpreted. If the "law of necessity," the law of contrast and analogy, were to disappear from the work in its dialectical continuity, and were no longer a concern of the interpreter, then we would no longer be dealing with a question of interpretation, but rather with the creation of a work of art based on a set of given materials (this is the case, for instance, of improvisation of a given theme, as in the *cadenza).* Perhaps the reproduction, or re-creation, of the work of art involves the presentation to a present subject of an object from the past that now exists in an inert state. The presence of the object in that case presents the risk to the artist of remerging with the creative flow of interpretation. This reproduction would consist of a confrontation of the work and the artist; yet the judgment of the adequacy of interpretation is not based on the dualistic position of confrontation, but rather evolves from within the creative act. Thus, we would not be dealing with reproductive interpretation, but rather with an original creation, which in fact resolves and dissolves the confrontation, without residue, in the unity of past and present, form and content. This occurs without the work submitting itself to any other laws than those of its own intrinsic coherence.

Furthermore, interpretation, even in the case of reproduction, does not totally "resolve," but rather accepts and assumes in the present of the interpreting subject the object as it was originally intended, in its own being, in its coherent sequences, and as it remains in the temporal duration of memory (which suggests the possibility of the conservation of the past in the present, as discussed by Henri Bergson in *Matiere et memoire,* pp. 225–33, 268). The work must also be understood by the listener, who is called upon to assume an attentive and active relation to the performance. The interpretation must make the object understood according to the principle of autonomy and coherence, that we as receivers apprehend during the operation of interpretation. If the process of hermeneutic research leads the interpreter to intuit the principle of autonomy, leads him to place himself within the lyrical sustenance of the work, to become one with the author according to the ideal of identification, then we successfully move toward coherence and reproduction, and away from censorship. Only then can interpretation be judged appropriate.

The Resolution of the Antinomy of Interpretation

We earlier mentioned that the problem of the interpretation of the work of art faced two requirements: that of the actuality of understanding and that of adequacy to the object. Two equally unsatisfactory solutions were proposed to this antinomy, one resulting in mere technical activity and the other in the creation of an unrelated work. At this point there remains no other criterion with which to solve the quandary cited by Wagner except to inject reason itself into the equation. In this orientation it is necessary to grasp the hermeneutic question through an analytical procedure and to articulate it through two phases, the re-cognitive (philological and technical) and the reproductive. The first phase is intransitive and the second transitive, and together they constitute two ideal moments of the interpretive process.

The initial moment consists of the reading of the musical score and establishing a claim of technical precision, aimed at a full understanding of the objective reality of the text — the notes, color indications, durations, and so on. This moment concerns the translation of each graphic element into its specific phonic value and the discovery of the right sonority. With the passage from silent reading to the performance, we face the inseparable risk of adopting the physical means of interpretation as a vehicle of expression. This is not to suggest that from a simple intellectual phase we move to a free "creative" phase, similar to that of the original invention.

The risk we face is that when we move from the silent reading of a poem or play to its declamation or recitation, we may fail in the correspondence and coherence that should be exact in the reexpression. There is presumed in this statement a comparison, the relationship of the performance with a model or paradigm that is established by reason. It is true that such a model (e.g., the form fixed and crystallized by the composer in the musical score) is, in relation to the original conception, a sketched and minimal form, a result of the process of objectification. From its living being in the subjectivity of the composer, it is reduced in certain aspects to a simple signpost toward the realization of its sonic potential. However, this does not in any way minimize the pregnant value of the form, in its generative potential, as well as in its artistic coherence and structure. It opens the way to recover the living equivalent form that aims to replace the original. It is significant only that the interpreter aiming at reproduction intends to integrate the musical score with his sensibility and taste, absorbing its meaning, and thereby staking his personality through being called to bring into life the wholeness of the form.

This encounter of the personality of the interpreter with that of the author, aiming at the integration of what is lacking in the written score, bringing it to life again, characterizes the second moment of interpretation, a dialectical moment. What is at stake here is to remake the totality of the creative process, of adjudicating that which was the expressive problem posited and resolved by the author, or rediscovering, on the basis of a stylistic intuition, the givens of the artistic creation, and of confronting the solutions given by the author with those not given by the interpreter. Such a confrontation is weighted with respect to taste, the expression of historicity, and the spirituality that is historically determined. The technique that is prevalent in the initial moment (noted above) is only the key to opening up the work of art, to making explicit that which is implicit, to recovering through a kind of divination the apparent hermeticism from the printed page, in which lyricism is implicit and which pulsates in silence. Interpretation as re-creation is at base a synthesis of results, a reconstructive interpretation, located in the dialectics of fidelity and renewal (and not necessarily perfect in its fidelity to the original creation). It is certainly not the original, because we no longer have a content without mediation, but rather a form which is already virtually completed. The interpreter is always in that dialectical context, turned toward a closed end, which must be dealt with continuously. His identification with the author is by definition an impossible ideal. On the part of the listener, however, reconciliation is possible, because the interpreter reveals himself and the music in a coincidence that, although imperfect, enables one to always recognize the two strands of author and performer. The infinite variety of interpretation thus depends on the variety of possible projections, but they do not replace, by themselves, the same object.

These are the preliminary, aesthetic questions to be raised in the context of reproductive interpretation. The problem is to understand the peculiar character of beautiful music. One of the traditions in this regard is to consider the musical work as an object that is simply indifferent to feelings. These might be present originally in the creative acts of the composer (which would call for a theory of emotions in reference to the author, but not in reference to the object). Similarly, attention to feelings may call for theories of performance (regarding the interpreter), or theories of reception (regarding the listener). All of these possibilities are external to the object.

Betti argues that with regard to feelings, music cannot represent anything else than the dynamic moment, the movement of the psychic facts that can be given in the increasing or decreasing presentation of a given sound, note, or chord. Moreover, the symbolic meaning of certain states emerges in accordance with our own subjective grasp. This thesis is not, of course, applicable to "pictorial music," in which tempo, strength, time, and rhythm are oriented to give us the basis for an analogy with the intended visual perception, to the extent that such an analogy can work through different sensations. Also, in the case of vocal music, the lyrics underline and comment on the musical text, giving value and focus to the symbolism of tonality, or even overriding the musical element in modalities such as that of the recitative.

If we move from the critique of the foundation of music as "feeling" to the specific positive character of what is aesthetically musical, we find the synthesis of sounds, the movements of sympathy and repulsion, of fugue and coming together, and of primordial elements such as rhythm, or as an alternate movement of single elements in the measure of time (melody). What must be expressed with such sound material (content) must be done through a musical idea, a sound form in movement. It is important to note that the forms constituted by sounds are not simply linear constructions, which means that music cannot be expressed by words or translated into concepts. We must also recognize that musical materials maintain "elective affinities" that constitute the nature of music according to its own structural relations, such as that of harmonic progressions. Considering that the art of composition consists in the elaboration of subjective elements into a material capable of receiving meaning according to the peculiar character of creative imagination, the hermeneutic task becomes immanent, in the sense that it grasps the musical idea from the sound elements. This it can do by accentuating the particular synthesis of the musical factors and the corresponding impressions, the unity of melody and harmony that redirects subjectivity, and the musical invention of the composer. Thus, whereas in language, subjectivity is nothing but a sign expressing something alien within the specificity of the medium, in music it is an entity unto itself, referring to itself, and not subjected to the absolute control of thought. There is in its center of gravity something other than language. If composing is a translation of subjectivity into style, e.g., the "speech" of a character, such translation goes beyond the requirements of a spoken or written language. That is the key difference that must be dealt with in the process of reproductive interpretation — to grasp and assimilate the structure that overflows the written signs.

The Transition from Classical to Postmodern Interpretive Modalities

To the capacity of assimilation that is required in the reproductive interpretation of a work of art, it seems that modern musical works raise further requirements than those of more traditional music. It is as though the earlier call forth the spontaneity and sensibility of the interpreter, whereas the others depend much more on "style." But such differentiation can be misleading; they are all structural phenomena that place emphasis on different vocabularies and rules of construction, and that call for different technical and stylistic demands on the part of the interpreter.

These differences do not announce a deeper contrast with reference to their respective generational processes, but rather to different synchronic structures. Thus, in the music of Beethoven, the central element is conceived and configured as one with the totality of which it is a part, and generates its full coherence through its logical structure. In modern music, "inspiration" leads to the expression of more elemental motifs (psychologically, one could characterize them as primitive, alienated, or expressive of angst), without embracing the more "epiphanic" level. Moreover the historical process of transformation of Western music created in the modern period a mutation of the way one experiences the music of the past.

In each historical period there is, at least partly, a correspondence and a correlation regarding the style of artistic production and reproductive interpretation of the works of that period. "Classical" music has a constructed coherence (certainly with exceptions, even in the repertoires of Bach or Beethoven), a cohesion and stylistic consequence that is parallel to discursive thinking. Musical elements express a musical "logic" that is pervasive to the totality of the work. Then, in the historical process, this logic loses energy and clarity. For instance, in programmatic music, coherence and cohesion appeal to extrinsic grounds, which order and establish the program, as in Honneger's *Pacific 321,* which presents the movement of a train from start to stop. One can argue that more recent music becomes more abstract and turned upon itself (Schönberg), or even appeals to visual (Cage) or spacial elements (Stockhausen). These other interests emerge as key elements for the ordering of the musical context. Thus, in the case of Western music, from an organic basis (the medieval monody), musical expression moved over time to a combination of single elements in an increasingly abstracting and purifying process, reaching in composers such as Alban Berg the tightest and briefest of compositions (cf. Theodor W. Adorno's *Alban Berg).* Even more recently, the "postmodern" trends in music reflect a contrary movement of enlargement and complexity, through the superimposition of traditions and elements (i.e., some of the works of George Rochberg). Such a process of historical change and differentiation could not remain external in its influence on reproductive interpretation. Emphasis on technical skills and the underlying technological infrastructure of performance, preoccupation with the detail and its role in the totality, constructive coherence and musical logic — all of these came to be reflected not only in compositional processes but also in reproduction.

Thus sensibility, which assumed a central position regarding emotional and psychological attributes in Romantic music, is at least partially replaced by technical accuracy, the reproduction of the particular modality of musical consciousness brought out by the composition, or the pertinence of the performance to the musical problematic of the text as revealing a specific "research program" of the epoch. In this way, the question of reproductive interpretation must remain attuned to shifts in compositional interests and requires that the interpreter account for the technical concerns of the context of the work. This situation announces a particularly difficult problem for the interpreter; in the stylistic coherence of the work, we cannot conflate its dynamic content, or what earlier would have been called the work's lyricism, with technical, expressive instrumentality. The lyricism of the former builds intuitive rapport between composer and interpreter, and the latter, in modern times, can reach exceedingly high levels of refinement and complication. If the musical content is to be expressed, however, the interpreter must be able to unveil that which is beyond the technical level, as complex as it might be. One is reminded here of Michel Foucault's "preliminary" announcement of the death of the subject in the *Archaeology of Knowledge,* or of Stravinsky's music for a mechanical piano, which cannot be played by a pianist. But the decentralization of the composer (as intended by Cage), or of the interpreter (as with Stravinsky's piano), or perhaps even of the audience (the next logical step) disseminates the musical phenomenon and loses its being (cf. Ingarden 1986).

One of the modern tendencies in music is not to put aside the intrinsic demands on the style of the work, or even to appeal to an extrinsic technical reconstruction of it, but rather to conceive the technique as something independent of the subject. Such a position continues the traditional dichotomy of the subject and object and moves interpretation to the level of the constructed intrinsic technical demands of the musical text and out of the subjectivity of the reconstruction of this text by the interpreter. This is clearly a shift from subjectivism to materialism (e.g., technology). It appears to be the case, however, that in the process of reproductive interpretation, we cannot depend for support on either the subject or the object. Both are discontinuous in reference to the musical event, and what makes music is the action of performance that connects both.

The "linguistic" event here is the "conversation" between interpreter and text, a quasi-dialogical situation in which neither can take precedence. It might be cast as the three structural stages of Hegel's phenomenology — knowledge, self-knowledge, and action. The first is an opening up of the interpreter to the world, in this case the actual musical score, but also the world that it establishes. The second stage is the self-knowledge, or self-discovery that the work brings to the consciousness of the interpreter. And the third stage is "making music together," as the interpreter and text intertwine in the act of performance. The first moment is primarily technical-practical, one in which the interpreter "opens" himself to the text. Interpretation at that moment is grounded in past training and practice. In this giving of oneself to the text, the interpreter becomes the instrument through which the text can speak again. Moreover, if it is true that the aim of interpretation is to understand and make something understood, namely, the language of the work of art in its intrinsic coherence and necessity, it is clear that such language is also a subjective language, beyond the simple technical and practical level. Thus, while technique begins as an instrumental extrinsic activity, one separated from the personality of the interpreter, in its opening to the text the performance becomes part of the text, bringing into it also the personality of the interpreter. Thus, in this contrary movement of text as understood by the interpreter, the text becomes part of him, as a dimension of his own self-knowledge, and it is through such a process that the interpreter and the text finally merge in action, in performance.

The General Project of the Interpreter

For Betti, in general, the activity of interpretation occurs when there is a break in the understanding that goes on in the process of communication. Interpretation serves as a corrective that provides for continuation of the communicative process. Interpretation is seen as a stepping stone toward reaching an understanding; the interpretive process thus aims at a higher level of comprehension, which attempts to capture the object in its complex field of meaning. This interpretive process, however, is not singular, but includes a number of dimensions, all of which warrant the practitioner's attention:

1. the elementary data of the interpretive process, such as the relationship between speaker and listener in an oral or written discourse
2. the actuality of speech and the objectivity of language, which calls for an analysis of the problem of the relationship between language and discourse
3. the question of the genesis of error and misunderstanding, two crucial instances of a break in communication
4. the premises referring to the requirement of the identity of signs among cocommunicators

5. the question of surrogates of the interpretive process present in mass society
6. the problem of artificial languages, which are ostensively developed to "solve" the question of ambiguity of meaning
7. the clarification of the notions of interpretation and understanding
8. the clarification of action and event in the process of communication, in particular taking the context of discourse as a totality
9. the understanding of meaning and its synthesis in knowledge through a phenomenological analysis of the predicative function of judgment and linguistic expression
10. the role of affective functioning (empathy) in recollection and its place as preparatory or integrative regarding the requirements of recognition or reproduction

In order to adequately fulfill the demands of the hermeneutic canon, any interpreter, at any time, must be cognizant of these preliminary mandates. It thus appears that Betti's interpretive project involves a psychological dimension, a cultivation of interior sensitivities, which one might indeed expect from its genesis in the work of Dilthey. Betti's agenda, however, also led him to Kant and the possibility of transcendentalism in interpretation. Dilthey worked on the problem of trying to identify fundamental categories of historical interpretive reason, but his appeal to a descriptive psychology grounded on empathy meant that the activity of interpretation remained historically variable. Betti sought a form of transcendental hermeneutics that held true across time and space, and thus was truly "canonical." The appeal to Kant accomplished part of his aim, in that he was able to develop a transcendental position, but the consequence of that position, as revealed earlier, becomes a dichotomy of science and life-world, of technique and emotion. Betti thus is led to formulate a hermeneutics along Platonic lines, citing the possiblilty of a realm of unending meanings from which the creator of the text receives her or his inspiration. What one wishes for in Betti's work is a critical dimension, one that investigates the structures of power and demand that link the text and its interpreter, a position that will be explored by Adorno and Habermas in successive chapters.

6

Humanist Interpretation: Hans-Georg Gadamer

Hans-Georg Gadamer was born in 1900 in Marburg, Germany, and studied philology, history of art, and philosophy at the Universities of Breslau, Marburg, and Munich. While at Marburg, he studied with Paul Natorp until graduating in 1922. At that time, Gadamer directed his attention to classical philology and became widely recognized for his contributions to the field. In 1929 he began his association with Martin Heidegger, with whom he shared a relationship as both student and colleague. In 1939 Gadamer was appointed Professor of Philosophy at Leipzig, where he also served as rector of the university from 1946 to 1947. He then moved to Frankfurt, where he taught from 1947 to 1949, at which time he went to the University of Heidelberg as the hand-picked successor to Karl Jaspers. Currently he is Professor Emeritus at Heidelberg.

Gadamer's scholarly production has been extensive and well regarded, consisting of numerous articles, books, and monographs. His best-known works are *Truth and Method* (English version, 1975a) and *Philosophical Hermeneutics* (English version, 1976). While he finds the basic tenets of traditional hermeneutics acceptable, Gadamer chooses a different starting point for his own inquiry. He writes in *Truth and Method:*

My real concern is . . . not what we do or what we ought to do, but what happens to us over and above our wanting and doing (Gadamer 1975a, xvi).

Later, he further defines his position:

My purpose is not to offer a general theory of interpretation and a differential account of its methods . . . but to discover what is common to

---

1. In this chapter, we shall use a terminological distinction that has become customary for readers in the Heideggerian tradition. The term "Being" will refer to the ontological dimension of human existence, while "being" will refer to the everyday, or ontic, level of lived experience. The term "Dasein," while used infrequently, will refer to the essential character of the individual human being as "being-there."

all modes of understanding and to know that understanding is never subjective behavior toward a given "object" but toward its effective history
— the history of its influence: in other words, understanding belongs to
the being of that which is understood (Gadamer 1975a, xix).

From this, one may conclude that Gadamer is not concerned with methodological questions pertaining to scientific understanding, as we find in Schleiermacher and Betti. Neither is Gadamer concerned with the kind of hermeneutics found in the *Geisteswissenschaften*. Indeed, he suggests that these arguments
have distorted the phenomenon of the universality of hermeneutics by focusing on the methodological aspects of the broader processes of understanding.
By attending exclusively to questions of interpretive methodology, one loses
track of the understanding that occurs everywhere in human life, including domains beyond inspection and scientific self-control. Like Heidegger, Gadamer
would have us deal with the ontological rather than the methodological in order
to examine what are, at least for him, the more important questions.

Gadamer's primary contribution to hermeneutic theory is his attempt to
shift the focus of discussion away from the methodology of understanding to a
clarification of understanding itself. *Truth and Method* shows how a method for
understanding that assumes self-conscious reflection can evolve (or be transcended) into a clarification of meaning. This clarification is by nature episodic
(the interpretation is an event in itself) and transsubjective (e.g., the mediation
and transformation of the present and the past are not under the control of the
actor). This is the fundamental difference between Gadamer and other hermeneutic theoreticians. Where others stress the examination of the phenomenon,
Gadamer examines the process as well. In this way we can note that for Gadamer,
"hermeneutics no longer means to provide rules for understanding, but to lay
bare the ontological structure of the process of understanding, specifically the
understanding of tradition" (Hogan 1989, 4). Gadamer provides a systematic account of philosophical hermeneutics, aimed at ontology, so that a clarification
can go beyond art and textual exegesis and toward aesthetics and history. Such
a transition would provide a foundation for truly sociological interpretation.

The more important and innovative aspects of Gadamer's work include
his extended discussions of the hermeneutic circle, the principle of effective
history, the conceptions of tradition and prejudice, and notion of the fusion of
horizons. It is these concepts, and others used in association with them, that
provide the foundation of Gadamer's hermeneutics. And it is to these basic
characteristics of Gadamer's project that we now turn.

Gadamer's Hermeneutics and Interpretive Sociology

A good deal of the ferment in contemporary sociology focuses upon
the various critiques of positivist sociology. From the point of view of neo-

Marxism and radical sociology, the separation of subject and object, especially as embodied in a detached, value-free scientific stance, is ethically untenable. It disengages the observer from the social responsibility that should accompany his accounts, and it results in the status quo being presented as somehow natural and real, rather than as constructed and partisan. From the perspective of symbolic interactionism, the positivist quest for regularities among variables erroneously depicts society insofar as it fails to accurately portray interaction and the indeterminateness of the outcomes of interaction. Positivism leaves the human element out of the investigation and is especially forgetful of that element's subjective components. From the perspective of phenomenology, the positivist separation of subject and object fails to ground knowledge in experience because experience occurs in the relationship between subject and object rather than in the object itself (see *inter alia* Blumer 1969 or Husserl 1970 for arguments on this point).

While these critiques are well-founded, they have failed to produce alternative sociologies with any degree of consistency. Neo-Marxist accounts distinctively focus upon class, conflict, and ideology, but they do not always use these categories in a nonpositivist manner. Symbolic interactionist accounts often have the aspect of a qualitative positivism, and some versions lose sight of interaction in a quasi-structuralist situational determinism. Even phenomenology has at times been applied as a positivist account of ethnoknowledge. The problem in all three cases is that nonpositivist traditions are being employed in a positivist problematic of rendering accounts of an object-world. Such work, of course, is self-defeating.

Despite the evolution of alternative theoretical approaches witnessed in recent sociology, there remains a depressing unity in the work that sociologists do. Few people still advocate macrofunctionalism, which once provided such unity, and no other theoretical approach has achieved a hegemony among theoreticians. Hence the sameness of sociological research cannot be explained by a sameness of theoretical conceptualizations. Indeed, one might argue that the irrelevance of much past theory for researchers has left the latter in a state of affairs wherein they have to rely upon something other than theory to provide an implicit paradigm for their work.

Consider the tendency of Marxism to degenerate into positivistic studies of stratification, of phenomenology to turn into "dust bowl empiricism" of a qualitative variety, and of symbolic interactionism to degenerate into curious ethnography. The problem seems to be that these three fine theoretical traditions have been subjected to a positivistic, empiricist, verificationist problematic. While they focus on interesting matters — class consciousness, dialectics, structures of awareness, processes of definition, and the like — they are forced into the introductory methods of science, into the "I told you so," hypothesis-testing version of the philosophy of science.

Thus, the human concerns that truly matter, the concerns that inform observables, the concerns around which the social world is structured, are ignored, while a game of prediction-and-observation provides its hypnotic distraction. The sociologist becomes a little child watching a puppet show, not inquiring about who is pulling the strings and, more importantly, for what reason.

The hermeneutics of Gadamer provides us with a fresh opportunity in sociology, precisely because it is not another theoretical tradition, which can be subjected to verificationist trivialization. To see hermeneutics as theory is to misconstrue it. Instead, hermeneutics is comprised of three related problematics, each of which is compatible with and useful for a variety of theoretical traditions. In fact, Gadamer developed his thought under such diverse influences as existentialism, dialectics, and the array of interpretive disciplines (the *Geisteswissenschaften)* present in Germany in the early decades of the twentieth century. Approaching sociology as a hermeneutic enterprise yields an array of problematics that open up the sectarian lines of scholarly traditions (cf. Blasi, Dasilva, and Weigert 1978, Habermas 1973, Radnitsky 1973).

The first problematic that Gadamer addresses is "understanding," or the process of establishing the meaning of a text. For the scientist this entails an Ego-to-text relationship. Understanding is never complete, in the sense that it cannot stand alone, for a knowledge that ignores the context in which a meaningful text comes to life and that ignores actions implied by the meaning of the text is not adequate knowledge of meaning. Understanding that does not go beyond mere understanding is not, paradoxically, understanding at all. Thus, Gadamer goes on to consider two issues: interpretation, or uncovering the contextual relevances of a text, and application, or the use of the text as a precedent. Interpretation focuses on the relationship between an environment and a text; the concern is no longer a simple Ego-to-text relation. Application thus proceeds from text to action.

An example can be given from the domain of aesthetic appreciation. This form of hermeneutic experience exists in contradistinction to the form of hermeneutic experience central to the social sciences. Gadamer describes those aspects of aesthetic appreciation that are central to it *qua* hermeneutic experience in order to draw a parallel with what he proposes for the human sciences. Like Betti in the previous chapter, and following an inquiry similar to one of Adorno's, Gadamer sees the role of the social scientist as parallel to that of the artistic performer who does justice to a text by mediating it through his or her own being and expressive activity.

A work of art is understood in terms of commonalities found both in the world of the original creator and in that of the appreciator. The sharing of commonalities is explained by the force of tradition. Thus, understanding a poem may require calling to mind an image that had meaning both in the epoch of composition and in the epoch of appreciation. This is not to be taken in some internal, psychological sense, but in terms of the simple cultural meaning. The

Occidental tradition, for example, may prevent a modern critic from understanding a poem by Sappho. It is important to realize that there are true and false understandings; the poem may call to mind one image and not another. Appropriate understanding cannot be arbitrarily set by an individual through an act of will. This, though, does not deny the possibility of purely subjective experiences occasioned by the text, either on the part of the creator or that of the reader. However, the meaning of the text resides in the reading and not in any purely private state of mind. Thus, understanding is not a matter of intuition or of duplicating the mental state of the creator, but of seeing what anyone standing within the tradition can see. The creator may have failed to carry out his or her intent or may have inadvertently produced something more or less than what was intended.

Interpretation goes beyond what the text says, through analyses of the text's grammar, the historical situation that contributed to its materials, the occasional situation that may give it a symbolic or memorial value beyond its meaning, and so on. A musicologist, for instance, may interpret a work in terms of its idiom or style, its place in the composer's career, etc. Such factors do not comprise the meaning of the text but certainly help comprise the text itself. A knowledge of such factors obviously enriches the aesthetic experience.

The notion of application pertains to changes suggested by the text for the appreciator. Gadamer refers to it in a discussion of law and morality rather than aesthetics, but clearly applications can and do occur in the fine arts. Hearing a musical work or watching a drama alters the expectations that the appreciator brings to other texts and even to second or third experiences of the same text. The experience may even have an impact on future creative activity, as in the case wherein a writer's style has been influenced by an exposure to the work of some other literary figure.

The experience of a work of art, be it understanding, interpretation, or application, involves a complicated relativity. The creation of the work is wrapped up in the prevailing cultural and situational context of the time and setting of the creative activity. The reader of any work is wrapped up in the prevailing culture and situational context of his or her own biography. In the case of the hermeneutic experience, the "wrapping" is unique to the experience itself, comprising a unique juxtaposition of the two contexts, thereby constituting a conjunctural context that will not be exactly duplicated again. Each hermeneutic experience thus speaks to a larger whole of an entirely occasional nature. One's first hearing of "La Donna è Mobile," for example, is unlike any later hearing, and one's own hearing will be contextually different from that of someone whose life entails different musical expectations and whose biography contains different musical experiences. This relative or conjunctural context is particularly important in music, dance, and drama, where it is embodied in a separate performance role but is, of course, coextensive with social action, in which different actors follow similar norms, i.e., scripts.

It is worthwhile pausing a moment to consider the dialectical nature of Gadamer's conceptualization of such aesthetic events. The hermeneutic experience that he describes resides in the interchange between text and reader (to use literary terms in a synecdoche for wider categories) but not in any long-term fashion as attributes of either the text or of the reader. This is particularly true of understanding, and also true of interpretation and application, to the extent that they have no sense apart from understanding.

This dialectical dimension of the hermeneutic experience gives it a peculiar ontological status. Gadamer likens it to play. In play there is a repetitive to-and-fro process in which the individual loses himself. There is a "truth" in the demands of play that is semiautonomous from the ontological reality of the player. "This gives the full meaning to what we call transformation into a structure. The transformation is a transformation into the true" (Gadamer 1975a, 101). In the case of the hermeneutic experience, there is a second presenting of a meaning, a second presenting that is a true process, in itself, and that stands in a dialectical tension with the unchanging aspects of that which is being interpreted. A text has some permanent features that endure many readings, but these meanings obtain only in the process of being read. In the later sections of *Truth and Method,* Gadamer takes this to be the ground of the eternal philosophical problem of the one and the many.

Prejudices and the Moments of Hermeneutic Inquiry

The hermeneutic project for understanding, as developed by Gadamer, can be succinctly conceptualized as a single unified process involving three interrelated and mutually dependent moments of analysis. As previously indicated, they are interpretation, understanding, and application. We now turn to the character of the structural nature of these moments in order to demonstrate how historical foremeanings (in Gadamer's terminology, "prejudices") are a central element in each moment. It is possible to do this by examining the three moments and then by directing attention to Gadamer's notion of prejudice and its relationship to hermeneutic understanding.

Traditional hermeneutics, according to Gadamer (1975a, 274–76) regarded the act of understanding as basically a two-step process. From this early position, hermeneutics was viewed as encompassing an understanding dimension *(subtilitas intelligendi)* and an interpretation dimension *(subtilitas explicandi).* Later, with the rise of Pietism, another dimension was added to the notion of hermeneutic understanding, namely, application *(subtilitas applicandi).* In both of these historical instances, however, hermeneutics was viewed as divided into different phases. Gadamer, on the other hand, argues that interpretation, understanding, and application were all part of hermeneutic understanding, but that they are inseparable moments and not distinct phases. Building upon and beginning with the phenomenological hermeneutics of Martin Heidegger, Gadamer's central concern was with establishing these unified moments as "existentials" in an ontological mode of inquiry. His position, like that of Heidegger, was to reject any notion of hermeneutics that began with the assumption that hermeneutics is, or could be, an ontic inquiry (Gelven 1970, 19–24).

Gadamer's rejection of the notion of separate categories of analysis must be considered as a theoretically significant event in at least two respects. First, it was Gadamer's position that hermeneutics was not, nor should it be, concerned with augmenting any "ontic" inquiry, a decision that denies the possibility of assigning hermeneutics to any special discipline. Furthermore, he argues that the factual and truth claims of ontic inquiry are in diametric opposition to the claims of ontological hermeneutics. The theoretical integration of these three moments was, therefore, designed to negate any tendency to posit hermeneutics as yet another "scientific" methodology or technique that could address a level of social existence that previous disciplinary approaches had failed to comprehend. Second, by maintaining that interpretation, understanding, and application were moments in a single unified act of hermeneutic understanding, it was possible for Gadamer to argue that no moment was more important theoretically or methodologically than any other moment. Furthermore, it was possible then for Gadamer to posit each moment as an ontological level of inquiry, as essential in explicating and disclosing the world of being (or, in other words, as the life-world of the human being as a historical world, rooted in the commonalities lent history by tradition).

It should be noted here that Gadamer's hermeneutics, in keeping with the tradition of ontological hermeneutics established by Heidegger, takes Being (Sein), and not an object or thing, as its target of inquiry. Therefore, while ontic forms of inquiry have historically sought to distinguish between cognitive, normative, and reproductive dimensions and kinds of understanding, as with Emilio Betti, Gadamer's hermeneutics makes no such distinction. Instead, Gadamer maintains that these and similar categorical distinctions are nonsensical, serving little purpose in elucidating the act of hermeneutic understanding which is grounded in Being itself (Gadamer 1975a, 276–77).

For the most part, hermeneutics as practiced prior to Gadamer, and here one must include even the hermeneutics of some of Gadamer's contemporaries (i.e., E. D. Hirsch, Jr.), focused on the problem of attaining "truthful" interpretations of historical and classical texts. However, as Hoy notes, Gadamer's hermeneutic selected a radically different objective:

Traditional hermeneutics from Schleiermacher to Hirsch is concerned with the knowing relation, and specifically with the problems of preventing misunderstanding of texts. The task of Gadamer's ontological hermeneutics is more fundamental in that it raises questions about the very possibility of coming to understand at all (Hoy 1978, 47).

Gadamer's primary concern is not with establishing factual interpretation (although he has indeed published a number of substantive works of interpretation) or with reducing interpretive results to the status of facts or factual claims. Furthermore, Gadamer is not particularly concerned with the methodological issues underlying truth and validity (that is, truth and validity in the ontic sense of essential categories of reality; it certainly is possible to consider them along the lines of existentials such as "care" and "fall," etc.). Gadamer's objective is to render the hermeneutic act of understanding as something more than simply the process of culling and gleaning systematically correct information from a text. Instead, the act of hermeneutic understanding must produce "knowledge" that has a value (i.e., a use-value) for the interpreter, which is in part predicated upon previous acts of understanding. Moreover, and this point will be made more clear below, Gadamer does not necessarily want to delimit his hermeneutics to textual analysis.

The process of attaining hermeneutic understanding is possible only to the extent that the interpreter can base the interpretation on her previous knowledge or misunderstanding. This, then, is the famous notion of the "hermeneutic circle." Interpretation is a historical act, or process, that takes previous understandings and the social meanings derived from them in order to achieve a new understanding, that is, an understanding generated through their application. This new understanding, coupled with the understandings (now modified) that predate it, then provide the foundation for even further acts of interpretation. Understanding, accordingly, is specifically set in the situation of interpretation and is therefore inseparable from interpretation. Gadamer contends, however, that understanding is not to be thought of as an exclusively subjective process or act:

> Understanding is not to be thought so much as an action of one's subjectivity, but as the placing of oneself within a process of tradition, in which past and present are constantly fused. This is what must be expressed in hermeneutical theory, which is far too dominated by the idea of a process, a method (Gadamer 1975a, 258).

Gadamer does not end his notion of hermeneutic understanding with the idea of a dialectical interplay between interpretation and understanding, however. Rather, he goes on to integrate the third moment of "application" into the theory. In many ways, it is almost impossible to even crudely differentiate what Gadamer has to say about the moment of understanding from those comments he offers regarding application. In point of fact, the two moments are so closely related that they are not only inseparable, the point that Gadamer wants to make, but also that they actually *appear* identical. There is a subtle distinction that Gadamer makes between the two moments, which is very important for the act of hermeneutic understanding. Application refers to the utilization of understanding for the purpose of reflection upon the experience and the world of the interpreter. In this sense, application is the understanding induced through the generation of self-consciousness, the establishment of new thoughts, new ways to think, and new lines of inquiry. Application, then, is the act of hermeneutic understanding that through the moment of understanding generates self-clarification for the interpreter. In other words, application is the act of increasing the interpreter's consciousness of Being. Gadamer does not intend to imply that the interpreter can ever achieve "full consciousness," as did Hegel, since that would, in essence, short-circuit the hermeneutic process. Application, then, is a continuous dynamic that flows from interpretation and understanding.

In another vein, Gadamer sometimes uses the notion of application in a manner that makes it almost a form of mediation between the moments of interpretation and understanding. Here it is instructive to recall that Gadamer maintains that interpretation is directed at tradition, i.e., at the world. Tradition, furthermore, is not an entity that has set horizons or boundaries that an interpreter can ascertain once and for all. It is not something that the interpreter experiences once, and then through that experience comes to "understand" in the sense of comprehending a totality. For Gadamer, understanding is experience. Understanding is a continual process or series of acts. The impact of tradition is constant throughout all acts of understanding; its importance for the interpreter is never-ending. Thus, application is the dialogue with tradition such that the value is given to understanding by letting tradition "speak" to the interpreter through the interpretation. This notion of application basically involves the idea of a fusion or meshing of the interpreter's situation with his tradition such that the commonalities between the two are allowed to surface. Application, therefore, is the action represented by grasping what is necessary and important to the particular situation of the interpreter and this situational relationship with the tradition.

It is the relationship of these three moments that gives Gadamer's hermeneutics its rather unique, and frequently misunderstood, position regarding truth. Gadamer does not intend to offer claims concerning the *factual* contents of either the interpreter's situation or its relationship to tradition (in a significant sense, one's interpretation speaks to one's own Being and as such is ontologically truthful; this is more important to consider than its status as ontically truthful). His hermeneutics is not a reconstruction or reproduction of the historical contents of tradition. Truth, for Gadamer, to the extent that one wants to argue its position of importance in his hermeneutics, is ushered into existence in the form of a dialogue with the interpreter's tradition. Truth is not, therefore, the imposition of the interpreter's meanings on an event or text. Nor is truth the process of systematically and objectively "letting" an event or text speak its own real truth content. These two conceptions of truth constitute subjective-relativism and absolute-relativism, both of which Gadamer wants to reject.

A good way to comprehend Gadamer's conception of truth is provided by Hoy (1978), in his comparison between psychoanalysis and Gadamer's hermeneutic. With psychoanalysis, the goal is not to discover what is objectively true for the client in terms of biographical development. Nor is the goal of psychoanalysis to let the client offer just any random account of his biography. Instead, the goal is to establish new openings in the realm of self and social perception whereby the client can expand upon existing alternatives and advance beyond any blockages that render self-understanding and further development unlikely. Thus, in both psychoanalysis and Gadamer's hermeneutics the truthfulness of understanding is related to its usefulness *for Being*. These are merged into a single necessary quality of understanding and cannot be evaluated independently. In both cases the understanding that is generated is necessarily incomplete, based, as they are, not upon a sense of verification (again, an ontic form of inquiry), but upon a sense of situational validity, which thus implies a dynamic process.

The Idea of Effective History

A fundamental ground of Gadamer's critique of positivist hermeneutics stands upon his own hermeneutic reconstruction of the surrounding historical situations that led to positivism. Another ground is his phenomenological analysis of the event of interpretation per se. In the latter, the concept of *Wirkungsgeschichte*, variously translated as "effective history," "operant history," or "effects history," becomes central to the critique (cf. Hoy 1978). Gadamer criticizes two alternative positivistic approaches as partial accounts of the hermeneutic experience. One of them treats the past as an object that can be classified into properties, while the other treats it as some radically other time, which contains values that the present can no longer share. Gadamer's analysis, under the influence of Heidegger, shows that neither of these conceptualizations can be completely tenable. We can review the details of the dimensions of the hermeneutic "event" in order to uncover the sociological implications of the alternative conceptions and to highlight the innovations introduced by Gadamer.

The most general outline of the hermeneutic event would begin with an Ego (engaged in hermeneutic activity) and foreaspects of that Ego, found in his consciousness — such as prejudices, extant definitions, etc. Ego is part of a collective process in the development of historical consciousness, and through this process Ego is immersed in the collective tradition. Ego in the hermeneutic activity is intentionally oriented toward a text *(latu sensu)*, in such a way that preexisting categories and grammars are founded upon the tradition. The text itself has foreaspects; that is, among other things, it contains a set of values, with historical sedimentations that have accrued through the historical permanence of the text as a significant entity in the collective historical movement of consciousness. The intentionality of Ego regarding the text is itself historical, and includes value components, since it questions the text in order to speak to us as an identifiable Ego.

The outline of the structure of the hermeneutic event as delineated allows a conceptualization in which the terms of the structure can be viewed in the classical model of "subject-object" relations. It is in the critique of this structure of the event that Gadamer introduces significant modifications. These modifications are rooted in existential and phenomenological critiques of the history of modern Western thought. On the one hand, one can aim at positivist accounts of natural events, and quite possibly of history. As argued by Kierkegaard, such accounts have their interest, but they are also abstract and constitute "approximate knowledge" at best. The positivist orientation casts the knowing-event as a dynamic moving "from the things over the person to the things" and is able to secure the kind of objectivity appropriate to these disciplines.

In this situation, the classical framework of "subject-object" relations is transformed into "object-subject-object" relations. In such an account of the situation, we thus find a priority of the "object," which is the initial point of the process and which calls for the interest of a "subject" that will consider it. From this confrontation, explanations are constructed and are reimposed on the object again. When this structure is imposed on the interpretive event, the text becomes objectified, and the situation can be conceived in naturalistic (i.e., positivistic) terms, and so the process of knowing intrinsic to the natural approach can be transferred into and can dominate the hermeneutic activity. In other words, the past, as crystallized or objectified in the text, can be manipulated and technically acted upon following procedures similar to the methodology of the positive sciences.

Moreover, the text viewed as an object can also receive a status similar to that of other natural objects, which underlies the radical separation between its character and that of the analyzing subject. This separation, in turn, magnifies the gulf of history separating the subject and object. Gadamer reevaluates the structure of the hermeneutic event not as one of subject-object relations, but rather as a process that goes "from the person over things to the person," to recast Kierkegaard's phrase. This approach emphasizes the authenticity of the personal life enmeshed in the event. It is exactly in this reformulation that Heidegger's influence on Gadamer is crucial. Among the concepts developed by Gadamer under this influence is that of "effective history" and the key role it plays in the hermeneutic event.

As with Heidegger, what we find in Gadamer's approach is an account of the nature of the hermeneutic event from the standpoint of the person. This standpoint is not static, but involves a movement from the person outward to the text and back again. What we find in Heidegger is an account of existential events in which things and persons become blurred and existences themselves become fluid, intermingling and interpenetrating each other. Thus, for example, Heidegger gives a characteristic definition of a hammer, not in terms of wood and steel, but in terms of its nature as a tool, its relation to human purpose. One of his descriptions for that type of existence is that of "being-ready-to-hand" *(zuhandenheit)*. Or, in general, "the tool, related to other tools in an elaborate system of regular, serviceable, but modified relations, is the typical thing or object in the world. . . . This is the primitive meaning of objects or things, and remains their fundamental concrete meaning . . . they are constituted by their relations to other things in the world and to an existent of the nature of Dasein" (Blackham 1952, 89–90). Thus, by appealing to Heidegger's conception, Gadamer reformulates the description of the hermeneutic event to shift it from a frame of "subject-object" relations into one of "I-Thou," in which the text becomes a mediative component.

From the side of the I as being-in-the-world, the interpreter must be understood as the being with a realized selection of possibilities in her past, and a realizable selection of possibilities in her future. Moreover, this existential process of realized and realizable possibilities occurs fundamentally in-the-world, with other subjects (Heidegger's *Mitman)*. Two consequences are immediate from Gadamer's formulation. First, the actuality of being in any present is a result of the effective selection of possibilities made in the past, so that one could say that one's present existence is a result of the effective history of the selection of possibilities that came about in the various contexts of one's human existence. Second, each situation in the ongoing process of existence represents the convergence of possibilities open for effective selection by the subject. The situation is a horizon that delimits fields of possibilities; and the subject moves with other subjects and related objects from horizon to horizon.

Furthermore, much of the same can be said about the object, which is in the narrow sense a text. At its place of historical origin, it was the result of effective selections of its author, also a being-in-the-world, with the same fundamental attributes of being as the subject-interpreter. Later, as the text travels through time, it becomes a process of relations to other things in the world and to other subjects. In this case, the process of historical sedimentation surrounding the text can be seen as depositions of usages (which include interpretations) that the text receives as a part of the horizons of subjects-in-the-world in their histories of selections of possibilities. This reinterpretation of the hermeneutic event yields two significant results.

First, the position of the interpreter is reinstated as crucial to the development of any hermeneutic activity, and the interpreter is viewed in active, existential interaction with the text. Second, the text itself comes to be understood not as a crystallized, static thing, but rather, at any given moment, as a selection of possibilities delimited by the present horizon, including the horizon of the interpreter and the text in a human community, and by the horizon of similar constitutions that make up its transit through time.

One of the more interesting outcomes of Gadamer's hermeneutics is the disappearance of the individual from philosophical hermeneutics. By virtue of the phenomenological-existential analysis of the Heideggerian orientation, the earlier monadic character of the individual is dissolved into his situations, events, and the life-world. Such a reformulation of life processes, inasmuch as it relates to similar reformulations from Habermas (in his critique of advanced capitalism) and Foucault (identifying a possible transitional moment in the transformation of the present episteme developed in the nineteenth century), might be one of the most fundamental issues that, willing or not, Gadamer has brought to philosophical hermeneutics.

Belongingness-Correspondence

The analysis of this issue in the hermeneutics of Gadamer emerges from the Heideggerian conception of the relationship between Being and its objects. Thus, as objects in general are conceived as being-ready-to-hand, the relationship of the interpreter to the text is expressed by the conception of the ways in which the interpreter *belongs* to the text. Viewed from this perspective, the existential linkage between subject and text is placed within the context of tradition and history and in the frame of the effective history of the subject, where the text becomes a constitutive dimension of the being of the subject.

The character of this belongingness is based on the linguistically constituted experience of the world by the subject. An inspection of the problematic surrounding belongingness discloses that in metaphysics, for instance, the term refers to the transcendental relationship between being and truth. In that case, truth is an element of being itself, and not an attitude of the subject. The identification of knowledge as a constitutional aspect of being is fundamental to all classical and medieval thought. Conceived in this fashion, the question of truth is transformed into an existentialia, with the focus on its nature as it is present before the mind. In such a conception, thought does not start from the idea of a subject that exists in its own right and makes everything else an object. On the contrary, cognition is an aspect of true being, and truth belongs to the same sphere of being as the Idea. To such thinking there is no question of a self-conscious spirit without a world, which then must find its ways to worldly being. Both belong originally to one another, and thus the relationship is primary.

In modern science this metaphysical conception of the way in which the knowing subject is adequate to the object of knowledge is without justification. Science's methodological ideal ensures for every one of its stages a return to the elements from which its knowledge is built, while the teleological units of significance of the types "thing" or "organic whole" lose their justification. As a consequence, the critique and reformulation of such conceptions in modern thought has dissolved the old association between humans and the world.

Nevertheless, modern science has never entirely denied such classical traditions, however much it has become critical and analytical. And, philosophical hermeneutics leads back to the classical formulations. Classical thought did not seek to base the objectivity of knowledge on subjectivity, but rather always saw knowledge as an element of being itself. This classical model is taken over in the modern period by Hegel. Both his dialectic of the determinations of thought and his dialectic of the forms of knowledge explicitly repeat the total mediation between thought and being that was formerly the natural element of classical thought. Thus, hermeneutic theory seeks to show the interconnection of event and understanding.

If we consider the concept of belongingness as a character of the relationship between subject and object and then draw the parallel with the classical framework, it must be noted that we are not simply renewing the classical conceptions regarding the intelligibility of being, nor are we merely transferring the classical notion to the modern world. Such a re-elaboration would be tolerated by neither the experiential standpoint of modern science nor the critique raised by Kant. Instead, a reformulation can be accomplished through the perspective of existential hermeneutics, which admits an internal necessity of the thing itself, while at the same time going beyond the idea of the object and the objectivity of understanding, toward the idea of the coordination of subject and object.

From the perspective of language, the concept of belongingness between subject and object is no longer seen as the teleological relation of the mind to the ontological structure of extant being. A quite different problematic emerges from the fact that the hermeneutic experience is linguistic in nature, that there is a conversation between the tradition and its interpreter. The fundamental point in such a context is that something is happening. The mind of the interpreter is not in control of what words of the tradition reach him, nor can one suitably describe what happens as the progressing knowledge of what exists evolves. Seen from the point of view of the interpreter, "event" means that he does not, as a knower, seek his object, "discovering" by methodological means what was meant, and what the situation actually was. Such a conception would at best be simply an external aspect of the actual hermeneutic event. The actual event is made possible only because the word that has reached us through tradition, and to which we are to listen, really encounters us and does so in such a way that it addresses us and is concerned with us.

On the side of the object, the hermeneutic event means the coming into play, the working itself out, of the context of tradition in its constantly new possibilities of significance and resonance, newly extended by the other person receiving it. Inasmuch as the tradition is newly expressed in language, something comes into being that had not existed before and that exists from now on.

The idea of belongingness between subject and object must take into account the particular dialectic that is contained in hearing. It is not just that the person who hears is also addressed, but that there is also the element that the person who is addressed must hear, whether the person wants to or not. The primacy of hearing is the basis of the hermeneutic phenomenon (although

Jacques Derrida establishes the opposite position, but perhaps not in the context of hermeneutics). There is nothing that is not available to hearing through the medium of language. Hearing, then, is the fundamental expression of the linguistic experience of the world. The significance of this is not only that everything can be expressed in language, but rather that, in contrast with all other experiences of the world, language opens up a completely new dimension, the profound dimension by which tradition comes down to those now living.

Thus, the concept of the belongingness between subject and object is determined in a new way. We belong to elements in the tradition that reach us, and everyone who lives in a tradition must listen to what reaches her or him from that tradition. The truth of tradition is like the present that lies immediately open to the senses. This mode of being of tradition, though, is not sensible immediacy. It is language, and in interpreting its texts, the hearer who understands it relates its truth to the linguistic attitude she has toward the world. Linguistic communication between present and tradition is the event that takes place in all understanding. The hermeneutic experience must take as genuine experience everything that becomes present to it.

Furthermore, language is something other than a mere sign system used to denote the totality of objects. The world is not just a sign. In a manner that is difficult to grasp, the world is for the interpreter something akin to an image. We need think only of the other extreme possibility of a purely artificial language to see the relative justification of such an archaic theory of language. The word has a mysterious connection with what it represents, a quality of belonging to its being. This is meant in a fundamental way; it is not just that mimesis has a certain share in the creation of language, for no one denies this. However, language is too often taken to be something wholly detached from the considered object and to be, rather, an instrument of subjectivity. This is to follow a path of abstraction at the end of which stands the rational construction of an artificial language.

For Gadamer, this takes us away from the nature of language. Language and thinking about objects are so bound together that it is an abstraction to conceive of the system of truths as a pregiven system of possibilities of being, with which the signs at the disposal of the signifying subject are associated. A word is not a sign for which one reaches, nor is it a sign that one makes or gives to another. It is not an existent thing that one takes up and to which one accords the ideality of meaning in order to make something else visible through it. This is a mistake on both accounts. The ideality of meaning lies in the word itself; it is meaning-full already. But that does not imply, on the one hand, that the word preceeds all experience and simply joins up with an experience in an external way, by subjecting itself to it. The experience is not wordless to begin with, which then becomes an object of reflection by being named, or by being subsumed under the universality of the word. Instead, it is part of experience itself that it seeks and finds words that express it. One seeks for the right word, that is, for the word that really belongs to the object, so that in it the object comes into language. Even if one holds the view that this does not imply any simple copying, the word is still part of the object in that it is not simply alloted to the object as a sign.

The interpreter trying to understand a text in terms of the situation of its historical origin cannot disregard the continuance of its validity. It presents the interpreter with questions that must be asked of historical tradition. Inasmuch as the actual object of historical understanding is not merely a set of events but their significance, it is clearly not a correct description of this understanding to speak of an object existing in itself and of the approach of the subject to that object. The truth is that there is always contained in historical understanding the idea that the tradition reaching us peaks into the present and must be understood in this mediation, indeed as this mediation.

This is one of the fundamental conditions of understanding and belongs itself to tradition. The way in which the interpreter belongs to her text is like the way in which the vanishing point belongs to the perspective of a picture. It is a matter of looking for the vanishing point and adopting it as one's standpoint. The interpreter similarly finds her point of view already given and does not choose it arbitrarily. Thus, it is an essential condition of the possibility of hermeneutics that the rule system ordering the text is binding on all members of the community in the same way.

The meaning of the connection with tradition, in other words, the element of tradition in our historical, hermeneutical attitude, is fulfilled in the fact that we share fundamental prejudices with tradition. Hermeneutics must start from the position that a person seeking to understand something has a relation to the object that comes into language in the transmitted text, and has, or acquires, a connection with the tradition out of which the text speaks. On the other hand, hermeneutic consciousness is aware that it cannot be connected with this object in some self-evident, unquestioned way. There is a polarity of familiarity and strangeness on which hermeneutic work is based. This polarity is not to be considered psychologically, though, as a tension that conceals the mystery of individuality; rather, it must be considered as truly hermeneutic. That is, it has to be considered with regard to what has been said, the language in which the text addresses us, the story that it tells us. Here too there is a tension. The place between strangeness and familiarity that a transmitted text has for us is that intermediate place between being a historically intended, separate object and being part of a tradition. The true home of hermeneutics is in this intermediate area.

Because historical knowledge receives its justification from the forestructure of Dasein, there is nevertheless no reason for anyone to interfere with the immanent criteria of what is called knowledge. For Heidegger as well as Gadamer, historical knowledge is not a planning project, the extrapolation of aims at will, an ordering of things according to the wishes, the prejudices, or the promptings of the powerful; instead, it remains something adapted to the object, a *mesuratio ad rem*. This object is not a *factum brutum*, something that is merely at hand, something that can simply be established and measured, but it is itself, ultimately, of the essence of Dasein.

Furthermore, it is important to understand this often repeated statement correctly. It does not mean simply that there is a resemblance between the knower and what is known, on which it would be possible to base the special character of this psychic transposition as the "method" of the human sciences. This would make historical hermeneutics a branch of psychology, which was indeed the result of Dilthey's meditations. In fact, however, the coordination of all knowing activity with what is known is not based on the fact that they (knower and known) are essentially the same, but draws its significance from the peculiar nature of the mode of being common to both of them. Knowledge consists of the fact that neither the knower nor the known are present-at-hand in an "ontic" way but in a "historical" one; in other words, they are of the mode of being of historicality. Hence, everything depends on the generic difference between the ontic and the historical. The fact that a contrast can be made between "similarity" and "correspondence" reveals the problem that Heidegger was the first to develop in its full radicality. We study history only insofar as we are ourselves "historical," which means that the historicality of the human being in its expectancy and forgetting is the condition of our being able to represent the past. What appeared thus at first as a simple barrier that cut across the traditional concept of science and method, or a subjective condition of access to historical knowledge, now becomes the center of a fundamental inquiry. Correspondence is not a condition of the original meaning of historical interest because the choice of theme and inquiry is subjected to extrascientific, subjective motivations, in which case correspondence would be no more than special case of emotional dependence, of the same type as sympathy. Correspondence with traditions is an original and essential part of the historical finitude of Dasein, as its projectedness towards future possibilities of itself. Heidegger was correct to insist that what he called "thrownness" belongs together with that which is projected. Thus, there is no understanding or interpretation in which the totality of this existential structure does not function, even if the intention of the knower is simply to read "what is there" and to discover from sources "how it really was."

The correspondence between the interpreter and her object acquires a significance that is concretely demonstrable, and it is the task of hermeneutics to demonstrate it. That the structure of Dasein is thrown projection, that Dasein is, in the realization of its own being, understanding, must also be true of the act of understanding within the human sciences. The general structure of understanding acquires its concrete form in historical understanding, in that the commitments of customs and tradition, and the corresponding porentialities of one's own future, become effective in understanding itself. Dasein that projects itself in relation to its own potentialities-for-being has always "been." This is the meaning of the existential of "thrownness." The main point of the hermeneutics of facticity and its contrasts with the research into the constitution of the transcendental found in Husserl's phenomenology was that no freely chosen relation towards one's own being can go back beyond the facticity of this being. Everything that makes possible and limits the project of Dasein preceeds it absolutely. This existential structure of Dasein must find its expression in the understanding of historical tradition as well.

The Concept of Experience (Erlebnis)

The life-philosophy of our own day follows on its Romantic predecessors. The rejection of the mechanization of life in contemporary society puts such an obvious emphasis on the word "life" that its conceptual implications remain totally hidden. We must understand Dilthey's coining of the concept of experience (Erlebnis) in the light of the previous history of the word among the Romantics and remember that Dilthey was Schleiermacher's biographer. It is true that we do not yet find the word "Erlebnis" in Schleiermacher, nor even the word "erleben." But there is no lack of synonyms that cover the range of meaning of Erlebnis, and that background is always clearly in evidence.

Thus, both in Dilthey and in Husserl, in life-philosophy and in phenomenology, the idea of experience is primarily a purely epistemological one. It is used by them in its teleological meaning but is not conceptually determined. That it is life that manifests itself in experience means only that it is the ultimate to which we return. The history of the word provided a certain justification for this conceptual construction of performance. For we have seen that the word "experience" has a condensing, intensifying meaning. If something is called or considered an experience, its meaning collapses it into the unity of a significant whole. An experience is as much distinguished from other experiences, in which other things are experienced, as from the rest of life, in which "nothing" is experienced.

An experience is no longer just something that flows past quickly in the stream of consciousness; it is meant as a unity, and thus attains a new mode of being. Thus, it is quite understandable that the word emerges in biographical literature and ultimately stems from its use in autobiography. What can be called an experience establishes itself in memory, by which we mean the lasting meaning that an experience has for someone who has had it. This is the reason for talking about an intentional experience and the teleological structure of consciousness.

However, in the notion of experience there is also a contrast of life with mere concept. The experience has a definite immediacy that eludes every opinion about its meaning. Everything that is experienced is experienced by oneself, and it is part of its meaning that belongs to the unity of this self, and thus contains inalienable and irreplaceable relation to the whole of this one life. Thus, its being is not exhausted in what can be said of it, and what can be grasped as its meaning. The autobiographical or biographical reflection, in which its meaning is determined, remains fused with the whole movement of life and constantly accompanies it. It is practically the mode of being of experience to be so determinative that one is never finished with it. Experiences are not soon forgotten; it takes a long time to assimilate them, and this, rather than their content, is their real being and significance. What we emphatically call an experience thus means something unforgettable and irreplaceable, that is inexhaustible in terms of the understanding and determination of its meaning.

Considered philosophically, the ambiguity that we have noted in the concept of experience means that this concept is not wholly exhausted by its role of being the ultimate givenness and basis of all knowledge. There is something else quite different in the idea of "experience" that needs to be recognized and that reveals a set of problems that have still to be dealt with — its inner relation to life.

There were two starting points for this important theme of the relationship between life and experience. If one examines more precisely what is here called "life" and what part of it is active in the concept of experience, one sees that the relationship of life to experience is not that of a universal to a particular. Rather, the unity of experience determined by its intentional content stands in an immediate relationship to the whole, to the totality of life. It was primarily Georg Simmel who analyzed the idea of life in this regard as the "reaching out of life beyond itself," a version of the hermeneutic circle in which parts and whole constitute a mutual totality (Simmel 1918).

The representation of the whole in the experience of the moment obviously goes far beyond the fact of its being determined by its object. Simmel, who was largely responsible for the word "Erlebnis" becoming fashionable, sees the important thing about the concept of experience as being "that the objective does not only become, as in knowing, an image and idea, but an element in the life process itself." He even says that every experience has something about it of an adventure. But what is an adventure? It is by no means just an episode. Episodes are a succession of details that have no inner coherence and for that very reason have no permanent significance. An adventure, however, interrupts the customary course of events but is positively and significantly related to the context that it interrupts. Thus an adventure lets life become felt as a whole in its breadth and in its strength. Here lies the fascination of an adventure. It removes the conditions and obligations of everyday life; it ventures out into the uncertain. But at the same time, it knows that, as an adventure, it has an exceptional character and thus remains related to the return of the everyday, into which the adventure cannot be taken. Thus, the adventure is "passed through," like a test, from which one emerges enriched and more mature.

There is an element of this, in fact, in every experience. They (experiences) are taken out of the continuity of life and at the same time are related to the whole of one's life. It is not simply that it remains a living experience only until it is fully integrated into the context of one's life-consciousness, but the very way in which it is preserved through its being worked into the whole of life-consciousness goes far beyond the "significance" it might be thought of having. Because it is itself within the whole of life, in it too the whole of life is present.

Dilthey most directly confronted the question of how historical experience takes place, with a view toward establishing the scientific foundations of the cultural-historical sciences. Thus, in a clear analogy with the program of Kant, he sought to discover the categories of the historical world that would be able to support its construction within the human sciences. Dilthey is critically important here because he does not forget that experience in life is something quite different from what it is in the investigation of nature. In the latter, verifiable discoveries arising from experience are all that matter; in other words, that which detaches itself from the experience of the individual and constitutes part of the reliable stock of experiential knowledge is valued. The categorical analysis of this "object of knowledge" had been, for the neo-Kantians, the positive achievement of transcendental philosophy.

Simply to adapt the construction and apply it to the field of historical knowledge, as neo-Kantians did in the philosophy of value, was for Dilthey an inadequate solution. He considered the critical philosophy of neo-Kantianism as itself dogmatic. For the structure of the historical world is not based on facts taken from experience that then acquires a value-relation, but rather on the inner historicity that belongs to experience itself. It is a living historical process, and its paradigm is not the discovery of facts, but that strange fusion of memory and expectation into a whole that we name experience and that we acquire through experience. It is, in particular, the suffering and instruction given by the painful experience of reality to the person who is growing in insight that preshapes the mode of knowing of the historical sciences. They only continue what has already been thought in the experiences of life.

Thus, the epistemological question here has another starting point. In some ways its task is easier. It does not need to inquire into the grounds of the possibility of the fact that our ideas are in agreement with the "external world." For the historical world, the knowledge of which we are concerned with here, is always a world that is constituted and formed by the human mind. For this reason Dilthey does not regard the general synthetic judgments of history as any problem, a notion with which Vico agrees in *Scencia Nuova*. We can recall that, in reaction to Cartesian doubt and the certainty of the mathematical knowledge of nature based on it, Vico asserted the epistemological primacy of the human-made historical world. Dilthey repeats the same argument and writes: "The first condition of possibility of a science of history is that I myself am an historical being, that the man who is studying history is the man who is making history" (Dilthey 1976, 183). It is the homogeneity of subject and object that makes historical knowledge possible.

This, however, is no solution to the epistemological problem that Dilthey posed. Rather, this condition of homogeneity contains the real epistemological problem of history. The question is how the experience of the individual and the knowledge of it comes to be historical experience. In history we are no longer concerned with connected wholes that are experienced as such by the individual or that are reexperienced as such by others. Dilthey's argument applies only to the experiences and reexperiencing done by the individual, and his is the starting point for his epistemological theory. Dilthey elaborates the way in which the individual acquires a continuity of life in order to obtain the constitutive concepts to support at the same time historical continuity and the knowledge of it.

Unlike the categories for the study of nature, these concepts are drawn from life. For Dilthey the ultimate presuppositon for knowledge of the historical world, in which the identity between consciousness and object is still demonstrable reality, is experience. This is where immediate certitude is to be found, for experience is no longer divided into an act, or a becoming conscious, and a content, or that of which one is conscious. It is rather indivisible consciousness. Even to say that in experience something is possessed is to make too great a division. Dilthey then investigated how continuity is created from the elements of the world of the mind that are immediately certain and how the knowledge of this continuity is possible.

The self-evident starting point for Dilthey's analysis is that it is life itself that unfolds and forms itself in intelligible units, and it is in terms of the single individual that these units are understood. The continuity of life as it appears to the individual (and is reexperienced and understood by others through biographical knowledge) is created through the significance of particular experiences. Around them, as around organizing centers, the unity of life is created. Like the continuity of a text, the structural continuity of life is determined by a relation between the whole and the parts. Every part expresses something of the whole life and has significance for the whole, just as its own significance is determined by the whole. This is the old hermeneutic principle of textual interpretation, which can be applied to the continuity of life inasmuch as this assumes the unity of a significance that is expressed in all its parts.

The important step for Dilthey's epistemological groundwork for the human sciences is the transition from the structure of continuity in the experience of an individual life to historical continuity, which is not experienced by any individual at all. For that transition it becomes necessary to replace "real subjects" with "logical subjects." Dilthey considers that it is permissible to make this transition on the basis of an existing similarity between individuals that share the communalities of the same historical context, which thus becomes to a large extent a common spiritual reality that can be recognized as such. The crucial question nevertheless becomes how statements about such a collective reality can be justified epistemologically. Gadamer provides some illumination here.

Gadamer, among others, argues that Dilthey never reached complete clarity in his formulations on this point, one that fundamentally refers to the transition from a psychological (i.e., individual cases) to a hermeneutics (i.e., the collective history) that would ground the human sciences. Gadamer sees that it is significant that from the start, Dilthey's efforts were directed toward separating the relationships of the historical world from the causal relationships of the natural order, and so the concepts of understanding and expression were always central to him. Such a separation could prove problematic, since it would lead to a bifurcation not only of experience, but also of consciousness. In order to avoid this, we may turn to another influence on Gadamer's work — Edmund Husserl.

Dilthey's concept of the structural quality of the life of the spirit corresponds to the theory of the intentionality of consciousness introduced in Husserl's *Logical Investigations,* in that it is not merely psychological fact but the phenomenological description of an essential determination of consciousness. Every consciousness is consciousness *of* something; every relation is a relation *to* something. The correlative of this intentionality, the intentional object, is not, according to Husserl, a psychic feature but an ideal unity, and it is meant as such. Thus, Husserl's first "logical investigation" defended the concept of the one ideal significance against the prejudices of logical psychologism. Like Brentano, Husserl sees an essential difference between physical things and consciousness, although Husserl's principle of differentiation is not the same, being drawn strictly from the reflective analysis of these affairs, without relying on any uncritically accepted assumptions about "real" physical things.

Briefly, Husserl points out that a physical thing cannot be experienced in any possible process of consciousness as a *really immanent component of consciousness* (Husserl 1962, sec. 42). Consciousness, a stream of ongoing processes (in other words, *Erlebnis),* cannot by essential necessity have anything in it; it is only "things," if you will, that are processes of consciousness. To speak of mental activities as "intentionally inexistent," or as "images," "copies," etc., is either a fatal ambiguity or outright nonsense. Rather, the objects of consciousness are *all other than the activities having them as objects* ("intending activities"). Negatively, the objects are nonimmanent; positively, in Husserl's technical term, they are "transcendental" to the stream of mental activities, where transcendent means only that these objects are not themselves immanent components of the stream of mental life itself.

As contrasted with the transcendent status of its objects, every process of consciousness is given reflectively as immanent to some consciousness, as a really inherent component of that consciousness. Being thus essentially different from the status possessed by objects of consciousness, the processes of consciousness differ also in their modes of givenness, and Husserl draws this distinction with great care. On the basis of these analyses, we are able to see what Dilthey construes to be a difference between "structure" and causal continuity.

Dilthey can now examine the meaning of the notion of the continuity of life. Continuity is not given in the immediacy of an experience, nor is it simply constructed as the resultant of operating factors, on the basis of the "mechanism" of the psyche. Rather, the theory of the intentionality of consciousness provides a new foundation for the idea of givenness. One can no longer derive continuity from atoms of experience, or explain it in that way. Consciousness is always involved in continuity and has its own being in its conception of that continuity. One must note, however, that Dilthey shifts certain of the conceptions from the *Logical Investigations* to his own problematic. For him significance is not a logical concept but is to be understood as an expression of life, which represents a shift from phenomenology to life-philosophy. Life itself, flowing temporally, is ordered towards the formation of permanent units of significance. Life interprets life. It has itself a hermeneutic structure. Thus, life constitutes the real ground of the human sciences, and Dilthey's hermeneutics of life seeks to retain, at its foundation, the historical view of the world.

Historical consciousness extends into the universal, in that it sees all data of history as manifestations of the life from which they stem, or as Dilthey notes, "here life is understood by life." Hence, for historical consciousness the whole of tradition becomes the self-encounter of the human mind, a notion important to Gadamer. Still, an important question remains, though at another level. That is, how is infinite understanding possible for finite human nature? Dilthey did not object to the inner infinity of the mind, which was positively fulfilled in the ideal of a historically enlightened reason. For him, the awareness of finitude did not mean that consciousness was made finite or limited in any way; instead, it bore witness to the capacity of life to rise in energy and activity above all limitations. The awareness of finitude represented the potential infinity of the mind, though it is, not in speculation, but in historical reason that this infinity is realized. Historical understanding extends over all historical data and is truly universal because it has its firm foundation in the inner totality and infinity of mind. Dilthey sees one's world of experience as the mere starting point for an expansion that, in a living transposition, fills out the narrowness and fortuitousness of one's own experience by the infinity of what is available in the reexperiencing of the historical world.

In the examination of experience as the basis of the epistemology of historical understanding, and through the detailed analyses of the contributions of Dilthey, Vico, and Husserl, Gadamer still concludes that the epistemological question must be asked in a different way. Crucial to this problem for Dilthey was his inability to overcome traditional epistemology. His starting point in the awareness of experience was not conducive to a bridging between that beginning and the historical realities. Major historical realities, such as society and the state, have a predeterminant influence on any "experience." Self-reflection and autobiography — Dilthey's starting points — are not primary and are not an adequate basis for the hermeneutic problem, because through them history is made private once more. In fact, history does not belong to us, but rather we belong to it. Long before we understand ourselves through the process of self-examination, we understand ourselves in a self-evident way in the family, society, and state in which we live. The focus of subjectivity is a distorting mirror. The self-awareness of the individual is only a flickering in the closed circuits of historical life. And Gadamer concludes:

> That is why the prejudices of the individual, far more than his judgments, constitute the historical reality of his being. (Gadamer 1975a, 245).

In his contributions to both theoretical and applied hermeneutics, Gadamer demonstrates a thorough control of the hermeneutic tradition and its problematic. He also coins and renews concepts that issue from that tradition and that receive a new and central locus not only in his work, but also in contemporary discourse. Beyond that, Gadamer establishes a position that is critically important, but that was discarded by Betti in his concern with scientism and truth and was also discarded by Habermas, who considers hermeneutics as an important, but only partial component of research in the human sciences. That position involves the shift from the ontic to the ontological, to foundational matters in hermeneutics that begin with Gadamer's interest in the meaning of Heidegger's ontology.

For Gadamer, the important work of interpretive social science is the exploration of the terrain upon which *any* interpretation can take place, rather than, as for Habermas, the appropriation of hermeneutics as a method aimed at the adumbration of a critical political disourse. Gadamer's viewpoint accomplishes a resolution of a conflict noted in our discussion of Weber, namely the controversy between the methods of the *Geisteswissenschaften* and the sciences of nature. That controversy becomes a derivative issue to the more essential discussion of prejudices, effective-history, belongingness, experience, and the site-specific parameters of art, conversation, and games.

Nevertheless, Gadamer is unable to avoid or resolve a problem that appears not only in his hermeneutics, but also in the philosophy of the early Heidegger. That is, both positions seem too involved with a kind of description that resurrects the notion of the analyst found in the classical model of "subject-object" relations, in which the subject inquires about the object but is not really in conversation with it. Such a kind of relationship expresses aspects of control (of the object, of the topic, etc.) that lends a flavor of conservatism to the inquiry. In such a project, there is the temptation to vest the status quo with undeserved importance, or, to put the issue in another way, there is the temptation to evade or ignore the critical dimension. The strength of Gadamer's position, however, is that he emphasizes the significance of *application* in hermeneutics, and it is this issue of application, in a critical vein, that we now turn to as we explore the significance to hermeneutics of Adorno and Habermas.

7

Critical Interpretation: Theodor Adorno

Theodor Wiesengrund-Adorno was born in Frankfurt in 1903. His father was a wealthy wine merchant married to a woman of Corsican origin, who happened to be a celebrated singer. Adorno's father was intellectually oriented and promoted the younger Adorno's intellectual development. Another person who significantly influenced Adorno's education was his aunt Agathe, who was also a musician and who Adorno considered to be a second mother. Adorno studied at the University of Frankfurt, where much of his work was dedicated to a thesis on Edmund Husserl, part of which was later included in the volume *Against Epistemology*. In 1924, Adorno moved to Vienna, where he studied musical composition with Alban Berg and piano with Steuermann. During this time he was primarily concerned with cultural issues, particularly analyses of contemporary music. From 1922 to 1925, Adorno published a number of articles on music, including "Bela Bartok," "Three One-act Operas of Paul Hindemith," "Richard Strauss: zum 60 Geburtstags, 11 Juni, 1924," "Bela Bartoks Tanzuite," "Alban Berg: Zur Uraffuhrung des Wozzeck," and "Zeit genossiasche Musik in Frankfurt."

Adorno himself began to compose music, notably string trios and quartets, based on the texts of poems by Stephan Georg, Trakl, Kafka, and Brecht. He thought about composing an opera, a project that he dropped at the urging of Walter Benjamin, who did not like the libretto. Until 1930, music remained Adorno's primary interest, even though he had earned his doctoral degree in philosophy in 1922 and had been affiliated with the program of the Institute for Social Research in Frankfurt since meeting Max Horkheimer in 1919. The institute was formally created in 1924, and after the tenure of Carl Grünberg as director, Horkheimer assumed the position of Professor of Social Philosophy and Director of the institute in 1931. Adorno joined the Institute as a professor in 1925.

When the institute was threatened by the rise of National Socialism, members established a branch in Geneva (1933), where activity was less restricted. Other members of the institute migrated to Paris, where they were affiliated with the Ecole Normale Superieure, and to New York, where the most important branch of the Institute was established at Columbia University. Adorno decided to write a new doctoral dissertation, and so he moved first to England

(Oxford), where he dropped his plans, and then to New York, where he resumed work on that project.

While still in Germany, and facing the rise of National Socialism, the institute started a major research program on authoritarianism, and Adorno became one of the chief contributors to that project. Adorno addressed the authoritarian personality and its effects on youth and the development of values. Although the journal of the institute was reestablished in New York as *Studies in Philosophy and the Social Sciences,* Adorno did not publish very much under his own name. Instead, he devoted much of his time to collaborative efforts with Max Horkheimer, among which is the book, *Dialectic of the Enlightenment: Philosophical Fragments,* published in 1947. Adorno completed his study, entitled *The Authoritarian Personality,* and published it in 1950. Parts of the work included contributions from other members of the institute.

At the invitation of the postwar German government, Horkheimer and Adorno returned to Germany after the armistice, and they reestablished the Institute at Frankfurt. Following that renewal, Adorno published a number of works on issues concerning the culture and politics of advanced capitalism. By 1968–69, when he found himself in the middle of the polemics that characterized the student revolutions of those years, Adorno had gained an international reputation as a commentator on social and political issues. The student movements bolstered his interest in such issues, although he had never relinquished his devotion to music. Indeed, he taught musical composition at the music research center in Cologne, and among his students there was Frederick Stockhausen. Adorno became a celebrated author and intellectual and received several major awards for his work. He died at Zermat, Switzerland, on August 6, 1969.

The Origin of Adorno's
Hermeneutics of Society and His Aesthetic Theory

Adorno's hermeneutics are particularly evident in works dealing with the processes of transformation of advanced societies (including the critique of modernity) and in works exhibiting a critical evaluation of the position and role of aesthetics, especially music, in contemporary societies. His sociology of artistic (e.g., cultural) production and aesthetic theory is perhaps one of the most original and important contributions to the critical tradition (see our Introduction for a discussion of the critical mode of science). The study of aesthetic issues has emerged as a focus of the hermeneutic position, as noted earlier in the discussions of Betti and Gadamer. For Adorno, the focus on aesthetics can be viewed as a consequence of theoretical considerations:

It wasn't that Adorno favored transforming philosophy from a scientific inquiry into an art form. Rather, he rejected the dichotomy between science and art, which he considered not necessary, but the product of a particular historical era (Buck-Morse 1977, 122).

The aesthetic experience is first and foremost knowledge, and as knowledge, the aesthetic experience is a fundamental mode of encounter and a critical mediating force. Historically, this approach to knowledge has been subjected to prejudicial devaluation by scholars since the genesis of the scientific revolution in the seventeenth century. Indeed, a basic consequence of the Enlightenment was to deny aesthetic knowledge its validity. When not denigrated as a mystical, nonscientific, and irrational subjectivism, it has been naively celebrated as an ultimate form of truth (cf. Buck-Morse 1977). In its objective form, replete with bloated claims to truth, it promised much and was unable to deliver. In its prejudged subjectivist form, it was hailed as a means of mystifying the world, rather than as a means of rendering the world comprehensible.

To view the aesthetic experience as either unbridled subjectivism or an ultimate form of truth is to misunderstand both its nature and its potential. Moreover, such an attitude implicitly accepts as viable the subject-object dichotomy upon which positivism and Romanticism share a common philosophical ground. If there is a crisis in Western thought, and much suggests that there is, then perhaps the crisis is attributable to this commonly shared bifurcation between subject and object, in its numerous manifestations.

The aesthetic experience, when freed of the debilitating influences of subjectivism, emerges as a vital model of knowledge encompassing both subjective and objective aspects, considering these as a unity, unencumbered by the domination of either. Moreover, the aesthetic experience unites both understanding and interpretation while simultaneously representing the world, a perspective similar to that of Gadamer. Within the aesthetic experience, creativity, the activity of human production, merges with criticism, the activity of an enlightened grasp of the world. Rather than reducing the world to *a priori* categories of cognition and foisting upon reality a prefigured order, purpose, and character, the aesthetic experience is intimately predicated upon that which it endeavors to render meaningful. That is, the aesthetic experience engages the world and Being in an intentional act of critical production. It is, beyond all else, an edificational activity. The aesthetic experience produces through involvement, it instructs through criticism, and it does this without exempting itself from either creativity or critique.

There are, however, important issues that need to be resolved before we can accept the aesthetic experience as a tenable source for or kind of knowledge. For example, aesthetics is grounded in the "art object." It has been suggested, though, that a serious question might be raised as to whether art exists, or can exist, in the modern world. If this were the case, then the positivist's objections to the aesthetic experience must be entertained. If art can exist, however, then the employment of the aesthetic experience as a model of knowledge

remains an alternative open to exploration.   To avoid risking oversimplifica-
tion, the issue of the existence of art must be approached historically. Here,
then, it must be presupposed that the existence of an object of art entails a relationship with a particular society. This relationship is not self-evident or trans-
parent. Moreover, the relationship, the object, and the society are not without
a dynamic interplay. The object is not simply an inflexible reflection of society, nor is society a reflection of the object. The relationship, or stance, of the
object to society is transformed when the conditions of its existence are changed.
This leads to the observation that art must function differently as its context of
existence changes since its stance and the conditions of that stance fluctuate.
The question of meaning is not raised at this point.

It is from the vantage point of *stance* that the question of the existence
of art in the modern world can be addressed. The autonomy of art, or for that
matter of any cultural form, is ultimately a matter of both its function and meaning. To the extent that artistic creation is merged with ritual and ceremony, and
thereby made indistinguishable from a use-content, it can be said to lack autonomy. Under these conditions, art exists only as an instrument for expressing culture and is thereby firmly wed to a principle of use. Art achieves at least
a potential for autonomy only under those sociohistorical conditions in which
the art object is freed from an exclusive use-context and develops, in conjunc-
tion with use, a value-dimension. This value, then, must not be overdetermined
by use if the object is to remain autonomous and/or an object in itself.

The conditions for autonomous art are best met under a capitalist mode
of production. With capitalism, the art object is transformed into a commodity
and thus develops a concrete exchange-value. The art object can now truly stand
as an object. Moreover, capitalism, unlike previous modes of social organization, universalizes culture, thereby imbuing the art object with a potential for
knowledge generation beyond that of other objects, under conditions where use
determines function and meaning.

It would be unwise, however, to suggest that art is singularly circumscribed by the social context of its origin. Art objects are not to be thought of
as distorted in the sense that they merely reflect dominant economic and/or political forms. Perhaps this becomes more clear if the discussion is framed in a
distinction between "forces of production" and "relations of production."

Concerning the objects of art, the forces of production are the sum of the
compositional activity. They include the skill of the artistic community, the
technical and "technological" underpinnings of the artistic activity, and the totality of other inputs, regardless of purpose, that go into the creation of the object. On the other hand, the relations of production refer to those dimensions
of consumption (e.g., lifestyle and patterns) and consciousness that form the
receptive aspect of the object. Under capitalism, then, art is managed by certain forces of production that give rise to certain relations of production that
are based upon the exchange character of the art object. Simply stated, a social

dynamic is generated between (a) the organization of composition and (b) the concomitant organization of reception (consumption).

While capitalism provides art with certain favorable conditions, it also places restraints upon art that tend to be counterproductive to its newly discovered artistic potential. Freed from the artificiality of an exclusive use-function, art is capable of both presenting and representing (i.e., displaying and critiquing) the context of its origins. This dynamic of function and significance is the fundamental knowledge component of art. Historically, this has been a component characterized more by its potential than by its objective expression. Yet, capitalism assaults, in a most direct manner, the very potential it imbues in art by positioning composition (the critical-creative component) against the industry of culture (an authoritarian mode of exchange between composition and consumption). Under these circumstances, art becomes entangled in an abstract process prefigured by the forces of its production. In addition, these forces are themselves grounded in a newly acquired abstract commodity character which, by definition, negates critical potential *vis-à-vis* a hyperbolic celebration of the presentation of form. It could be said that a preoccupation with production exists. The history of the aesthetic experience thus moves from function as art, to art as potential, to art as function.

Under the influence of modern capitalist culture, art is horizontalized and made indistinguishable from real life. It is, in other words, subjugated to identity thinking. There emerges a power of assertion that renders even the pretense of art's critical-creative function unnecessary, and indeed, improbable. The novel, film, radio, and music succumb to reduction; outwardly, each becomes a feature of commodity production. No apology is offered. What is gained is the standardization of form and function. In this case, each consumer of culture is all but guaranteed the ability to appropriate each artistic product, because art is naturalized — it becomes the equivalent of everyday life and becomes knowable through everyday language. The "obligations of the natural idiom" are swiftly fulfilled, and efficiency becomes the order of the day. What is lost is only the art (i.e., mass-media) consumer's power of imagination, creativity, and critique. Of course, the consumer must also suffer a loss of spontaneity, though spontaneity itself is saved through its ascription to the objective nature of the artistic products themselves. This is the irony of the modern aesthetic experience.

There is no longer a need to differentiate high from low culture. The counter- and contracultures can rest easy in the company of the dominant culture, which they once ostensibly opposed. Art is art. The principle of "unity" is pervasive; it is hegemonic. Productive rules, structural obligations and forms predetermine formats. Each instance of artistic production is assured that it will be received as art, and what remains is for specialists (namely, connoisseurs and critics) to hazard evaluations. Does the product please? Does the art object articulate contemporary standards? Does the finance company's jingle blend at the appropriate moments with Beethoven's *Fifth?*

Style is not an issue. The culture industry exists as the negation of style, and to raise considerations is to disregard the facts. Art is life and cannot be reduced; art is pure and should not be corrupted. This is what the culture industry proclaims as truth. Thus, to raise the issue of style is to do more than challenge the culture industry; it is to raise challenges to the integrity of life as we know it.

The objection is occasionally voiced that within the modern aesthetic experience there are, however infrequent, true instances of creativity. Yet these moments of "realistic dissidence," which seem to imply radical breaks with the normative order, generally receive rapid reconciliation with the prevailing forms of production. Permitting analogy, monopoly markets find few threats in innovation when it is easily assimilated or viewed as an aberration of little significance to the industry as a whole. Innovation that is tolerated does not embrace a powerful critical capability. It is with this understanding that it can be said that true innovation in the culture industry is best characterized by its complete lack of existence.

Critical thinking is a burden. It is a labor requiring considerable effort and time, as noted by Jacques Lyotard in *Post-Modernism for Children* (1989, 47). In the capitalist mode, therefore, art should be praised as a relief from a burden. Art today is fraught with pleasure precisely because it exempts consumers from thought. Indeed, there is no need to expect that the consumers of artistic production will be enticed by independent thought. Such will not be their predilection. Moreover, to anticipate that they will actually think is to mystify what has become of the aesthetic experience. The culture industry is predicated on the assumption that consumers' reactions can be known in advance, that they are predictable.

While this may sound cynical, the fact is far from remarkable, since the reactions of consumers of art in capitalist society are prescribed. This is the playful outcome of the capitalist semiotic. The whole is meaningless. Each segment of the artistic object is vivified by its predecessor. Meaning is elicited by signs, signs are conjoined to form sequences, and sequences are arbitrary. Meaning for the consumer is thereby assured throughout — it cannot be lost or misapprehended since it does not exist.

It would be inaccurate here to presuppose a state of complete and total passivity on the part of consumers. Such is certainly not the case. There is demand as well as supply, and both are essential considerations of the culture industry. Both are carefully calculated, for the consumer has his taste and the producer has her standardized product. Taken together, the situation has developed that the consumer is free to feast among the range of standardized products. This, then, is the supply and demand of contemporary society.

All systems have open points. All points represent contradictions to systems predicated upon closure. If the aesthetic experience has been standardized through repetition and abstraction, and if it has been drafted into the service of identity-thinking, then it also expresses opposition to these nodal points. The same mechanization that ruthlessly advocates and imposes pseudo-individuation in the aesthetic experience also suggests its own negation. If an art object can function to perpetuate an abstract commodity exchange system, then it can also function against such a system. Art can confront *or* comfort. The viability of the aesthetic experience as a model of knowledge in interpretation is possible only if these contradictions and potentials are made explicit (recall here that the need for interpretation emerges from within a rupture of understanding). The focus must be upon the relationship between the subject and the social object that structures it.

To judge art and aesthetic experience on the basis of the degree to which it assumes a critical posture is to necessarily separate potential from production. It is to reverse the emphasis away from production by taking it up as a primary point of analysis. This is not to suggest a return to the examination of artists' intentionality, the immanent structure of the art object, or the art object's social meaning. It is, however, to approach the entirety of the aesthetic experience with the foreknowledge of its potential and to examine that potential from the historical vantage of both function and significance. Here significance and function must be viewed as relational properties located between subjectivity and social objectivity. This perspective prevents the substitution of the illusion of reality and intelligibility in the place of understanding. Moreover, it negates the tendency to transform the aesthetic experience into an entertainment value or abstract exchange-value.

Minima Moralia as Interpretive Sociology

In a radical fashion, Adorno's *Minima Moralia* posits an alternative sociology, one that emerges from a series of aphoristic reflections. Not only the sociology, but also the aphoristic style, even in its "decoded" form, are thoroughly antiscientific. The alternative sociology consists of four dimensions, that appear as four rogues on the "one-way road," to use a notion from Walter Benjamin. The first dimension is that of the individual, the real individual, a singular reconstruction, in contrast to the abstracted structure to which the social totality is reduced, both in mainstream sociology and in those "revolutionary analyses" that become emptied under the form of a "theory of reproductive forces." The second dimension is that of everyday life, understood as a properly historical dimension toward which the individual orients himself. The risk of this encounter is that the individual becomes reified within traditional sociology, which presents only abstract alienated everyday life. To avoid reification, the individual must become conscious of the abstractions involved in instrumental formalization, the consequence of traditional sociology. The organization of pessimism, which is radically opposed to liberal optimism, can be produced and perpetuated in the encounter by the consciousness of the inexorable reification of individuality at the core of the fetishized everyday-ness. In fact, the opposition between the analyses of the macrostructures of economic and political power and the analyses of everyday life, of its "nexus" and of its immediate modalities, yield the possibility of determinist tempta-tions as much as teleological optimism. Everyday life presents itself in a prob-lematic fashion in its ambiguity and in its enigmatic character. This enigma provides the stimulus and privileged ground for a permanent assault against the permanent repression of social reality intrinsic to instrumental science.

Because of these conflicts, reflection about everyday life opens the pos-sibility for a continuous methodological and conceptual de-structuration, an "epistemological catharsis" that is not only the intellectual crisis, but also the moral and existential crisis that corrodes the "signifier" and the "signified," that is, a crisis that moves beyond the essential form of the exposition and the discourse itself. Adorno establishes a sort of "sociological extra-territoriality" with a surrealistic "uprooting" of the banality of everyday social objects. This "semioclasty" is the third dimension of *Minima Moralia.*

The fourth dimension of the work is that of the "perspective," or, in Adorno's memorable term, "prophecy," in opposition to the statistical meth-ods of "precision." This is a prophecy completely "internal" to the organiza-tion of the pessimism and that resides within the shelter of teleological vision. This prophecy is implicit in the "utopia of theoretical work" and is, like every-thing else, reduced to falsehood but rails nonetheless against the falsehood of the world of commodities and can thus represent a kind of political practice that conjures up a vulgar practical materialism with its total abandonment to reification. These four dimensions of a radical sociology are maintained in a close dialectical relationship and continuously illuminate each other in the apho-risms of *Minima Moralia.*

Adorno's repositing of the individual dimension, of the definitive soli-tude of the individual at odds with instrumental ideologies trying to fit her or him into a universe completely given and finished, tears the individual away from the activity of being manipulated and assigns her or him to the halluci-nated contemplation of everyday reification and banalization. The simple con-tact of the individual with everyday objects, which try to establish the per-spectives "where the world finds itself disrupted, is dispossessed, shows its fractures and its crevices as it will appear one day, deformed and empty in its messianic light" (Adorno 1954), is perhaps the only means by which the indi-vidual may escape the process of "total socialization" that envelopes the per-son and collectivity in the false security and terrorized intimacy of "universal formalization and quantification." The process of formalization removes from the individual the framework of self-consciousness and the internalized sense of collective responsibility, leaving only the act of reason to verify the already-existent. Once the self has been driven back, it experiences both the anguish of the distance and the fading of the properly dialectical tension between the object and its own concept. This dialectical tension is the source of "critique" (cf. Horkheimer and Adorno 1966, 23–24), and its loss means that the abandonment of self that occurs in objective thought yields an "absolute tautology." For Adorno, "madness" is the last refuge of the subject who has exchanged the autonomy of his own personality for a state of dispossession and annihilation. In a fragment from *Minima Moralia,* Adorno writes:

> The completely pure reason of these that have rid themselves from the capacity to represent an object away from its presence converges with pure unconsciousness, with madness strict sense, because by rapport to the absurd realist ideal of the pure given, free from any category, every knowledge is false, and what is only true is why the question of the truthful and the false cannot be any longer posited. Such tendencies have made enormous progress, and constantly appear in scientific activity which, by definition, consists in submitting also the last remains of the world, such ruins without defenses (Adorno 1954, 159).

In the rarefied, closed, voluntary, and necessarily provincial realm of the social sciences, it is imperative that nothing foreign to the "given" must trouble the slow crystallization of the scientific "modules" of the abstract codes capable of accomplishing the work of formalization of everyday social action that evaded the efforts of political economists.

The foundation of an abstract and mystified pseudo-totality must entail the replacement of the social actor, the real subject oriented toward objective practicality, with an abstract and fetishized object, such as the "autonomic" movement of the structures of which the totality is known as "social reality." In the social sciences, the mystification of the totality of social and collective acting starts with the process of formalization and abstraction that originates with the "discovery" of the laws of the market. The process then veils human reality with laws of political economy and constructs schemes of the interior of monopolized labor (e.g., "abstract alienated labor") as it is extended to the totality of everyday life, the specific framework of the "social sciences." The fundamental historical operation of capitalism, the process of abstraction that leads to the foundation of a "pseudo-reality" of social acting, is reinforced by the dual effects of the movement toward totalization: market and labor. For the sociologist, work changes into "occupation" and "task," that is, into a function, and thereby reveals itself as the means of access into the total fetishization of social relations, themselves reduced to "functions."

Such sociologically objective phenomena are in fact alienated aspects of praxis. From the basis of abstract alienated labor, the social sciences (and especially sociology) construct the abstract alienated "everyday" that is then submitted to the manipulative practice of instrumental rationality. In this way, the sociology of labor and its corollaries, the sociology of organizations and

industrial sociology, become an important stage in the process of formalization effected by political economy, a process that led to the development of
other special sociologies and human sciences, all of them dealing with pieces
of a broken social reality.

For example, if we force the meaning of Habermas' phrase, "interaction
mediated by the everyday discourse," we note that the domain of nonstrategic
action, in which domain belongs the "general social knowledge," or Marx's
"general intellect," is that focus of historical concretizations of collective memory and imagination that is alleged to be understood "authentically" only by
social scientific "specialists." The meaning of mediated interaction is translated into cumulative, specialized codes, interpreted as the "reality" of the phenomenon, and these codes, called "sociology" or the like, are used to support
the notion that social knowledge constitutes a private property accumulated by
scientific practitioners. Such property may be controlled at all levels, creative
interpretation can be squelched, and the process results in the legitimation of
the "power for technical disposition" over people and nature (Habermas 1973,
85–87).

This slow crystallization of cumulative knowledge, nevertheless, by its
nature, does tend to close, little by little, all of the strategic horizons of bourgeois society. While the statistical methods of forecasting, based on the calcu-
lation of probabilities, were being developed and refined, they became incapable of forecasting the erosion of the Western and capitalist symbolic world.
The great cultural revolution begun by the European intellectual avant garde
at the time of the First World War became an explosive political mass by 1968.
This historical development constitutes the most significant verification of the
"pathological professional stupidity" cited by Adorno in *Minima Moralia*. And
for Adorno, such a flaw characterizes above all the sociologists. But such stupidity is also a comfortable refuge:

> Far from resenting anything hostile in the interdictions of thinking, the
> bureaucratic apprentices — and all scholars are that — feel relieved. Be-
> cause thinking would impose on them a subjective responsibility that the
> objective situation that they have in the process of production would pre-
> vent them from assuming. They renounce them raising their hands, and
> unhappiness of thinking becomes incapacity for thinking; and the same
> persons that know how to investigate the most refined statistical objec-
> tions when it is necessary to dispute a knowledge, are not in the position
> to formulate *ex-cathedra* the most simple concrete predictions. They at-
> tack speculation and kill in it the common sense (Adorno 1954, 161).

As noted, in the early years of the twentieth century, the radical critique
of what Roland Barthes calls the "relationship with the significant" commenced.
This attack was waged simultaneously against the "signified," the everyday

world as both fetishized and reified, and against the "signifier," the symbolic world of the West, which in its bourgeois use tended to become frozen as objective universal nature. After 1968 the critique of the "relationship with the signifier" that revealed the frailty of sociology's portrait of everyday life also disclosed the shallowness of the concepts of exchange-value and use-value, concepts that also achieved reified status during the formalization of sociology.

Why is this disclosure important? Its significance refers to the realization that already in the concept of use-value we find the relationship of subject-object, as indicated, for instance, in the opposition of human beings and nature. This nascent formalization grows along with bourgeois social science, until it reaches its fully developed posture, at which point, use-value and exchange-value are discovered to be equivalent. The revolution of 1968 will propose (again) the conditions of interaction of subject and object as "nonstrategic action," at the base of which is posited a relationship between individuals free from the subject-object domination. This is a *concrete utopia,* exactly because it is grasped in the depths of the everyday in its enigmatic and essential reality, as opposed to its abstract appearance in crystallized, codified, and cumulative science.

The annihilation of "universal functionalization" (the process of formalization and abstraction of everyday social action), the denial of such a locus for the encounter of individual history and collective-political creation, becomes the duty of sociology. Thus, authentic sociology essentially becomes cultural terrorism. It assumes an ideological duty to bring about from the beginning a de-ideologization that eliminates every residual space between individual and objective reality. Similarly, sociology depopulates the social world of "instruments." The subject thus finds herself reduced to the anguish of everyday choices, both individual and collective. She is assigned a serene death, in the limbo of maintenance, heterodirection, and permanent consensus, in which the regression to infantilism, the abode of instrumental rationality, is consummated. With reference to this point, Adorno is convinced, as was Horkheimer, that capitalism does not any longer need any "ideology," in the sense of "justification." The disappearance of ideology leads to the emergence of the totally reified individual with the total reification of her everyday environment.

Toward a Renewal of Sociology

According to Horkheimer and Adorno, the origins of capitalism did accomplish a historically important operation, that of providing a cultural-historical space for the emergence and efficacy of ideology, now viewed not as a power that is exerted in an immediate fashion, but as mediated by capital itself. Domination in such a scenario is based upon abstraction, as instrumental formalization. Ideology emerges and is propagated at the schisms of social life, where objective reality is covered by the veil of formal values. As it grows, ideology becomes the ghostly reminder of original reality, muffling the authentic human's cries of conscious unhappiness. In this hallucinating agony of early capitalism, the line between truth and untruth, between concrete and abstract, is covered over. Any residue of creativity, of knowledge still intimately rebellious to domination, will be concealed by the logical barbarism of Buchenwald and Auschwitz. In the development of late capitalism, reification and its instruments of quantification attack and penetrate everyday life, and the relative autonomy of the occasional residues of unhappy consciousness becomes further suppressed.

In contemporary society, and social science, there is no longer any pretention to ideological autonomy; there is no separation of ideology from bourgeois society and no separation of ideology from its own object. Ideology can no longer be talked about but is constantly lived. Consequently, the world of spirit dissociates into two existential foci. On the one hand, critical questions that aim at truth are stripped of their signification, isolating critique from social relations. On the other hand, the planned administration of ideological concepts is not possible, because ideology becomes the ground of social relations and action. Ideology has ceased to be an interpretation of the world and has become the world's accepted image (Horkheimer and Adorno 1966, 225).

With the dissolution of the last residue of unhappy consciousness within the cloak of ideology, individuality itself seeks its own dissolution in the pseudototality of the everyday. Individuality corroded by reification is simply an encrustation on the world of objects. This annihilation of individuality is not just a result of the processes of construction undertaken by the social sciences (e.g., the replacement of individuality by the movements of structures and the replacement of practice by function). It is also a result of other forces, dressed in the facade of liberalism, that reconstruct human reality as, for instance, "productive forces," thus replacing the reality of political and historical creativity and the tensions emanating from shifts in the relations of production with abstract concepts. Consequently, political processes, such as the dissolution of the Soviet Union, are unexpected and underestimated in their significance as processes of ideological groups.

Generally, sociology is criticized on the basis of specific formulations or small points of practical utility and rarely is the enterprise addressed globally. Its epistemological foundations are substantially unchanged and seem to presage the development of new social sciences, such as social engineering and social code enforcement. It could not be otherwise, given that capitalist accumulation and private appropriation of social knowledge could not lead to the creation of a sociology absolutely opposed to the goals that have led to the creation of such bourgeois social science. The search for another "sociology," therefore, corresponds to the search for a political economy that is different and not related to the present usages of such science.

This search, obviously, must begin with the acknowledgement that there is an intrinsic validity to the study of political economy (e.g., the breakdown of the Soviet Union is essentially a consequence of economic issues) and that political economy is a science that may serve any political orientation. In this light, the ideology of the dominant class can be identified by its fundamental relationship to the ideology of all other classes. Economic foundationalism, however, suppresses alternative programs and confines research entirely to the technocratic and nonpolitical role of the special cadre of political economists, who, impotent to choose really alternative roles for their own action, because they are closed within their own problematic, must limit themselves to the selection of means and instruments they deem technically appropriate. Within the spectrum of dominant regimes, authentic sociology would be submitted to what Horkheimer terms "subjective reason." This shift from instrumentality, this search for a different sociology, does not advocate the disappearance of the state, but rather the appearance of another state in which the constraints of the present one are absent or overcome.

If the process of abstraction and instrumental formalization of all social action is successful, the result is the annihilation of the individual. Any vestige of individualism is subordinated to the world of objects, and the person becomes an object among others, manipulable and reified. Against this objectification at the hands of science, the subjective person remains ambivalent:

The reduced and degraded essence rebels with tenacity against the enchantment that transforms it into a facade. The mutation of these same relations of production depend in a large extent upon what goes on in the sphere of consumption which is a simple reflection of production and a caricature of real life; that is, the conscious and the unconscious of the individuals. Only in the contrast with production, in what they are not yet entirely controlled and absorbed by the order, men have the potential to create a new order. If the appearance of life would erase definitively, protected even by bad reasons, the sphere of consumption, then the nonsense of absolute production would triumph (Adorno 1954, 4).

Perhaps individual consciousness is still an open fissure of the "total socialization" into which the scalpel of critique can penetrate. This indeed is the promise of Adorno's critical theory. His work reaffirms the irreplaceable value of the individual to repel every form of paralysing objectivism, including the objectified and reified dialectics of orthodox Marxism. This reaffirmation, however, does not authorize a replacement metaphysics and remains completely tactical. The hermeneutic subject is situated at the base of the object but is not posited as an originator of the object's identity. If the identity or activity of the object calls for the intervention of the subject, that subject in turn reveals itself as incapable of grounding the object and refers back to the object for determination (e.g., "It was not me; it is my job."). In fact, the subject discovers in himself or herself, in the process of his or her own constitution, the object. In turn, the object requires that the subject transcend him- or herself in order to attain self-knowledge, but the knowledge of the object is not based on the subject; its constitution is independent, made by others, such as specialists or scientists, etc.

At exactly the moment that capitalist logic annihilates the individual in total reification, it confers to him, nevertheless, a pseudo-existence. Individuals become in everyday life the "spectres that menace with misfortune," which refers to a kind of recuperative operation. The values of individualism have always been at the center of the bourgeois worldview, but at the culmination of capitalism they take on a double function. On the one hand, the individual is but a simple agent of the law of value. On the other hand, it is necessary that the individual have consciousness of her- or himself, as being-it-itself, because only such a conviction will enable the person to intensify her or his own productivity.

As suggested earlier, the successful abstraction of the "real individual" and the recuperation of pseudo-individuality by instrumental reason is carried out in the process of abstract, alienated everydayness, the locus of the fission of the person with fetishized objectivity. Here, in the fire of such a tragic fission, and especially because it is not perceived as such, Adorno explores the field of negative thinking. This combination of words — negative thinking — captures the tragedy in its abstraction and organizes the potential for the resuscitation of unhappy consciousness "around pessimism." Consequently, the collective rites and infatuation, the most used iconographies, the most common stereotypes, the most minimal habituations, the most banal objects and everyday kitsch — that nausea, that disgusting and apparently insignificant rumination, that continuous miscarriage and refusal of everyday existence, each of these constitutes a summary of all the attributes of the political-economic system that brings to life and reproduces everyday pseudo-reality. At its core, then, Adorno's conception engages a struggle aimed at opening fissures in the Western symbolic universe.

For Adorno, the everyday object that is subjected to careful observation loses its banal meaning, like a word that is repeated obsessively. The resulting transformation places the subject and object in a clash of dissonances, opening a field for analysis that can remove the subject from the reified universe of exchange-value. The subject can be thrown beyond or under use-value, in a context of nonstrategic action ruled by noninstrumental reason. This is a world of negative aphorisms . . . the world of *Minima Moralia*. In the abstract world of "evident appearance," dominated by the instrumentality of the principle of presentation, interaction and gratuity can only *erupt* sporadically and provincially, as improvisations. In the light of such an enigma, however, the abstract universe of reification is revealed as an absurd absolute. Such a moment demonstrates how, within a social system characterized by the cumulative knowledge of instrumental formalization, noninstrumental reason and its transcendence imply both exchange- and use-value. The meaning of an interaction liberated from the domination of instrumentality can emerge only within a field in which the knower's social knowledge has been fractured by enigma. Adorno's aphorisms in *Minima Moralia* attempt to present sparks that suddenly illuminate, or sometimes burn, that which we take to be familiar. They open onto an enigma, in which what is absurd is presented as if it were completely evident, thus suppressing its power. The evidence of the everyday is transformed into something quite other — "the irreality of despair" (Adorno 1974, 247).

At the center of this deconstruction of the everyday is the actualization of an "organization of pessimism," to which Benjamin attributes the character of an exorcism against the omnipotence of pseudo-reality and the pseudo-totality of the everyday (Benjamin 1962, 23–24). In the alienated everyday, abstract images and language collapse into their own objectifications. In the solitude of the individual facing the reified order of objects, elements for an ideological critique are born and become honed. This is accomplished when we focus on the rights and happenings of the collectivity, on the iconography, habituations, and banal objectivities that are the tangible signs of the substantial abstractions of blind, bourgeois everydayness.

Postmodernism/aesthetics

Adorno's contribution to the theory of postmodernism, which is often overlooked by critical theorists, cannot be separated from his work on aesthetics. Nor can it be abstracted from his writing on political theory at the level of the subject *(Aesthetic Theory,* 1984). Thus his theory of postmodernism is directly tied to his entire critical theory of society and its philosophical underpinnings of negative dialectics (Adorno 1973b). Our discussion will be limited to three central areas of Adorno's theory, namely:

1. the negation of the intellectual division of labor
2. the negation of the Hegelian conception of historicity
3. the negation of the bourgeois notion of art

These three themes form the core of his conception of postmodernism. In addition, from a discussion of these themes, it is possible to disclose how Adorno envisioned aesthetics as a form of life-praxis and as a potential resolution to the problems posed to human existence by capitalist society.

From the outset, it is necessary to insist upon a differentiation between Adorno's position on postmodernism and what at first glance appears to be two parallel postures — the "end of ideology" speculation and the thesis of the "postindustrial society." Although all three of these notions pay some homage to the theories of Marx and Hegel, Adorno's position eschewed politically conservative proscriptions in favor of a fundamentally radical critique of society.

Specifically, the political role that Adorno accords aesthetics runs directly contrary to the evolutionary fatalism of the other two positions. Adorno intends to avoid a materialist account of modern society, in which the subject is left without accomodations. In this regard, it should be noted that the place of the subject, sometimes referred to as the "recovery of the subject," is a central theme not only to Adorno, but also to such scholars as Michel Foucault, Martin Heidegger, and Hans-Georg Gadamer. At least in this view, these thinkers represent a common tradition.

In order to better comprehend Adorno's position, it is advisable to recall his critique of Hegel's *Philosophy of History* (in the *Jubulaeums Ausgabe*, ed. by H. Glockner, Vol. XI, 1928). A second relevant text is Adorno's critique of orthodox Marxism, which is systematically presented in *The Dialectic of Enlightenment*, written with Max Horkheimer (1972). In this volume Adorno and Horkheimer endeavor to enliven Hegel's metaphysics by recasting it in the more sociohistorical framework of critical theory. Basically, Adorno and Horkheimer take exception to Hegel's conceptualization of humanity and history, wherein both are presented as denuded of all vestiges of autonomy and self-determination (cf. Rosen 1982). Their argument calls for a return to open systems of thought that feature human praxis as a central feature. In a similar vein, they object to orthodox Marxists' accounts of society; that is, Adorno and Horkheimer deny the notion that humans represent little more than objects within the sphere of manipulation of an "overdetermined" history. The term "overdetermined" comes from the work of Louis Althusser and is not used by Adorno; it is this notion of history represented by Althusser (and Stalinism in general) that Adorno rejects. In both of these cases, i.e., in Hegel and in orthodox Marxism, it is the closure of the accounts and the loss of the subject within history that prompts the critique issued by Horkheimer and Adorno.

To illustrate Adorno's objection regarding both the Hegelian and orthodox Marxists accounts, we need only briefly reflect upon his views concerning the political inability of the proletariat to overturn the bourgeois state in Germany. His account, shared and developed jointly with Horkheimer, posits the idea of a breakdown of the class structure of society; a breakdown that is most clearly evidenced in early capitalist society. Predicated upon this breakdown, two structural levels of social integration emerge.

The first is the *state,* replete with a powerful bureaucratic, economic, and military apparatus. The second is the *family.* While granting that historically this social configuration resulted in the family being little more than an appendage of the state (i.e., subject to its indoctrination and authoritarianism), the issue, for Adorno, was not to be reduced to a simple matter of infrastructural domination. The family's subjugation was a historical reality and not an empirical case for the absolute domination of the infrastructure relative to all other spheres of society for all times. The fact that few social spheres, the family included, remained as viable arenas for critical reflection on society was not for Adorno a *prima facie* case for the nonexistence of such arenas. Moreover, if one encounters a paucity of such arenas, which in fact is the case, this lack cannot be translated into a nonexistence of critical or potentially critical spheres.

On this point of avoiding *ad hominem* arguments, Adorno was adamant. In his view, the failure to identify potential arenas of opposition and critical reflection was for the most part a failure of positive science, and especially of the prevailing positivistic sociologies. In this sense, Adorno's theory includes an indictment of any social theory that does not, or cannot, develop the necessary intellectual capabilities to identify and act upon the potential arenas of critical reflection (cf. Frankfurt Institute for Social Research 1972).

In opposition to orthodox Marxism, Adorno and Horkheimer argued for the quasi-independence of both superstructure and infrastructure. In a characteristically uncharitable manner, they argue not only for a measure of independence, but also on behalf of the superstructure, which position offers the greatest potential challenge to the historical domination of the infrastructure. Here the orthodox Marxist position is not only challenged, but is also inverted. The inversion, however, was agreed to only in general terms, as Adorno and Horkheimer did not agree as to what aspect of the superstructure represented the most salient challenge. Horkheimer singles out religion as the focus of challenge, while Adorno advocates a focus on aesthetics.

Horkheimer's argument centered on the idea that religion was the fundamental caretaker of basic human values (cf. Dasilva and Faught 1991; also Ponsetto 1981). These values referred both to the freedom of the subject and to universalistic human judgments. On these grounds, religion constituted the primary source of opposition to the totalitarian and authoritarian aims and practices of the modern state.

Adorno was not given to optimism concerning the critical potential of religion. Instead, he turned to aesthetics as one of the more promising sources of opposition. In his theory, aesthetics represented one area that presupposes a radical critique of society and of the positivistic (i.e., instrumental) knowledge base that underlies all action within the modern state. We can begin to comprehend Adorno's thinking as to this potential when he writes:

The truth content of works of art is inseparable from the concept of mankind. They are always images of a new mankind, their negations and mediations notwithstanding. Just looking away from that change does not help them find peace. Art is more than praxis because by turning away from praxis art denounces the narrow-mindedness and untruth of practical life. Praxis here and now does not want to hear anything about that as long as the practical ordering of the world has not yet come to pass (Adorno 1984, 342).

While Adorno and Horkheimer selected different spheres around which to develop their arguments, the logic each employed was remarkably similar. In their way of thinking, aesthetics and religion constituted primary critiques of instrumental reason. From their somewhat phenomenological vantage points, aesthetics and religion were antithetical to instrumentality as it had become manifest in capitalist society. Beginning with Horkheimer's post–World War II essays and continuing through Habermas' recent work, the critique of instrumental reason has been a central component of most critical theory programs. For critical theory in general, and most especially for Adorno, instrumental reason, because it dominates all forms of human action in the modern world, has become the primary source of alienation and the ground for reification and fetishism.

It is important to understand that for Adorno, aesthetics is not a specialized intellectual discipline reserved for scholars specifically trained in aesthetic theory and the conduct of aesthetic inquiry (Adorno 1984, 478–81). On the contrary, aesthetics is a holistic realm of life, patently historical and intricately tied to the process of becoming human and entering into human relationships. Moreover, aesthetics involves the actual horizons of Being (in the sense of Husserl's later writings, e.g., *The Crisis of European Sciences)* and their dynamics, as these horizons expand and modify to transcend both situational and epochal crises. For Adorno the aesthetic experience is both a product *of* and an independent force *in* society. This contrasts with Hegel, in that aesthetics is not just one more sphere of life to be transcended in the historical evolution of consciousness. Furthermore, aesthetics is not another phase of the alienation of consciousness. To transcend aesthetics, to eclipse the aesthetic experience, would for Adorno be tantamount to negating life itself.

From this argument one can begin to detect a certain metaphoric homology between Adorno's notion and use of aesthetics and Horkheimer's notion of religion as critique. If, as Adorno claims, aesthetics is a basic aspect of being human, which aspect is then acted upon throughout history (i.e., aesthetics as a universal), then aesthetics clearly has religious connotations. In short, aesthetics furnishes the roots of man's "lost paradise" and suggests the crucial context for its retrieval. In addition, aesthetics is infused with a "messianic" quality that provides human actors with signposts for their life-projects.

In Adorno's account it is impossible to begin with categories of judgment, as we find with Kant, and as is common to conventional aesthetics. For Adorno, any category involves the whole of Being. Thus, a traditional aesthetic category, such as "beauty," represents a loss of truth, for it seeks to delimit and close horizons, rather than facilitate their expansion and reinterpretation. In this example, beauty operates as a category without any reference to the real-life practices of the subject and his or her relationship to either society or the object. For Adorno the aesthetic sphere provides people with an unfinished system, replete with openings for breaking down form into life. One might note that on this point Adorno shares a number of commonalities with Simmel (cf. Simmel 1923, 31–64).

This resistance to formal systems remains a guiding principle of Adorno's work on postmodernism. As with his other writings, his position is that the most faithful sociological accounts are those that do not nest themselves in a prefigured system of categories and interpretations. He celebrates the nonsystem or antisystem approach, because life itself is a continuous process of negation and transformation. Life indeed repels the claims of validity proffered by techniques designed to fabricate explanation through categorical juxtaposition. Life and its realization are predicated upon the dynamic of decomposing the very crystallizations generated by formal analysis.

Underlying this account is a sense of history wherein aesthetics, as one component, is the individual and collective practice of "acting out" and transcending all the social barriers to self-becoming. Contrary to Hegel's conception, the historical plane is essentially open, with a critical tension placed upon human action. It is human action that can, and must, in concert with aesthetics, react against the quasi-naturalistic processes imposed upon the subject by society. Aesthetics becomes the precondition and ground for projects of human liberation.

This is the theoretical backdrop against which Adorno composes his critiques of Stravinsky and Wagner, his optimistic portrait of the serial music of the Vienna school, and his strong denunciation of American jazz. In each of these instances, and especially in the case of jazz, the early seed of negation and any hope of freedom were soon confined to the straightjacket of the commerciality of the "cultural industry."

All forms of aesthetics and artistic production are subject to incorporation into the culture industry in a capitalist society. In fact, most of what is taken to be art is defined and promoted by this industry in the process of transformation of art into commodity. Those productions standing outside the industry (a feat that is quite difficult to accomplish, e.g., as in the case of Christo) retain their maximum critical potential. Those products captured by the industry become part of the bourgeois conception of art, which ranges from "high art" to the artistic products of mass or popular culture. While the cooptation of art can and does occur, the process is never total. The autonomous aspects of art resist complete assimilation into the prevailing corporate mentalities and productive arrangements. Unlike politics, for example, aesthetics contains a self-constituting quality that cannot be transformed to meet the requisites for the survival of either ideology or economy.

The aesthetic judgments of good/bad, beautiful/ugly, innovative/traditional, high/low, etc., are not inherent in the art objects themselves. Instead, these and similar dualities emerge as the property of intellectuals whose position and interests within the division of labor have given them special, if not exclusive, rights to criticize aesthetic objects and activities. It is on account of the confirming of this privilege upon intellectuals, or "experts," that certain modalities of art have become "great art," and in turn great art has become fixed at particular points of "high civilization." Thus we have art classified into overtly normative categories, such as "classical Greek," "Renaissance," or "pop." Similarly, we also discover periods of history in which no art of significance was believed to exist (e.g., until recently, the art of the mid-nineteenth century). In Adorno's formulation there are neither great civilizations nor great objects of art, or the misunderstandings thereof (note his critique in "Bach Defended Against His Devotees," in *Prisms* 1981, 133–46). Most certainly, for Adorno it is illogical to assume that a great civilization (however that might be defined) is any more likely to spawn great art than some historically weaker period. In his account, aesthetics has existed continuously since the expulsion from Paradise in the expression of unmediated communication between human beings and nature, down to the most contemporary of artistic statements. All artistic experience and expression possesses the potential to transcend both its own sociohistorical circumstance and previous modalities of artistic expression. Here, then, the question of critical theory is simply the demand that one need only understand the realization of such a potential is a step on the way to freedom.

From this viewpoint on aesthetics, one realizes that it is impossible to negate the implicit political dimension of all art. Every instance of art represents, at least on the theoretical level, the act of a human being capable of and attempting to break through the disabling constraints imposed by social convention. Previous notions of aesthetics, and much of what passes as contemporary philosophical aesthetics, are obsolete. Since Adorno, we can no longer seriously entertain the idea of an artistic expression transferring messages via a form and content to a waiting subject. The subject does not wait, is not passive. Aesthetics is a praxis, and therefore the subject both anticipates and involves itself (that is, involves Being) in the object. Moreover, the art object cannot be thought of as an empirical record or storehouse of meaning from which the subject can shop for the correct interpretation. If the art object can be said to be a record at all, and the metaphor borders on reification, it is the record of a continuous historical struggle wherein humans are laboring to actualize more and more freedom.

Aesthetics as life and life as aesthetics. This is postmodernism for Adorno. Aesthetics is not some quadratic set of subjects and objects, encompassing the object, the viewing subject, an expert subject, and a medium of presentation for both (namely, the mass media). Rather, aesthetics is a fundamental dimension of each nonexpert subject, a way of relating to self, others, and the world. As with the Heideggerian hermeneutic circle, aesthetics maintains the tensions between the sedimentations of our past and the possibilities of our future. Moreover, aesthetics furnishes the critical ground from which we can begin to resolve these tensions within the existential moment of the present. Aesthetics is one of relatively few social spheres in the modern world in which subjects are free to attempt political (in its widest sense) decisions. To renew the religious metaphor used earlier, aesthetics allows for the differentiation of the Fall from the Resurrection. And in the context of life's praxis, the ability to render such a differentiation frequently spells the difference between political domination and freedom.

Postmodernism for Adorno is not something that can be theoretically, or for that matter, methodologically, assigned to attributes of the superstructure, as is advocated in the "end of ideology" argument. Furthermore, postmodernism is not an end product, quality, or characteristic of the infrastructure, as is proposed by the advocates of the thesis of the postindustrial society. Aesthetics is very much a part of the dialectics of real beings in a real social context. The analytical separation of infrastructure and superstructure makes sense only because both are essentially unified in the existence and fabric of Being itself.

Finally, there is an additional dimension to Adorno's concept of an immanent aesthetic analysis or criticism (i.e., an analysis that does not impose external models on aesthetic judgments). Adorno locates his aesthetic theory at the point of the subject, a real historical being. For Adorno, postmodernism is the joining of the critical being in an authentic subject/society totality. Aesthetics is that space or field of mediation within which the subject can pursue the most basic of human practices — the critical project of reaching for freedom.

8

Critical Interpretation: Jürgen Habermas

Jürgen Habermas was born on June 18, 1929, in Düsseldorf, Germany. From 1949 to 1954, he studied philosophy, history, psychology, and German literature at the universities in Göttingen, Zurich, and Bonn, where he wrote his dissertation on *The Absolute and History* (a study of certain aspects of the work of Schelling). In 1956 he became an assistant at the Institute for Social Research in Frankfurt, where he conducted research on the political knowledge of students, which led to the publication, in 1961, of *Students and Politics*. From 1951 to 1961, while still at Frankfurt, Habermas worked on his Habilitation, published in 1962 as *Structural Change of the "Public Sphere."*

After teaching philosophy at the University of Heidelberg, and then teaching philosophy and sociology back at Frankfurt, Habermas became the director of the Max Plank Institute in Starnberg, where he led a research program concerned with the human condition in a technical and industrial age. His work became widely recognized, and he received a number of awards, including the Hegel Prize from the city of Stuttgart (1973), the Sigmund Freud Award from the German Academy of Language and Literature at Darmstadt (1976), and the Adorno Prize from Frankfurt (1980). In 1982 Habermas returned to the University of Frankfurt, where he is a professor of sociology and philosophy. He is considered to be one of the major figures in contemporary social thought and the most far-reaching contributor to neorationalist theory.

Habermas' research program has been oriented toward the development of a theory of society that includes a practical intent, namely, the self-emancipation of people from systems and structures of domination. He has observed a degeneration in the sociopolitical contexts of socialist and capitalist societies, such as the disappearing proletarian consciousness and the tendency of advanced societies to be dominated by bureaucracy. As a consequence of these perceptions, Habermas judged that it was time to radically reformulate some of the major traditions in social thought.

This project is still in the process of unfolding. However, Habermas has produced a significant body of work on his wide-ranging "theory of communicative action." He argues that at the level of social theory, the increasing tendency to define practical problems as technical issues, which is the decided inclination of positivist sociology, threatens an essential aspect of human life.

For Habermas, technocratic consciousness justifies class interests and domination. Therefore, there is a need to go beyond the level of particular historical class interests in order to discover the fundamental interests of humankind as a whole. Thus, one of his first investigations concerned the domination of instrumental reasoning in contemporary science. He believes it is necessary to counteract the unidimensional tendencies of positivism and the consequences of such an orientation. He begins the attack with a systematic investigation of the nature of human interests and the kinds of knowledge that correspond to those interests. The argument refers to classical Greek philosophy, German rationalism, and a diverse range of philosophical traditions.

Habermas' contention is that knowledge is historically grounded and is also interest bound. Such boundness he terms "cognitive interest," or (later) "communicative competence." The theory of cognitive interests is an attempt to uncover the conditions for the possibility of knowledge. For Habermas, history, social reality, and nature are all a product of the constituting labor of the human species, the effort to produce one's existence and reproduce one's species-being. Thus, Habermas rejects the Kantian approach of locating such an enterprise in an ahistorical, transcendental subject. (Such a foundationalism, however, returns later in Habermas' work, in a modified form, to the structure of the process of communication and language itself.)

The cognitive interests are "quasi-transcendental," in the sense that they have a transcendental function, i.e., self-reflective and self-determining, and this function arises from actual structures of human life. The cognitive interests include the technical, the practical, and the emancipatory. These three interests unfold in the media of: work (instrumental), interaction (language), and power (asymmetrical relations or constraints and dependency). These give rise to three modes of science: the empirical-analytical, the historical-hermeneutical, and the critical. Habermas' central claim in this context is that these three sciences systematize and formalize the procedures required for the success of human activity.

Discourse, Science, and Society

Habermas traces the origin of the emergence of public opinion from the eighteenth century, when state and civil society began to separate themselves. This division increased with the growth of capitalism. Habermas notes that two trends have become increasingly marked in advanced industrial societies. First, there has been an increase in the intervention of the state in people's economic activity, intervention ostensively designed to stabilize economic growth. Second, there has been an increase in the interdependence of research and technology, to the extent that one seems to presume the other.

The first, state intervention, has altered both economic activity and political life. It has altered economic activity by restructuring the market and manipulating tendencies for economic crises. Similarly, it has altered political life by transforming the structure of ideology and communication. For example, the classic capitalist ideology of fair exchange and the free market is disrupted when economic life increasingly operates under direct political regulation, which attempts constantly to "fine tune" the market. However beneficial such intervention is intended to be, though, the consequences are ultimately self-defeating. There is an urgent need to rethink many of our practical problems, in particular those that are directly affected by such market manipulation.

Habermas identifies four levels of progressive rationalization of technical control:

1. the application of scientific techniques to social problems to achieve specific goals (note the similarity between this and the increasing reconstruction of everydayness by the social sciences, discussed in the section on Adorno)
2. the competing technical solutions for the realization of specific goals; here the technical values of efficiency and economy, in addition to the internal politics of the expert establishment, tend to dominate the selection of means
3. the technical rationality is extended directly to the basic formalized value-survival or self-assertion of interest groups
4. a process of decision making centered on statistical forecasts and the use of computerized manipulation of data

As a whole, these types of cybernetic systems theories are becoming the bases for the automatic analysis and steering of action systems in complex environments. The solution to the problems caused by these unilinear perspectives, according to Habermas, began and begins with Marx.

Marx incorporates an analysis of the way human beings reproduce the material conditions of their lives in his theory of structural transformations. This reproduction is accomplished by people interpreting and altering their institutions through historical struggles, a dialectical process that incorporates both economic and cultural traditions, and that brings about "epochal inventions." Habermas argues that Marx had a tendency to reduce practical to technical activity, which is productive labor, or instrumental action, an emphasis on instrumentality that lends positivistic overtones to Marx's work. Later, in the works of Engels, Lenin, and Stalin, this emphasis became even more dominant, leading to the well-known reliance on economic determinism of orthodox Marxism. Such determinism culminates in a centralized bureaucracy dominated by a party and its "security" apparatus, accompanied by a concomitant decrease of freedom. Thus, science in the form of dialectical materialism (or DIAMAT) legitimizes technocratic activity and centralized management by "experts" supported by an extensive system of coercion and domination.

Habermas' critique of such developments in Marxism, as well as his critique of the developed societies, leads him to attempt a reformulation of the philosophical and methodological foundation of these trends. He focuses his discussion of historical materialism, for instance, on two basic concepts, social labor and the history of the species. For Marx, the concept of "socially organized labor" specifies the way human beings reproduce their lives; for Habermas, social labor is their form of social organization, and he emphasizes that language is one of the crucial media through which social life unfolds.

The critique and reformulation of Marxism, and the incorporation of cognitive dimensions into the project, emerge in particular in *Communication and the Evolution of Society* (1979). That work contains a number of essays that are critical for an understanding of Habermas' mature research program. In it he works out his project regarding the theory of communication in human interaction. In addition, the book introduces a critical reevaluation of Kohlberg's theory of moral development with a view toward establishing the bases for a description of personal and societal moral development within his own theory of socialization. Furthermore, the work delineates Habermas' theory of social evolution through a reformulation of Marxism that pays particular attention to the development of law and morality, and it concludes with an elaboration of arguments regarding the modern state, which he earlier presented in *Legitimation Crisis* (1975).

Habermas argues that European capitalism was not conditioned by productive forces, but rather followed their development. He contends that social evolution is a "learning process" that can be reconstructed on the basis of developmental logic. Borrowing concepts from social psychology, Habermas explains, by analogy, the stages of development, which include Ego-development and the evolution of worldviews, the development of Ego-identity and group identity, moral judgments, and actions of individuals regarding legal and moral systems.

For Habermas, the core dimensions of interaction are law and morality. These represent arrangements and orientations taken by people to resolve action-conflicts by constructing agreements, and they also link these arrangements to three levels or stages in the development of human moral consciousness: the preconventional, conventional, and the postconventional. (The best formulation of these stages is in L. Kohlberg 1969. For a recent critique, see Cortese 1990.)

Briefly, the preconventional level of morality occurs at the stage of childhood, the conventional at adolescence, and the postconventional at maturity. At the preconventional level, the subject has not yet come to full knowledge; it is an egocentric and egoistic position, and the tendency is to manipulate the social and natural environment to one's own ends. At the conventional level, symbolic meaning-systems begin to operate, and the subject starts to realize the expected standards to follow in social interaction. At this point the process of social relations becomes a commonality of norms that structure social interaction. Moreover, since at this level the underpinnings of relations stand on a symbolic universe, the problems are particular to specific contexts, or "social environments." The postconventional level is a stage of the collective sharing of norms; the central criterion is given by the group, which possesses abiding transcendental values and which leads the individual to universalistic orientations.

Like Marx, Habermas allows that the developmental dynamics of normative structures are conditioned by economic circumstances, and thus the learning process becomes merely a reaction to such circumstances. In this sense, culture remains part of the superstructure, although for Habermas it plays a more prominent role in the transition to new developmental levels. This notion was central to the work of the early Frankfurt School, in particular the considerations of Adorno and Horkheimer. Habermas' reconstruction of capitalism includes a treatment of the question and character of a "postmodern" society, as well as the emergence of social crises unique to advanced capitalist societies. In these contexts, two concepts assume great significance — the notion of life-world and the idea of self-regulated systems.

The world presupposes human life, and the human life-world can never be completely analyzed (of particular salience to this point is Husserl's *The Crisis of European Sciences*). Nevertheless, such a life-world can be thematized, particularly through its horizons, i.e., subjects and things. One can look at a text as a complex picture of a life-world, and can view such a life-world as a construct emerging from the centrality of its subjects. Moreover, the life-world can also be viewed from the perspective of the other person, as an intersubjective phenomenon. Much of Western thought has been classically based on the dyad of subject and object, a construct that is overly egocentric. Thus, there is a need to reconstruct a basic unit of analysis, and a fundamental way of effecting this construction is to focus on language, which links the two poles of the unit in intercommunication, and distorted communication, which is also derived from the basic unit and which implicitly makes the subject active and the object passive.

The reconstruction of historical-materialism recognizes stages of formation brought about by the internal characteristics of the social formation itself. It is a result of the whole dynamism of an ongoing self-regulated system (further discussion of this theme appears in Habermas' debate with Niklas Luhmann, in Habermas and Luhmann 1971; cf. Sixel 1976). In the system of advanced capitalism, Habermas sees three subsystems operating: the economic, the political-administrative, and the sociocultural. The first has a public sector (i.e., industries involved in armaments and space research), a private sector (oriented toward market competition), and a segment of the private sector that is free from market constraints (foundations, charitable organizations, etc.). A crisis in one is controlled at the expense of displacing and transforming the contradiction into another. Ultimately, the system's identity can only be preserved at the cost of individual autonomy, with the coming into being of a totally administered and manipulated world.

Interest, Knowledge, and Action

It is in this realm of thought that Habermas supplies his strongest critique of scientism, i.e., the ideology through which science has been identified with knowledge, rather than as one form (among others) of models toward knowledge. He centers his attack on positivism, in particular, because of its foundation in instrumental reason. One of the pervasive concerns of Habermas's critical theory is with the relationship between knowledge and human interests (Habermas 1971). Knowledge enterprises are seen as the result of three kinds of interests: information that expands our exercise of technical control, in particular of the natural environment; interpretations that make possible the orientation of action within common traditions; and analysis that frees consciousness from its dependence on hypostatized power.

Kant had understood science as one category of knowledge; Hegel sought to supersede Kant's project through a reflection on the forms of knowledge that emerge out of human experience. Instead of understanding the empirical sciences as one category of possible knowledge, Hegel dissolved its pristine status into a developmental and holistic process of knowing (individual and collective) leading to Absolute knowledge (in the Wise Man and Absolute Spirit). Habermas' critical evaluation of these theoretical formulations leads him to suggest that philosophical representation of a universal scientific knowledge is nothing but a fiction. It was Marx, of course, that demythologized such fictions and uncovered the basis for comprehending the epistemic subject as the knower *(The German Ideology* 1947), but he reduced "practical activity" to labor. For him, the labor process represented the perpetual natural necessity of human life, and in this process, knowledge increased the human's range of control over nature and enhanced the capacity to transform the world (a notion derived from Hegel's *Phenomenology of Spirit,* in the section on the "Master and the Slave"). But the instrumental relation to nature did not change. Furthermore, Marx also tied this principle to that of evolution as adumbrated by Charles Darwin, describing the modes of production as they develop according to an evolutionary, albeit dialectical, process.

Habermas criticizes Marx further for not distinguishing between the empirical-analytical and the human sciences. Habermas accepts that knowing-subjects play an active role in constituting the world they know. Thus, he proposes that hermeneutics become a key project in disclosing the reality of the human realm, and he borrows ideas from Gadamer and Dilthey toward that end (this approach led to what is known as the Gadamer-Habermas debate in hermeneutics, which is described below).

Dilthey's position toward understanding relied substantially on the philosophy of life and the question of human experience (Erlebnis), on the objectifications of the human mind (especially art), and on a psychological formulation of the relationships between investigator and created objects. Concerning the latter, one may recall that Dilthey requires that the researcher must place herself in the context of the creator of the cultural object so as to grasp the structure of experiential meanings that inform the creation of the object. For later proponents of hermeneutics, such a simplified version of the interpretive event cannot stand phenomenological and existential criticisms.

As noted in an earlier section, Gadamer constructed a hermeneutics that accounts for Dilthey's flaws. Here it is sufficient to summarize the main points:

1. Prejudices are an integral part of understanding.
2. Knowledge is generated within the framework of tradition, and hence there is no possibility of arriving at a final understanding of the phenomenon.
3. We are part of history and tradition, and therefore understanding contributes to our own self-formation (Bildung).
4. The process of understanding cannot ever be complete, since we are a part of history, and not vice versa.
5. Understanding is neither an ideal of human experience nor a method; it is rather "the original form of being in the world" (cf. Heidegger 1962, 78–168).

For Gadamer, the medium in which understanding itself is realized is language. Language transcends human beings and therefore has a universal character. Habermas goes a step further and suggests that the tradition that supports consensus provides the standards from which the experienced meaning is derived. One of the key forms of knowledge engendered on the basis of such standards, and most appropriate for the emancipatory interest of human beings, is self-knowledge, generated through self-reflection. What enables self-reflection is the process of "depth hermeneutics," a concept developed by Habermas from the domain of psychoanalysis. This is an attempt to reconstruct a portion of one's life history that has been systematically repressed. It is the mode of reflection that brings to consciousness those determinants of self-formative processes that ideologically determine a contemporary praxis and conception of the world.

This world, however, always involves discourse with other people, and such discourse requires a commonality of meaning that yields the possibility of understanding. Habermas asserts that "communicative competence" can be rationally reconstructed. The basis of this investigation rests in human utterances (or discourses) and their underlying validity claims. He recognizes four types of validity claims:

1. that the utterance is comprehensible
2. that its propositional content is true
3. that it is legitimate and appropriate in the context
4. that it is sincerely spoken

The goal of coming to an understanding requires the establishment of a genuine consensus. This involves the emergence of an agreement among participants that includes intersubjectivity, shared knowledge, mutual trust, and an accord with each other. Each speech act carries specific meaning and also puts forward general claims. Consequently, the listener can be "rationally motivated" to accept the content of the speaker's intervention. But if the accountability is presupposed, how do we account for systematically distorted communication? Habermas quickly points out that accountability is created through a legitimation of norms, world views, and power, which creates a sort of fictional accountability (for a parallel argument, see Michel Foucault's *The Archaeology of Knowledge and The Discourse on Language*). Habermas also emphasizes that an ideal speech situation must ensure equal opportunity for discussion, free from all domination and systematically distorted communication. He calls such a criterion a "rational consensus," and this is the ultimate criterion of the truth of a statement. In a systematic argument, the reality of an ideal speech situation is anticipated. Without such an anticipation, there would be no scope for a discourse. The anticipated situation can serve as a standard for the critique of systematically distorted communications.

The Habermas-Gadamer Debate

Earlier, we suggested that Gadamer's *Truth and Method* constitutes the most significant contribution toward an understanding of the cultural disciplines since Dilthey's essays on the historical method. It was these essays that were discussed and critiqued by Habermas in Part 2 of *Knowledge and Human Interests,* and part of the importance of Gadamer's work lies in the criticism that he raises against Dilthey's conception of hermeneutics. Gadamer's and Habermas' critiques are quite similar, and Habermas acknowledges Gadamer's significance to his own work. Nevertheless, there is a major disagreement between them as to the consequences of rejecting Dilthey's methodology for the cultural disciplines. This dispute was stimulated by Habermas' essay on "The Universality of Hermeneutics," which concerns both the status and the scope of hermeneutic inquiry.

In the context of his debate with Habermas, Gadamer raised the issue of the limitations of applicability of the psychoanalytic method (which was a perspective that contributed to the critical theory that grounds Habermas' work). In a postscript to the third edition of *Truth and Method,* Gadamer writes:

If the place of my work within the philosophy of our century were to be characterized, then it would be necessary to proceed from the standpoint that I have attempted to achieve a contribution which mediates between philosophy and the sciences and especially to advance in a productive manner the radical questions of Martin Heidegger, to which I am decisively indebted, upon the broad plane of scientific experience — so far as I am able to survey it at all. Of course this necessitates superseding the limited horizon of interests of the methodology of the philosophy of science" (Gadamer 1975b, xiii).[1]

This statement of Gadamer's intent lies at the root of his disagreement with Habermas. The title of Gadamer's major work *(Truth and Method)* heralds Gadamer's conception that these are two different subjects of investigation and that the preoccupation of the modern sciences with method has obscured the experiential awareness of the importance of truth. For him truth is the larger goal of inquiry, and it is the task of philosophical hermeneutics to disclose to us the totality of human experience within which truth can be understood. He calls our attention to this in the introduction: "The hermeneutic developed here is not, therefore, a methodology of the human sciences, but an attempt to understand what the human sciences truly are, beyond their methodological self-consciousness, and what connects them with the totality of our experiences of the world" (Gadamer 1975b, xiii).

The central notion that Gadamer develops out of Heidegger's philosophy and employs in his criticism of Dilthey is that of "effective history" (see the earlier discussion of this topic). For Gadamer, as for Heidegger, the medium within which tradition is transmitted is language. Thus, the paradigmatic hermeneutic activity is that of translation: "The translation process contains the whole secret of human understanding of the world and of social communication. Translation is an indivisible unity of implicit anticipation, of presumption of meaning in general and of the explicit determination of what one presumed" (Gadamer 1975b, xiv). Within the translation process, a linguistic equivalent in the "reception" language is sought for the foreign expression, since at no time can the translator stand outside of his own language in order to grasp the expression "directly." This characteristic is also true for the

---

1. Certain passages in this section are from the third German edition of *Wahrheit und Methode.* That edition contains material, such as this excerpt and the three following, that do not appear in the standard English translation. The English version of *Truth and Method* is a translation of the second German edition. Ironically, the English translation appeared in 1975, which was the same year of publication of the third edition in Germany. Hence the English version is listed as 1975a and the third edition as 1975b. The excerpts from the third German edition were translated by the authors, and any error of translation is ours alone.

hermeneutic situation in general, and Gadamer makes use of it in introducing the important term "horizon."

Effective-historical consciousness is primarily consciousness of the hermeneutic situation. . . . We define the concept of "situation" by saying that it represents a standpoint that limits the possibility of vision. Hence an essential part of the concept of situation is the concept of "horizon." The horizon is the range of vision that includes everything that can be seen from a particular vantage point" (Gadamer 1975b, xv).

Gadamer's criticism of Dilthey capitalizes on the notion of horizon by arguing that an essential feature of the hermeneutic situation is the horizon that the historical investigator himself brings to the investigation. Consequently, the historical investigator cannot attain a status of virtual simultaneity with the author of the text. This possibility is excluded by the fact that the text itself proceeds from a horizon of understanding that is different than the historian's. Not just the single elements of the text, but also the general cultural perspective within which the text arises must be projected as a horizon different from the horizon of the present if true historical knowledge is to be achieved. Therefore, historical knowledge is not acquired through the denial of the role of either horizon, but instead through the *fusion* of the two different horizons. Such fusion does not in itself present a remarkable or unusual achievement, but is something that occurs continually in the transmission of tradition:

There is no more an isolated horizon of the present than there are historical horizons which one would have to achieve. Understanding, rather, is always the fusion of these horizons which we imagine to exist by themselves. . . . In a tradition this process of fusion is continually going on, for there old and new continually grow together to make something of loving value, without either being explicitly distinguished from the other" (Gadamer 1975a, 273).

Historical understanding leads to an explicit awareness of the fusion of historical horizons and also of the role of tradition in making such a fusion possible. In itself historical consciousness is not structurally different from everyday experience; but, in being carried out explicitly, it can also make us aware of the role of the everyday, prescientific understanding, both historically and in our own present situation. It is within everyday experience that traditional meanings are mediated to a present context and that the truths of that tradition are disclosed. Habermas has few objections to Gadamer's description of hermeneutics and has even borrowed elements of it in his own critique of Dilthey. However, Gadamer does express a fundamental objection to Habermas' use of hermeneutics, in terms of the manner in which Habermas wishes to apply the hermeneutic method. Habermas

> . . . considers the hermeneutical description of the sciences relevant only to the sociohistorical disciplines. The hermeneutical dimension is not universal and all-inclusive, but subordinate to the even more reflective level of Habermas's own concern with *Ideologiekritik* — social criticism of ideologies modeled on the paradigm of psychoanalysis (Hoy 1978, 117).

Granted that this position is a particular kind of understanding of what sociological theory may be, Gadamer tends to assume a much broader and diverse sort of task for hermeneutics (setting aside, for instance, fundamental hermeneutic questions as they appear in historical sociology, ethnomethodology, symbolic interactionism, and etc., Gadamer is basically correct in his assessment of Habermas' use of hermeneutics, in particular within the context of a model for a critical theory of society). Habermas sees the model of translation as a scientific method for attaining understanding, and he interprets the consciousness of effective history to be the transcendental framework within which translation occurs. Therefore, although Habermas criticizes Dilthey's treatment of historical method, he does not abandon the methodological ideal altogether, but rather chooses to see a methodology operative within Gadamer's own work.

Gadamer believes that his analysis takes place at a deeper level than that of methodological discussions (Heidegger's "ontological," rather than the "ontic" level of the special disciplines such as sociology) and that it opens up important dimensions of the past of which social science, especially the emancipatory social sciences (e.g., "critical"), show no awareness. For the consciousness of effective history discloses the essential part that the horizon of the present plays in the formulation of historical analysis. One way that the horizon of the interpreter enters into the process of interpretation has been noted by many historical theorists, but also quite clearly by Gadamer himself:

> . . . a person trying to understand a text is prepared for it to tell him something. . . . The important thing is to be aware of one's own bias, so that the text may present itself in all its newness and thus be able to assert its own truth against one's own fore-meanings (Gadamer 1975a, 238).

Yet, from this worry Gadamer does not wish to extrapolate to the conclusion that all foremeanings or "prejudices" are bad. In his opinion, an increased estimation of the role of prejudices in hermeneutic understanding will also lead to a higher evaluation of the role of authority, which inculcates the prejudices that we have. Dilthey's historicism, but also the concern for methodology in general, take their historical roots from the opposition between authority and reason propagated by advocates of the Enlightenment (e.g., Francis Bacon and the *idolae* and the debate on "value-free" science, so prominent in the 1960s). Emancipatory social science continues often to accentuate the opposition of reason to authority, by propounding a critique of ideology that dissolves the dogmatic powers of authority through the self-reflective powers of reason. The paradigm for Habermas' emancipatory social science is given in psychoanalytic practice, in which the therapist offers an interpretation of the patient's unconscious motivations that stimulates a process of critical self-reflection. Yet, to the employment of psychoanalysis as a paradigm for the general understanding of social reality, Gadamer argues that hermeneutics is not such a methodological activity:

> The concerns of hermeneutics are distinct from epistemological or methodological ones. They are 'ontological'. The process of understanding, understood ontologically, is co-extensive with an experience of our world and history, in which we are not masters of either or both. . . . Knowing how to live is a form of wisdom and does not always and necessarily imply mastery of the conditions of life (Misgeld 1976, 173).

The systematic reasons that support Gadamer's argument flow from his concept of the role of prejudices in hermeneutic understanding. Yet, beyond seeking to eliminate "false prejudices," all efforts must be made to insure that the horizon of the text that is being interpreted is really disclosed. As Gadamer writes of historical consciousness:

> The task of historical understanding also involves acquiring the particular historical horizon, so that what we are seeking to understand can be seen in its true dimensions. If we fail to place ourselves in this way within the historical horizon out of which tradition speaks, we shall misunderstand the significance of what it has to say to us. To this extent it seems a legitimate hermeneutical requirement to place ourselves in the other situation in order to understand it (Gadamer 1975a, 270).

In addition, the applicability of the text to the present situation — its practical relevance as a part of the past tradition for the present horizon of the historical interpreter — must also be carefully examined:

> That which has been sanctioned by tradition and custom has an authority that is nameless, and our finite historical being is marked by the fact that always the authority of what has been transmitted — and not only what is clearly grounded — has power over our attitudes and behavior (Gadamer 1975a, 249).

As a result, if there is any disturbance in the symmetrical relationship between interpreter and text, it must necessarily fall in favor of the text as a part of the past tradition. Because the text must genuinely be seen as a source of possible truth from an authority within an earlier historical horizon, every step must be taken to insure that it is the text itself that is actually being interpreted.

In psychoanalysis the symmetrical relationship between interpreter and interpreted is slanted, only in the opposite direction. In this instance there is a superiority of the interpreter, the analyst, who is held to possess a greater knowledge of the patient's linguistic utterances than the patient herself. Moreover, in manipulating the interactional context in such a way that the transference neurosis results, the analyst is also in a position of being able to know his patient's behavior in advance (for an analysis of the psychoanalytic model as a model of hermeneutic investigation, see K. O. Apel, *Analytic Philosophy of Language and the Geisteswissenschaften,* 1967). Against this posture of the analyst, Gadamer has argued:

> The claim to understand the person in advance performs the function of keeping the claim of the other person at a distance. . . . A person who reflects himself out of the mutuality of such relationship changes this relationship and destroys its moral bond. A person who reflects himself out of a living relationship to tradition destroys the true meaning of this tradition in exactly the same way (Gadamer 1975a, 324).

The transition from psychoanalysis to the critique of ideology involves the sort of generalization from individual to group critique that is referred to in the final sentence of this above quotation, only Gadamer wishes to argue that such a generalization is neither desirable nor even possible, because of the constitutive role that tradition plays in the acquisition of moral values and of all knowledge. In other words, the authority of tradition serves as the source of the moral values, which are handed down in the socialization process, and also of the conceptual frameworks within which truth can be discovered: "Tradition is operative on us by forming our personal and social preoccupations before we can even pass judgment on the manner in which they are operative" (Misgeld 1976, 178). Yet Gadamer's emphasis is upon how this prejudicial force of tradition is not so much a limiting condition as an enabling one:

> The effect of a living tradition and the effect of historical study must constitute a unity, the analysis of which would reveal only a texture of reciprocal relationships. Hence we would do well not to regard historical consciousness as something radically new — as it seems at first — but as a new element within that which has always made up the human relation to the past (Gadamer 1975a, 251).

Because of this necessary relationship between knowledge and tradition, there can be no necessary opposition between reason and authority. Therefore, Gadamer holds hermeneutic reflection, a form of reflection that clarifies the important role of tradition for all human understanding, to exceed in scope the power of critical self-reflection or of any other method that would claim an access to truth outside tradition. As a consequence, psychoanalysis is also considered to be an inappropriate model for understanding the full contours of past and present social reality.

Gadamer attacks the applicability of psychoanalytic technique to the larger sphere of social reality, because Habermas has proposed it as a limitation to the scope of philosophical hermeneutics. Gadamer's response has the effect of admitting the exceptional status of psychoanalysis in respect to hermeneutics but also of restricting the scope of psychoanalytic method itself so that Habermas' claim is noticeably weakened. Since psychoanalysis can only have applicability with regards to individual cases that are institutionally defined and delimited, it offers a too-restricted approach to social reality and must be supplemented by a broader philosophical hermeneutics. Therefore, psychoanalysis, in Gadamer's view, represents a true exception to hermeneutics but not a damaging one with respect to its scope as a social approach.

At this point we can inquire as to Habermas' precise response to Gadamer's arguments. Habermas' original appeal to the "depth hermeneutics" of psychoanalytic interpretation was motivated by the consideration that it incorporated aspects of causal explanation in a manner in which historical narrations do not. Thus, in this respect at least, it was apparently broader than historical hermeneutics. Further analysis indicated how the "explanatory understanding" of such depth hermeneutics was the result of the "general interpretation" of the socialization process presented by the therapist to the patient in order to stimulate self-reflection. But subsequent, deeper analysis also revealed that the basis for such general interpretations does not lie within psychoanalysis itself, but is instead the product of reconstructive sciences, which examine the cognitive, interactional, and linguistic competence of the developing individual. Hence psychoanalysis itself became more limited in scope for Habermas, since it as a self-reflective science was seen to depend for its theoretical foundations upon the reconstructive sciences, especially upon the theory of communicative competence.

Thus, when Habermas refers to psychoanalysis in the later essay on the claim of the universality of hermeneutics, it is not primarily to argue for the greater scope of critical social sciences in comparison to philosophical hermeneutics — although he does indeed continue to hold this thesis — but instead to make use of a discipline with very clear ties to the reconstructive sciences in order to illustrate the quite similar foundations for hermeneutics itself. In other words, the primary limitation on the scope of hermeneutic inquiry is not any longer to be found in psychoanalysis, but instead within the new category of rationally reconstructive science. That this is the underlying significance of Habermas' later appeal to psychoanalysis in his dispute with Gadamer can be discerned from the following:

> . . . the collective background and context of speakers and hearers determines interpretations of their explicit utterances to an extraordinarily high degree. . . . Naturally this meaning could not be thought independently of contextual conditions altogether; for each type of speech act there are *general* contextual conditions that must be met if the speaker is to be able to achieve illocutionary success. But these general contextual conditions could supposedly be derived in turn from the literal meaning of the linguistic expressions employed in the standard speech acts. And as a matter of fact, if formal pragmatics is not to lose its object, knowledge of the conditions under which speech acts may be accepted as valid cannot depend *completely* on contingent background knowledge (Habermas 1984, 335–36).

Thus a theory of communicative competence is required to examine and adumbrate not only everyday speech acts, but also those systematically distorted speech acts found in the discourse of psychoanalysis. "The hermeneutical dimension is not universal and all-inclusive, but subordinate to the even more reflective level of Habermas's own concern with *Ideologiekritik* — social criticism of ideologies modeled on the paradigm of psychoanalysis" (Hoy 1978, 117).

Yet why should the theory of communicative competence also play an important role with respect to philosophical hermeneutics? In order to answer this question, Habermas turns his attention to the "systematic argument" he finds in *Truth and Method.* For Habermas,

> . . . critical theory demands the self-limitation of the hermeneutical approach on behalf of critical reflection, which cannot be thought of but as taking an interest in its own generation by emancipating itself from tradition. For it, reaching reciprocal agreement in the discursive examination of reciprocal and competing truth claims is a normative concept. A frame of reference is to be discovered which allows us to transcend the context of tradition as such. Only then tradition can also be criticized (Misgeld 1976, 181).

Gadamer, however, establishes the primacy of tradition through his development of the context of dependency of linguistic understanding. All legitimate understanding occurs in light of the "true" prejudices that promote the understanding of traditional texts. These true prejudices act as an implicit consensus between the two horizons of understanding that are being fused. Of course, it might be possible to question this consensus, but for Gadamer such questioning can be understood only on the basis of another common prejudice shared between the two horizons of understanding. It is not possible to prescind from all prejudices without interrupting the conversation within which hermeneutical understanding takes place; the conversation, which as Gadamer quotes from the Romantics as being "we are," cannot be transcended without destroying it completely. Therefore all human understanding can only be achieved on the basis of some antecedent consensus between the adherents of the differing horizons, which is also the reason "why prejudices of the individual, far more than his judgments, constitute the historical reality of his being" (Gadamer 1975a, 245).

Habermas finds the sciences of rational reconstruction relevant to this dispute, precisely because they do, in a certain sense, transcend the parameters of the conversational situation. They do so by inquiring into the subjective conditions, the individual and social competences, that make such an activity possible. This is not to say that the theory of communicative competence can totally explain the context of the conversational exchange. But it can point to certain formal structure, the dialogue-constitutive universals, which reappear in all acts of communication. Moreover, it can seek to relate these universals as they appear in one natural language to those of other natural languages so that a general and comprehensive theory of this competence is constructed. Admittedly, what is involved in this procedure is far more properly designated a reconstruction of a given natural language or natural languages than their transcendence, but the notion of reconstruction serves the same purpose with respect to Gadamer's argument. Rational reconstruction is based upon intuitive knowledge, which is implicitly bound not simply to the immediate linguistic context, but to a universal pragmatic context and ultimately to an ideal speech situation.

As might be expected, it is the normative aspects of the theory of communicative competence that are primarily relevant to the dispute over the scope of philosophical hermeneutics. Thus, Habermas agrees with Gadamer that all intersubjective understanding presupposes some antecedent background consensus, but he questions whether this consensus is necessarily rational. In particular, Habermas raises the question of whether the consensus was achieved in a situation free from violence and distorted communication or whether instead it was not a pseudo-consensus accomplished with the purpose that one partner in the communication could manipulate the other. Philosophical hermeneutics treats all linguistic interactions as acts of true communication and does not acknowledge the possible strategic use of language for ideological manipulation (cf. Hoy 1978, 124).

Psychoanalysis, on the other hand, does deal with such acts of pseudo-communication as it traces the power relationships between parents and child in the progressing process of socialization. When it does disclose such acts as pseudo-communicative, however, it must make clear reference to its theoretical presuppositions taken from the theory of communicative competence. Habermas' implicit claim in his dialogue with Gadamer is that philosophical hermeneutics must be similarly dependent upon this rationally reconstructive theory as well.

But what about Gadamer's argument that the appeal to the psychoanalytic model is totally misleading with respect to the larger sphere of social reality? What about his attack against the dogmatic antithesis between consensus accepted on the basis of authority and rational consensus? Here it is helpful to interject some of the important conclusions from the discussion of Arieti's notion of "paleosymbols." The systematic distortions of language expressed by the patient in psychoanalysis can be interpreted as a formal regression to an earlier stage of symbolic capacities, the paleosymbolic stage, which was superior to the levels of signs and images but antecedent to the stage of public symbols. Arieti chose the terms "paleosymbols" and "paleologic" to indicate that what is involved in schizophrenic utterances and dream symbols is not a totally irrational form of expression, but instead an archaic form of rationality. Consequently, the paleosymbolic stage of communication stands within a cognitively *developmental* scheme where each succeeding stage represents a progressive form of cognitive development.

The notion of cognitive development or of a developmental logic stands in latent conflict with Gadamer's emphasis upon tradition and authority, because implied within developmental framework is the notion that there can be an increase in the cognitive capacity or an improvement in rationality. This implication complements Habermas' criterion for truth as universal and unconstrained consensus, because this criterion is a feature of the ideal speech situation *anticipated* in every speech act. In other words, the notion of truth is future-oriented, and each progressive stage in the developmental process represents a closer approximation to it. Gadamer, on the other hand, goes to great lengths to emphasize the role of tradition as the source of knowledge and truth. There is no opposition between authority and reason, quite simply because reason is past-oriented toward the sources of tradition within which truth has been disclosed. If, however, there is such a phenomenon as the increase of rationality or the increase of knowledge, it is not immediately evident why this increase should be attributed to authority. Indeed it would appear more likely that the increase would be achieved in the face of authority or in opposition to the tradition.

When Gadamer states that tradition makes knowledge possible, this claim is indeed plausible with reference to the present stage of knowledge of the cultural tradition, but most implausible for any new developments that, in some sense or other, go beyond tradition. Psychoanalysis supposes the tenability of developmental models of cognitive, affective, and linguistic development for the individual, but are there any grounds for supposing a similar pattern with regards to social history? In short, can there be a theory of social evolution?

This, we can assume, is the real issue that Gadamer is raising in contesting the value of psychoanalysis as a model for social thought. For in emphasizing the general role of tradition in leading to the fusion between past and present horizons, he is at the same time establishing a bridge of continuity between any historical epoch and the present. This sense of continuity also extends to social institutions.

If an emphasis is placed upon mutual consistency, continuity, and resilience to institutional change, then one is led, as Habermas, to accuse Gadamer of defending an inherently conservative position. Gadamer tends to reject the application of the "conservative" label to his hermeneutics:

> However problematical the conscious restoration of traditions or the conscious creation of new traditions may be, the romantic faith in the "growth of tradition," before which all reason must remain silent, is just as prejudiced as and is fundamentally like the enlightenment. The fact is that tradition is constantly an element of freedom and of history itself (Gadamer 1975a, 250).

Even if this response from Gadamer is acceptable as a legitimate consequence of, or extrapolation from, his theoretical view, still it has the detrimental effect, in Habermas' estimation, of leaving the notion of tradition fundamentally unclarified. For fear that an exhaustive analysis of tradition might mistakenly be attempted, apparently no specific content at all is given to this key concept. Thus, if both changing the status quo and retaining it are forms of tradition, then tradition has been conceived so broadly as to exclude nothing from its scope. Habermas, on the other hand, seeks to distinguish the linguistic aspects of the tradition that express communicative understanding from those that serve to conceal power relationships. Moreover, he also separates the principles of social organization from the technical problems involved in economic production and technological change. In large part because of these categorical distinctions, he can plot significant changes in the mode of production and institutional structure that warrant the postulation of an evolutionary pattern. Within this pattern, tradition appears in the guise of stable factors of institutional organization that, however, are also susceptible to progressive changes under suitable economic and cultural conditions. Consequently, tradition for Habermas is not antithetical to reason, but is an insufficient source to account for what is a basically developing capacity on both the individual and the social levels.

Where the conflict between the views of these two theorists is most apparent is in the differing evaluations of the Enlightenment and modern science. For Gadamer, the historicism of Dilthey can be explained by his imitation of an inappropriate modern methodological ideal that led him to deny the continuity within the traditions of understanding. As a result, he assumed a great temporal distance between the modern epoch and its historical predecessors, which also reflected the Enlightenment's own estimation of itself. For Gadamer, "It would be more correct to take historical consciousness not as a radically new phenomenon, but as a relative if 'revolutionary' transformation within what has always constituted the relation of man vis-à-vis his past" (Habermas 1970, 285). For Habermas, however, the historical consciousness of the Enlightenment and historicism does represent a fundamentally new phenomenon, insofar as for the first time the role of authority in the transmission of tradition is actually recognized and methodologically understood. Thus the conscious awareness of authority means for Habermas something fundamentally different from the earlier unconscious role of authority, since the acceptance of tradition can now be called upon to justify itself rationally in a way that was not earlier possible. The justification ought not follow an ideal established by natural science. Instead, a methodological criterion appropriate for historical inquiry can be proposed in terms of a rational consensus among the participants in the inquiry. Hence, Habermas finds a change within the historical consciousness of the Enlightenment that has overall social evolutionary significance.

The question then arises as to whether in this historical instance the change in social consciousness involves a qualitative break with the tradition (Habermas), a question that goes beyond the current discussion. Still there does not appear to be any reason "in principle" why Habermas must be wrong in his historical judgment. To generalize, there appears to be no "in principle" objection to the larger project of developing a theory of social evolution to explain important social changes. In fact, the earlier discussion of Arieti's paleosymbols has lent credence to the step of invoking important evolutionary changes to explain the long and arduous transition from prehistoric forms of primitive social organization to the relatively recent forms of earlier civilization, so that at least the initial stages of a social evolutionary pattern have a high degree of plausibility. If there is indeed the historical basis for positing such a pattern, then there would also be the theoretical basis for a critique of ideology to discern the retrogressions in social development that have occurred in past and present constellations of social forces. Consequently, if there are grounds for accepting the theory of social evolution, there are also methodological reasons for rejecting Gadamer's argument concerning the limitations of psychoanalytic method because the same critical attitude also characterizes the activity of the critique of ideology. In fact, inasmuch as the inquiry into individual development would parallel the study of social evolution, to the same degree psychoanalytic investigation could complement a critical style of social analysis. Thus there is no systematic argument that in principle can exclude psychoanalysis from being a paradigm for inquiry within the field of social thought.

A final comment needs to be made about Gadamer's hostility to the methodological aims of Habermas and of modern science in general. Gadamer makes the ground for his antagonism clear in an early section of *Truth and Method:*

> The modern concept of science and the associated concept of method are insufficient. What makes the human sciences into sciences can be understood more easily from the tradition of the concept of *Bildung* than from the concept of method in modern science. It is on the humanistic tradition that we must rely (Gadamer 1975a, 18).

Gadamer reminds us that his essential task is aesthetic, that the goal of hermeneutics is the appreciation and understanding not only of works of art, but also of history and tradition. His diagnosis of the modern situation (or perhaps more accurately, the modern predicament) is that philosophers since Kant have denied these humanistic experiences any epistemological significance because they cannot be supported by scientific method. The danger is that because these civilizing influences have lost the dignified status of being considered as knowledge claims, they risk being dismissed or, in more contemporary parlance, commodified. Gadamer's project in *Truth and Method* is to rehabilitate these essential aspects of education as legitimate experiences of truth that transcend the sphere of control of the scientific method. If the primary modes within which authority and tradition are experienced are "prescientific," then so much the worse for scientific method. The moral and practical relevance of the humanistic tradition makes urgent the articulation of a philosophical hermeneutics that, if necessary, will oppose the methodological ideals of science and the predominant philosophical biases of the modern era.

As important as the humanistic ideals of Western education are for both a theoretical and practical analysis of the modern situation, as relevant as the message is for an Anglo-American intellectual audience in which philosophers are far more familiar with recent innovations in physics than the principles of literary criticism, and as eloquently as Gadamer's argument is formulated, still it is not unfair to point toward an important presupposition from which the argument gains much of its rhetorical force:

> However much Dilthey might have defended the epistemological independence of the human sciences, what is called "method" in modern science, remains everywhere the same and is seen only in an especially exemplary form in the natural sciences. *The human sciences have no special method* (Gadamer 1975a, 9, emphasis added).

Habermas has argued that the methodological ideal for the human sciences is significantly different than the ideal of the natural sciences, as the former is oriented toward consensus within personal communication and the latter is oriented toward technical control over nature. Admittedly this claim has been put into dispute by Gadamer, so that it might appear inappropriate to bring it forward as counterevidence. Still, there remains the case of the reconstructive sciences on both the individual and social levels. Is it so certain that the disciplined inquiry into the cognitive, linguistic, and interactive competences is diametrically opposed to the general tenor or contents of literature, history, or the arts? Is a methodological procedure that allows for the emergence of developing cognitive capacities and even ego-identity within the appropriate social environment so antagonistic to the view of human nature and morality expressed by the cultural tradition? At the very least it is not so immediately clear as the dichotomy drawn by Gadamer between *Truth and Method* would have it. It would seem quite plausible to suggest that such an inquiry also supports Habermas' project of a methodologically pluralistic taxonomy of the sciences.

IV

CONCLUSION

9

Conclusion: The Metatheory of Knowledge and Interpretive Programs

We began the foregoing presentation by giving a general frame of reference regarding orientations toward knowledge, in part derived from the work of Radnitzky, that attempted to give us, in a cohesive sketch, a metatheory of knowledge systems. Radnitzky's project identified three major orientations present in contemporary scholarship. They are: the naturalistic or positivistic, the hermeneutic or dialectical, and the critical. This scheme was presented as an attempt to single out the particular model that is operative in a interpretive orientation, taken in its narrow sense, since there are certainly interpretive moments in both the naturalistic and critical models.

Focusing on the interpretive orientation, we attempted to reconstruct that tradition in sociology by appealing to a selected number of crucial authors. We went back to the work of Max Weber, who as a classical sociologist was centrally concerned with the question of interpretation, so much so that he labeled his project *verstehende Soziologie*. We are very much aware, as discussed in our text, that Weber oscillated between the call for understanding and the demand for explanation, which in a very general sense reflects a humanistic and scientistic concern. Interpretation was a crucial thread in German thought, going as far back as Schleiermacher, and it was certainly a deep influence on the work of Dilthey. These were intellectual concerns that Weber could not avoid. Nevertheless, a case might have been made also to appeal at this classic stage to Simmel, Marx, or even Durkheim. There are, of course, primary reasons why we did not do so. In the case of Simmel, it is because the question of interpretation is much more grounded in the context of his philosophy than his sociology, which emphasized a formal approach, and resulted in a sociology of social forms. In the case of Marx, we may note that although interpretation is crucial to his program, it is fundamentally ancillary to his critical orientation. Interpretation, for Marx, is a strategy by which to clarify the sociopolitical attributes of a particular spaciotemporal situation so as to allow the subject to come up with decisions that will lead to enlightened political action. Finally, in the case of Durkheim, it seems that interpretation is significant, particularly since his model calls for a fundamental rupture between the subject and the object, thus putting the burden of interpretation-explanation in the consciousness of the subject. However, for Durkheim the question is not *per se* a major concern. In other words, interpretation itself must be explained sociologically. Thus instead of interpretation being the rule, the issue is shifted into the domain of epistemology.

Our focus on Continental thinkers is not to be construed as suggesting that there are no important contributions to hermeneutic theory that have been developed in American sociology. Certainly ethnomethodology, frame analysis, and social/symbolic interactionism are theories of interpretation that warrant inclusion and review in a general treatment of hermeneutics. In the contemporary interpretive perspective, however, the emphasis is on a concern with *roots,* and therefore we have intended to investigate the early and fundamental modes of interpretive sociology that have set the stage for later generations of interpretive sociologists, not only in the United States, but also in Japan, South America, Africa, and throughout Europe.

Now, the question to be confronted is of the possible order that one can identify within the approaches toward interpretation itself. In other words, one must search for a potential metatheory that will embrace all the possible existing or potential theories of interpretation. Historically, there have been three major attempts toward that synthetic goal: the original was that of Schleiermacher, who was concerned with practical purposes that brought together the work of jurisprudence, philology, and theological interpretation. A further expansion of that tradition in the work of Dilthey established interpretation as an epistemological foundation of the *Geisteswissenschaften.* More recently, the work of Emilio Betti aimed at a general theory of interpretation that would serve as an umbrella to all of its standing varieties.

Two fundamental questions might be raised to these programs: First, there is the question of the legitimacy of establishing an overall (and therefore closed) system to integrate all potential interpretative programs. It can be argued that such an intention involves an *a priori* that is grounded in the tradition of the Enlightenment and in a scientistic concern. That is, such a hope parallels the Enlightenment preoccupation of the encyclopedists, aimed at uncovering a universal method that would identify and locate all possible human knowledge, thus implying that knowledge is univocal and susceptible to closure. Possibly the best example of such a program comes from the table of atomic weights in chemistry. Unfortunately (or perhaps fortunately), no similar result has been forthcoming in the other natural sciences, and certainly not in the human fields. One of the correlates of that aim is to reach a kind of knowledge that is atemporal and universal, which was a strong argument offered on behalf of the natural sciences at least until recently. Such faith has been fundamentally challenged by the work of Einstein in physics, by Heisenberg, and in the realm of the character of scientific methodology, by philosophers such as Thomas Kuhn and Michel Foucault.

The more fundamental issue here is the second of these two questions, that of transcendentalism or foundationalism, a crucial issue that is playing havoc in contemporary thought, coming to the fore in the controversy between modernism and postmodernism. Indeed, it is because of these ongoing tensions and conflicts that we feel it is premature to take one or the other position. What is possible to say is that when we survey the literature of interpretation, and particularly as treated in the domain of sociology, we find a great deal of discontinuity of interests, aims, and methodologies, as well as significant cross-influences based on essentially different orientations. Thus, to start with the case of Max Weber, we see in his program both a neo-Kantian and a Rickertian (somewhat derived from Dilthey) influence, ostensively contradictory, and well captured in Weber's concern with reaching *causal-meaningful* interpretations. In the case of Alfred Schutz, we observe simultaneously the influence of Bergson, which is in many ways concerned with an existential context, and the project of Edmund Husserl, which grounds a phenomenology that is concerned with a view of science as an exact description of phenomena, thus bringing a scientistic and positivistic concern to Schutz' approach. Karl Mannheim's interpretative orientation pulls together the critical approach and background of Marx and the approach of German idealism — two conflicting relatives. Max Scheler creates his own conception of phenomenology and brings into it a fundamental concern with ethics that does not belong with the hermeneutics of description or explanation. And, as we have argued, in the contemporary trends we find positivist, humanist, and critical orientations simultaneously active. Thus, at least at face value, it is difficult for us to make an appeal to any transcendental or foundational ground for the interpretative orientation. In other words, it seems premature to identify at this point a metatheory of knowledge that could serve as an umbrella to various interpretative programs. Rather than providing for a closed theoretical system, the best one might do is take the position that one can identify a general problematic and in it certain central nodal points that, *a la* Adorno, create a constellation that loosely envelopes the interpretative interests.

To begin a description of this constellation, we might identify some of the nodal points as necessarily including the following categories of investigation:

1. *consciousness,* seen in particular as a dynamic reality characterized by intentionality and nonreducible to a natural entity (e.g., without the simultaneous determinants of space and time coordinates)
2. a *dialogical context* illustrated primarily by the model of conversation, incorporating the attributes that are characteristic of human conversation, such as engagement by the coparticipants, exchange of symbolic reference, development of at least a minimal community of meanings, and the natural, dialectical give-and-take of mutual exchange, conflict, and synthesis

3. a concern with the *crossing and conflict* of contrasting systems of signification
4. a *dependence* upon language *latu sensu* (That is, spoken language *simpliciter,* as well as gestures, and so on)

Methodologically, our constellation of elements constitutive of an interpretive project includes issues that have been somewhat more fully developed in earlier chapters of this work. Indeed, as one reviews our survey of interpretive techniques from Weber to Habermas, two primary methodological goals assume a central position — interpretation and understanding. Added to these, as a result of Gadamer's recommendation and in order to avoid the sublimation of the individual to an interpretive methodology, is the concept of practice. Practice is what moves hermeneutics from the confines of the isolated individual to the domain of the community and thus places hermeneutics in the center of any authentically "sociological" enterprise.

As we have attempted to point out, understanding and interpretation are not progressive or evolutionary notions. One does not necessarily precede the other as the practitioner goes about the hermeneutic project. Either of these "moments" can achieve a temporal priority, or, in other words, one can emphasize understanding as the primary moment (as with Dilthey) or one can emphasize interpretation as the primary thrust (as with the theoretical reconstruction of the psychoanalytic session). Each is implicated in the other, which means that not only is there no reason to cite a linearity between the two, but also that the play of interpretation and understanding is dialectical. The dialectic, of course, requires a synthesis, and in the play of interpretation and understanding this is the move from theory to practice, from adumbration to application.

This movement may be what Habermas fails to capture in his debate with Gadamer, because even in his own appeal to the universal structure of language, there is still a fundamentally hermeneutic dimension. That is, hermeneutics belongs to his project as an ontological substrate, rather than as a moment of the communicative process. Of course, the communicative process must continue, and on those occasions in which distorted communication occurs, hermeneutics is the site from which understanding and interpretation can lead to *un*distorted communication. This activity takes place on the applied level and not in an idealized frame. Therefore, Habermas is quite correct to state that this entails a political dimension of which we must always be aware. Any "practice" must face the resilience of a world in which power obscures the possibility of authentic conversation.

At this point, we find ourselves back at the classic model of an opposing subject and object, where the object is possibly another subject, and the standing challenge (for *us* as well as the participants) is the question of how to carry on a "conversation" between these two poles. The alternatives we have discussed in answer to this question involve "games," the "merging of horizons," "value structures," the activity of "being-becoming," or an agreement of a multiplicity of perspectives based on the activity of socialization (Mannheim, later explored by Gouldner). In this contest of conflicting possibilities, there are fundamentally two eternal alternatives. From the point of view of phenomenology, we may explore the essential/existential criteria by which interpretation can take place. This approach unveils the structures of consciousness that afford the possibility of interpretation in our everyday lives. On the other hand, we may appropriate the canonical approach, with a focus on the positive criteria by which interpretation is a feasible strategy of any linguistically experienced human being. The resolution of this competition is undecided and perhaps undecidable.

Another disturbing issue emerges, most clearly in the positions of Weber, Habermas, Gadamer, and Betti: Are the standards for interpretation, and the standards for the other moments of understanding and application, transcendental or immanent? If we adhere to the traditional view of the "great narratives" of Western culture, including the general project of the Enlightenment, the decision would favor the transcendental. On the other hand, more contemporary figures would call for an immanent standard in the relationship of context/object/conversation. This view leads to the controversy between the "modern" and "post-modern" approaches to social science, and the theoretical issues captured by both concepts have not yet been resolved. For example, Marcuse presents a model of a "global society," Horkheimer and Adorno deal with "advanced capitalism," and Lyotard presents a description of "postmodern society," each of which situates the interpretive ability in a different locus. Again, this question remains in the position of "undecidable."

Nevertheless, these conflicts do not mean that the question of interpretation should not be investigated. Such a decision would fall into the narrow trap of positivism, particularly as held by the Vienna Circle. Indeed, the issue is alive in our encounters with our own life-worlds. It is not because of the fact that our historical circumstances present us with lively symbols and texts that seem to be so translucent and unmediated that we ought to put the question of interpretation on the back burner. Rather, it is *because* of the press of unmediated communications that interpretation remains central to any critical and humanistic project.

In this imperative there lies the potential resolution of not only the conflict between immanence and transcendence, but also between the objective and subjective. This is because the hermeneutic drive resides within the life-world shared by each of us. We live in a world that is already "given" to us, a structure of practices and meanings that one must "understand" in order to go about the daily activity of living. Such structures of meaning have already been composed for us prior to our encounter with them. Hence, our book achieves a circle, in which we return to the question faced by Weber as he constructed his interpretive project — the question of history.

What is history? Our being, becoming? The structural processes that have contributed to the formation of our world? The details of living that are available for retrieval? This question is one of the key problems with Dilthey's hermeneutics, because any grand history is also the manifestation of the power of such persons as were able to "make it." As Adorno would ask: What about the histories of the unempowered? Where does one construct a history of suffering? We believe that this question rests at the core of any hermeneutic enterprise, if it is to be at all critical in character. Thus the questions of objectivity vs. subjectivity and immanence vs. transcendence are subsumed by the discussion of the relationship between hermeneutics as an ontic project and hermeneutics as an ontological mode of being.

Following the principle of the dialectic, the answer must be "both." History, and particularly "effective history," occurs within the contours of a life-world and in the presence of horizons for subjects and things. We find ourselves exposed simultaneously to subjective and objective aspects (of objects, culture, history, aesthetics, emotions, ethics, etc.), and in these situations we always have to cope with prepredicative meaning structures that are open to *a posteriori* reconstruction. The human community is incessantly "on the way," relating to each other and things in an ongoing, vibrant symphony. In this context, one can move within a taken-for-granted mode of relations that grounds preinterpretation (which is also called "common sense"). Or one can experience a point of rupture, which calls for a critical, reflective position, similar to that occurring in the psychoanalytic session. In this modality one can uncover existing, finite provinces of meaning — such as those of "science," the autobiographies of actors, and sociological constructions. Meanings are embedded in each such domain and constitute a background for any communication, an idea evocative of Gadamer's notion of "prejudice."

The process through which communication is carried out involves idealization (in a context characterized by the interchangeabililty of standpoints) and the constant reference to congruent systems of meaning that may hold relevance for the present context. This process exists on the ground of intentional consciousness and involves a witnessing of a constant application of meaning possibilities by the participants. One of the more formal constellations of meaning possibilities is the "ideal type" of Weber, which refers the actor to the typicalities drawn from the regularities of the life-world.

The ideas that are implicated in these interpretive contexts are always functions of social involvements, and as such they remain the result of articulations of conceptions of reality and modes of involvement in that reality. Understanding depends on the frame of reference of a "milieu," and that constellation depends on history as the system of classification of known types, goals, and elements of value criteria by which human beings order experience. No doubt people incorporate mystifications as a part of volitional life, which will always find resistance in the context of a practical attitude. But the preperceptive practical attitude, as argued by Max Scheler, always involves an ontological, loving orientation towards the world that opens up the vistas of understanding, and therefore, as a summarization of the foregoing, we may suggest that understanding is essentially grounded in intuition.

The very possibility of the objective understanding advocated by Betti is predicated on a subjectification of the frame of reference and, within that frame, an analysis of emergent and objective values. Because interpretation begins with intuition, we are reminded that hermeneutics is not a specialized province of knowledge and is not merely a methodology for disclosing knowledge — although both are accomplished — but is rather an practice that cuts across all knowledge domains. Against the demand of positivism that the hermeneutic enterprise be demonstrable and neatly closed in a wholistic package, the early Frankfurt School reminds us that the aesthetic experience is fundamental to the hermeneutic problematic and that the exploration of art and truth is enduring. The "hermeneutic problem" will remain with us, as a source of exhilaration and frustration, of fragile certainty and uncomfortable wonder, since it is implicated in the very character of being human.

REFERENCES AND SELECTED BIBLIOGRAPHY

Abel, Theodore. 1948. "The Operation Called Verstehen." *American Journal of Sociology* 14 (November): 218–38.

Adorno, Theodor W. 1984. *Aesthetic Theory.* Translated by C. Lenhardt. London: Routledge and Kegan Paul.

————. 1983. *Alban Berg.* Milano: Giangiacome Felrinel li Editore.

————. 1974. *Minima Moralia: Reflections from Damaged Life.* Translated by E. F. N. Jephcott. London: NLB.

————. 1973a. *Negative Dialectics.* Translated by E. B. Ashton. New York: Seabury Press.

————. 1973b. *Philosophy of Modern Music.* New York: Seabury.

————. 1970. *Asthetische Theorie.* Frankfurt: Suhrkamp.

————. 1968. *Berg: Der Meister des kleinsten Übergangs.* Wien: Österreichisher Bundesverlag.

————. 1967a. *Prisms.* Translated by Samuel and Shierry Weber. London: Neville Spearman Limited.

————. 1967b. *Prisms.* Cambridge: MIT Press.

————. 1964a. *Jargon of Authenticity.* London: Routledge and Kegan Paul.

————. 1964b. *Moments Musicaux: Neugedruckte Aufsatze, 1982 bis 1962.* Frankfurt: Suhrkamp.

————. 1963. *Dissonanzen: Musik in der verwalteten Welt.* Göttingen: Vendenhoeck and Ruprecht.

————. 1959. *Nervenpunkte der Neuen Musik.* Frankfurt: Suhrkamp.

————. 1955. *Kulturkritik und gesellschaft.* Frankfurt: Suhrkamp.

————. 1954. *Minima Moralia.* Frankfurt: Suhrkamp.

————. 1949. *Philosophy of Modern Music.* London: Sheed and Ward.

Alleman, Beda. 1967. "Metaphor and Antimetaphor." In Stanley R. Hopper and David L. Miller, eds. *Interpretation: The Poetry of Meaning.* New York: Harcourt, Brace and World, 103–23.

Allison, David B., ed. 1977. *The New Nietzsche.* New York: Dell Publishing Company.

Althusser, Louis. 1970. *For Marx.* New York: Random House.

Apel, Karl-Otto. 1974. "Wissenchaft als Emanzipation? Eine Kritische Wurdingung der Wissenschaftskonzeption der kritischen Theorie." In Winfried Dallmayer, ed., *Materialien zu Habermas' Erkenntnis und Interesse.* Frankfurt: Suhrkamp, 318–48.

————. 1967. *Analytic Philosophy of Language and the Geisteswissenschaften.* Dordrecht: Reidel.

Barnett, James H. 1958. "Research in the Sociology of Art." *Sociology and Social Research* 42: 401–5.

Barthes, Roland. 1972. *Mythologies.* Translated by Annette Lavers. New York: Hill and Wang.

————. 1971. *Sade, Fourier, Loyola.* Paris: Seuil.

————. 1970. *Writing Degree Zero.* Boston: Beacon Press.

————. 1967a. *Elements of Semiology.* London: Cape.

————. 1967b. *System de la Mode.* Paris: Seuil.

Beattie, John. 1968. "Understanding and Explanation in Social Anthropology." In R. Manner and D. Kaplan, eds., *Theory in Anthropology.* Chicago: Aldine, 115–23.

Becker, Howard S. 1945. "Interpretive Sociology and Constructive Sociology." In Georges Gurvitch and Wilbert E. Moore, eds., *Twentieth Century Sociology.* New York: Philosophical Library, 70–95.

Bendix, Reinhard. 1959. "Industrialization, Ideologies, and Social Structure." *American Sociological Review* 24: 613–23.

Benjamin, Walter. 1962. *Kaiserpaniorama (Einbanustrasse).* Frankfurt: Suhrkamp.

Bentley, Arthur. 1954. *Inquiry into Inquiries: Essays on Social Theory.* Boston: Beacon Press.

Berger, Bennet. 1971. "Audiences, Art and Power." *Transaction* 8: 26–30.

Berger, Peter, Brigette Berger, and Hansigfried Kellner. 1973. *The Homeless Mind: Modernization and Consciousness.* New York: Random House.

Berger, Peter, and Thomas Luckmann. 1966. *The Social Construction of Reality.* Garden City, N.Y.: Doubleday.

Berggren, Douglas. 1962–63. "The Use and Abuse of Metaphor." *Review of Metaphysics* 16 (December): 237–58; 16 (March): 450–72.

Bergson, Henri. 1896. *Matiere et Mémoire: Essai sur la Relation du Corps a L'ésprit.* Paris: F. Alcan.

Bergsträsser, Arnold. 1974. "Whilhelm Dilthey and Max Weber: An Empirical Approach to Historical Synthesis." *Ethics* 57 (January): 109–20.

Bernstein, Richard. 1986. *Philosophical Profiles: Essays in a Pragmatic Mode.* Philadelphia: University of Pennsylvania Press.

————. 1971. *Praxis and Action.* Philadelphia: University of Pennsylvania Press.

Betti, Emilio. 1955. *Teoria Generale della Interpretazione.* 2 vols. Milano: Dott. A. Giufre.

Bevan, Edwyn Robert. 1938. *Symbolism and Belief.* London: Allen and Unwin.

Birdwhistell, Ray L. 1970. *Kinesis and Context: Essays on Body Motion Communication.* Philadelphia: University of Pennsylvania Press.

Black, Max. 1968. "Metaphors." In Francis J. Coleman, ed., *Contemporary Studies in Aesthetics.* New York: MacGraw-Hill.

————. 1962. *Models and Metaphors: Studies in Language and Philosophy.* Ithaca: Cornell University Press, 216–32.

Blackham, H. J. 1952. *Six Existentialist Thinkers.* New York: Macmillan.

Blasi, Anthony J., Fabio B. Dasilva, and Andrew Weigert. 1978. *Toward an Interpretive Sociology.* Washington, D.C.: University Press of America.

Bleicher, Josef. 1982. *The Hermeneutic Imagination.* London: Routledge and Kegan Paul.

————. 1980. *Contemporary Hermeneutics.* London: Routledge and Kegan Paul.

Blum, Alan F. 1970. "Theorizing." In Jack D. Douglas, ed., *Understanding Everyday Life.* Chicago: Aldine, 305–19.

Blumer, Herbert. 1969. *Symbolic Interactionism.* Englewood Cliffs, N.J.: Prentice Hall.

————. 1931. "Science Without Concepts." *American Journal of Sociology* 36 (January): 515–31.

Bochenski, I. M. 1956. *Contemporary European Philosophy.* Berkeley: University of California Press.

Boelen, Barnard J. 1986. *Existential Thinking.* Pittsburgh: Duquesne University Press.

Brooks, Cleanth. 1965. "Metaphor, Paradox and Stereotype." *British Journal of Aesthetics* 5, no. 4 (October): 315–18.

Brown, Richard H. 1977. *A Poetic for Sociology.* Cambridge: Cambridge University Press.

————. 1973. "L'ironie dans la theorie sociologique." *Epistemologie Sociologique* 15–16: 63–96.

Buck-Morse, Susan. 1977. *The Origin of Negative Dialectics.* New York: Free Press.

Child, Arthur. 1947. "The Problem of Truth in the Sociology of Knowledge." *Ethics* 58 (October): 18–34.

———. 1941a. "The Problem of Imputation in the Sociology of Knowledge." *Ethics* 51 (January 1941): 200–19.

———. 1941b. "The Theoretical Possibility of the Sociology of Knowledge." *Ethics* 51 (July): 392–418.

Cicourel, Aaron V. 1974. *Cognitive Sociology: Language and Meaning in Social Interaction.* New York: Free Press.

Clifford, Derek. 1968. *Art and Understanding.* Greenwich, Conn.: New York Graphic Society.

Cooley, Charles Horton. 1926. "The Roots of Social Knowledge." *American Journal of Sociology* 12 (July): 59–79.

Cortese, Anthony. 1990. *Ethnic Ethics.* Albany, N.Y.: State University of New York Press.

Cuvillier, Armand. 1963–67. *Manuel de Sociologie, Avec Notices Bibliographiques.* Paris: Presses Universitaires de France.

Dasilva, Fabio B., and David R. Dees. 1976. "The Social Context of Music." *Revue Internationale de Sociologie* 12 (special issue, Summer).

Dasilva, Fabio B., and David Faught. 1991 "The Late Work of Max Horkheimer." In *Sociological Symposium,* special issue on theory and science, 63–82.

De George, Richard and Fernande, eds. 1972. *The Structuralists from Marx to Levi-Strauss.* Garden City, N.Y.: Doubleday and Co.

Deinhard, Hanna. 1970. *Meaning and Expression: Toward a Sociology of Art.* Boston: Beacon Press.

Dexter, Lewis A., and David Manning White. 1966. *People, Society and Communications.* New York: Free Press.

Derrida, Jacques. 1980. *Writing and Difference.* Translated by Alan Bass. Chicago: University of Chicago Press.

Diesing, Paul. 1971. *Patterns of Discovery in the Social Sciences.* Chicago: Aldine.

Dilthey, Wilhelm. 1989. *Introduction to the Human Sciences.* Translated and edited by Rudolf A. Makkreel and Frithjof Rodi. Princeton, N.J.: Princeton University Press.

———. 1977. *Descriptive Psychology and Historical Understanding.* Translated by Richard Zaner and Kenneth L. Heiges. The Hague: Martinus Nijhoff.

————. 1976. *Selected Writings*. Translated, edited, and introduced by H. P. Rickman. Cambridge: Cambridge University Press.

————. 1962. *Pattern and Meaning in History*. Edited by H. P. Richman. New York: Harper and Row.

Doroszewski, W. 1933. "Quelques Remarques sur les Rapports de la Sociologie et de la Linguistique, Durkheim et F. de Saussure." *Journal de Psychologie Normale et Pathologique* 30: 82–91.

Douglas, Jack D. 1977. *Existential Sociology*. New York: Cambridge University Press.

————. 1970. *Understanding Everyday Life*. Chicago: Aldine.

Douglas, Mary. 1973. *Rules and Meaning: The Anthropology of Everyday Life*. Baltimore: Johns Hopkins.

————. 1968. "The Social Control of Cognition." *Man* 3 (September): 361–67.

Dreitzel, Hans Peter. 1970. *Recent Sociology 2: Patterns of Communicative Behavior*. New York: Macmillan.

Dreyfus, Hubert, and Paul Rabinow. 1983. *Michel Foucault: Beyond Structuralism and Hermeneutics*. Chicago: University of Chicago Press.

Duncan, Hugh D. 1957. "Sociology of Art, Literature and Music: Social Contexts of Symbolic Experience." In Becker and Boskoff, eds., *Modern Sociological Theory*. New York: Dryden Press, 482–97.

Durkheim, Emile. 1965. *The Elementary Forms of Religious Life*. Translated by Joseph W. Swain. New York: Free Press.

Durkheim, Emile, and Marcel Mauss. 1967. *Primitive Classification*. Translated by Rodney Needham. Chicago: University of Chicago Press.

Edie, James. 1967. "Comments on Maurice Natanson's Paper 'Man as Actor.'" In Erwin W. Straus and Richard M. Griffith, eds., *Phenomenology of Will and Action: The Second Lexington Conference on Pure and Applied Phenomenology*. Pittsburgh: Duquesne University Press, 221–32.

Egbert, Donald Drew. 1970. *Social Radicalism and the Arts: Western Europe*. New York: Alfred A. Knopf, Inc.

Ehrmann, Jacques, ed. 1970. *Structuralism*. Garden City, N.Y.: Doubleday.

Ermarth, Michael. 1978. *Wilhelm Dilthey: The Critique of Historical Reason*. Chicago: University of Chicago Press.

Festinger, Leon, and John Thibaut. 1951. "Interpersonal Communication in Small Groups." *Journal of Abnormal Psychology* 46, no. 1 (January): 92–99.

Fingarette, Herbert. 1963. *The Self in Transformation*. New York: Basic Books.

Foucault, Michel. 1979. *Discipline and Punish.* New York: Vintage.

————. 1976. *The Archaeology of Knowledge.* Translated by A. M. Sheridan Smith. New York: Harper Colophon.

Frankfurt Institute for Social Research. 1972. *Aspects of Sociology.* Boston: Beacon Press.

Freud, Sigmund. 1955. *The Interpretation of Dreams.* New York: Standard Edition, 4–5.

Friere, Paulo. 1970. *Pedagogy of the Oppressed.* Translated by Myra Bergman Ramos. New York: Continuum.

Furfey, Paul Hanly. 1953. *The Scope and Method of Sociology: A Metasociological Treatise.* New York: Harper.

Gadamer, Hans-Georg. 1982. *Truth and Method.* New York: Continuum Press.

————. 1976. *Philosophical Hermeneutics.* Translated by David E. Linge. Berkeley: University of California Press.

————. 1975a. *Truth and Method.* Translated from the second German edition by Garrett Barden and John Cumming. New York: Seabury Press.

————. 1975b. *Wahrheit und Methode: Grundzüge einer Philosophischen Hermeneutik.* Third edition. Tübingen: Mohr.

————. 1964. "Aesthetik und Hermeneutik." In *Gesammelte Werke, Band 8.* Tübingen: Mohr (Paul Siebeck), 1993: 1–8.

Gans, Herbert J. 1961. "Hollywood Films on British Screen: An Analysis of American Popular Culture Abroad." *Social Problems* 9, no. 4: 324–28.

Garfinkel, Harold. 1967. *Studies in Ethnomethodology.* Englewood Cliffs, N.J.: Prentice Hall.

————. 1952. "The Perception of the Other: A Study in Social Order." Harvard University: Ph.D. dissertation.

Gelvin, Michael. 1970. *A Commentary on Heidegger's "Being and Time": A Section-By-Section Interpretation.* New York: Harper and Row.

Glaser, Barney, and Anselm Strauss. 1964. "Awareness Contexts and Social Interaction." *American Sociological Review* 29, no. 5 (October): 669–78.

Goffman, Erving. 1971. *Relations in Public: Microstudies of the Public Order.* New York: Basic Books.

————. 1967. *Interaction Ritual: Essays on Face-to-Face Behavior.* Garden City, N.Y.: Doubleday.

————. 1963. *Behaviour in Public Places: Notes on the Social Organization of Gatherings.* New York: Free Press.

————. 1961. *Encounters.* Indianapolis: Bobbs-Merrill.

————. 1959. *The Presentation of Self in Everyday Life.* Garden City, N.Y.: Doubleday.

Goldmann, Lucien. 1963. *Essais pour la lecture de Hegel.* Paris: PUF.

Gurvitch, Georges. 1971. *The Social Frameworks of Knowledge.* Translated by Margareth Thompson and Kenneth Thompson. Oxford: Blackwell.

Gurwitsch, Aron. 1966. *Studies in Phenomenology and Psychology.* Evanston, Ill.: Northwestern University Press.

Habermas, Jürgen. 1984, 1987. *The Theory of Communicative Action.* 2 vols. Translated by Thomas McCarthy. Boston: Beacon Press.

————. 1979. *Communication and the Evolution of Society.* Translated by Thomas McCarthy. Boston: Beacon Press.

————. 1975. *Legitimation Crisis.* Translated by Thomas McCarthy. Boston: Beacon Press.

————. 1973. *La technique et la science comme "ideologie."* Paris: Gallimard.

————. 1971. *Knowledge and Human Interests.* Translated by Jeremy J. Shapiro. Boston: Beacon Press.

————. 1970. "On Systematically Distorted Communication." *Inquiry* 13, 205–18.

Habermas, Jürgen, and Niklas Luhmann. 1971. *Theorie der Gesellschaft oder Sozialtechnologie.* Frankfurt: Suhrkamp.

Hartman, Geoffrey. 1970. "Structuralism: The Anglo-American Adventure." In Jacques Ehrman, ed., *Structuralism.* Garden City, N.Y.: Doubleday.

Heath, Stephen, Colin MacCabe, and Christopher Prendergast, eds. *Signs of the Times: Introductory Readings in Textual Semiotics.* Cambridge: Granta.

Hegel, G. W. F. 1977. *Phenomenology of Spirit.* Translated by A. V. Miller. New York: Oxford.

————. 1970. *On Art, Religion, Philosophy.* Edited by J. Glenn Gray. New York: Harper and Row.

Heidegger, Martin. 1979. *Nietzsche: The Will to Power as Art.* Volume 1. Translated by David Ferrell Krell. New York: Harper and Row.

————. 1971. *Poetry, Language, Thought.* Translated by Albert Hofstadter. New York: Harper and Row.

————. 1962. *Being and Time.* Translated by John Macquarrie and Edward Robinson. New York: Harper and Row.

Held, David. 1980. *Introduction to Critical Theory.* Berkeley: University of California Press.

Hirsch, E. D. 1976. *Validity in Interpretation.* New Haven: Yale University Press.

Hodges, H. A. 1952. *The Philosophy of Wilhelm Dilthey.* London: Routledge.

Hogan, John P. 1989. *Collingwood and Theological Hermeneutics.* Lanham, Md.: University Press of America.

Hollinger, Robert, ed. 1985. *Hermeneutics and Praxis.* Notre Dame: University of Notre Dame Press.

Holzner, Bukart. 1968. *Reality Construction in Society.* Cambridge: Schenkman.

Hopper, Stanley R., and David L. Miller, eds. 1967. *Interpretation: The Poetry of Meaning.* New York: Harcourt, Brace and World.

Horkheimer, Max. 1974. *Critique of Instrumental Reason.* Translated by Matthew J. O'Connell, et al. New York: Seabury Press.

Horkheimer, Max, and Theodor W. Adorno. 1972a. *Critical Theory.* New York: Seabury Press.

———. 1972b. *Dialectic of Enlightenment.* Translated by John Cumming. New York: Seabury Press.

———. 1966. *Le monde sociologie.* Turin: Einaudi.

Howard, Roy J. 1982. *Three Faces of Hermeneutics.* Berkeley: University of California Press.

Hoy, David Couzens. 1978. *The Critical Circle.* Berkeley: University of California Press.

Husserl, Edmund. 1973. *Experience and Judgment: Investigations in a Genealogy of Logic.* Translated by James S. Churchill and Karl Ameriks. Evanston, Ill.: Northwestern University Press.

———. 1970. *The Crisis of European Sciences and Transcendental Phenomenology.* Translated by David Carr. Evanston: Northwestern University Press.

———. 1962. *Ideas: General Introduction to Pure Phenomenology.* Translated by W. R. Boyce Gibson. London and New York: Collier Books.

Ichieise, Gustav. 1970. *Appearances and Realities: Misunderstandings in Human Relations.* San Francisco: Jossey-Bass.

Ingarden, Roman. 1986. *The Work of Music and the Problem of Its Identity.* Berkeley: University of California Press.

Jameson, Fredric. 1971. *Marxism and Form.* Princeton: Princeton University Press.

Jay, Martin. 1973. *The Dialectical Imagination.* Boston: Little, Brown and Company.

Jimenez, Marc. 1973. *Adorno, Art, Ideologie et Theorie de L'art.* Paris: Union Generale d'editions.

Kavolis, Vytautas. 1968. *Artistic Expression: A Sociological Analysis.* Ithaca, N.Y.: Cornell University Press.

———. 1965. "Political Determinants of Artistic Style." *Social Research* 32: 180–92.

Klein, Viola. 1948. *The Feminine Character: History of an Ideology.* New York: International Universities Press.

Kohlberg, Lawrence. 1969. "Stage and Sequence: The Cognitive-Developmental Approach to Socialization." In David A. Goslin, ed., *Handbook of Socialization Theory.* Chicago: Rand McNally.

Konk, Karl. 1970. *La Dialectique du Concret.* Paris: Maspero.

Laing, R. D. 1959. *The Divided Self.* London: Tavistock.

Lane, Michael. 1970. *Introduction to Structuralism.* New York: Basic Books.

Leach, Edmund R. 1970. *Claude Levi-Strauss.* New York: Viking Press.

———, ed. 1968. *The Structural Study of Myth and Totemism.* London: Tavistock Publications Social Science Paperback.

Lentricchia, Frank. 1973. *The Dialectical Imagination.* Boston: Little, Brown and Company.

Levi-Strauss, Claude. 1963. *Structural Anthropology.* New York: Basic Books.

———. 1962. *Totemisme Aujourd'hui.* Paris: PUF

Lindner, Burkhardt, and W. Martin Ludke, eds. 1979. *Materialien zur Asthetischen Theorie Th. W. Adornos Konstruktion der Moderne.* Frankfurt: Suhrkamp.

Linton, Ralph. 1945. *The Cultural Background of Personality.* New York: D. Appleton-Century Co.

Lipset, S. M., and Leo Lowenthal, eds. 1961. *Culture and Social Character.* New York: Free Press.

Ludweig, Friedeburg, and Jürgen Habermas, eds. 1983. *Adorno-Konferenz 1983.* Frankfurt: Suhrkamp.

Lukacs, Georg. 1971. *History and Class Consciousness: Studies in Marxist Dialectics.* Translated by Rodney Liningstone. Cambridge, Mass.: MIT Press.

Lyman, Stanford M., and Marvin B. Scott. 1970. *A Sociology of the Absurd.* New York: Appleton-Century-Crofts.

Lyotard, Jacques. 1989. *Post-Modernism for Children.* Barcelona: Horster.

Macksey, Richard, and Eugenio Donato. 1972. *The Structuralist Controversy: The Language of Criticism and the Sciences of Man.* Baltimore: John Hopkins.

Mandelbaum, Maurice. 1938. *The Problem of Historical Knowledge: An Answer to Relativism.* New York: Liveright.

Mannheim, Karl. 1956. *Essays on the Sociology of Culture.* London: Routledge and Kegan Paul.

———. 1952. *Essays on the Sociology of Knowledge.* London: Routledge and Kegan Paul.

———. 1950. *Freedom, Power, and Democratic Planning.* New York: Oxford University Press.

———. 1936. *Ideology and Utopia.* Translated by Louis Wirth and Edward Shils. New York and London: Harcourt Brace Jovanovich.

Manning, Peter. 1975. "Existential Sociology." *The Sociological Quarterly* 14: 200–25.

———. 1972. *Existential Sociology.* Mimeo. East Lansing: Dept. of Sociology, Michigan State University.

Maquet, Jacques J. 1951. *The Sociology of Knowledge: A Critical Analysis of the Systems of Karl Mannheim and Pitirin Sorokin.* Boston: Beacon Press.

Marle, Rene. 1976. *Introduction to Hermeneutics.* Translated by E. Froment and R. Albrecht. New York: Herder and Herder.

Marx, Karl. 1947. *The German Ideology.* Edited by C. J. Arthur. New York: International Publishers.

Maslow, A. H. 1950. *Meaning and Interpretation.* University of California Publications in Philosophy No. 25. Berkeley: University of California Press.

Mayenowa, Maria Renata. 1967. "Semiotics Today: Reflections on the Second International Conference on Semiotics." *Social Science Information* 6, no. 2–3: 59–64.

McCarthy, Thomas. 1978. *The Critical Theory of Jürgen Habermas.* Cambridge: MIT Press.

McKinney, John C. 1976. "Sociological Theory and the Process of Typification." In John C. McKinney and Edward A. Tiryakian, eds., *Theoretical Sociology: Perspectives and Developments.* New York: Appleton-Century-Crofts, 235–69.

Mead, George Herbert. 1967. *The Philosophy of the Act.* Edited by Charles W. Morris. Chicago: University of Chicago Press.

———. 1934. *Mind, Self and Society.* Chicago: University of Chicago Press.

Menger, Carl. 1984. *The Origin of Money.* Introduction by Anatal E. Fekete. Greenwich, Conn.: Committee for Monetary Research and Education, Inc.

——. 1981. *Principles of Economics*. Translated and edited by James Dingwall and Bert. F. Hoselitz. New York: New York University Press.

——. 1963. *Problems of Economics and Sociology*. Translated by Francis J. Nock. Urbana, Ill.: University of Illinois Press.

Merleau-Ponty, Maurice. 1969. *Signs*. Translated by Richard McCleary. Evanston, Ill.: Northwestern University Press.

——. 1967. *The Structure of Behaviour*. Translated by Alden L. Fisher. Boston: Beacon Press.

——. 1964. *The Primacy of Perception*. Translated by Arleen B. Dallery, et al. Evanston, Ill.: Northwestern University Press.

Messinger, Sheldon L., Harold Sampson, and Robert Towne. 1962. "Life as a Theater: Some Notes on One Dramaturgic Approach to Social Reality." *Sociometry* 25, no. 1 (March): 98–110.

Mills, C. Wright. 1959. *The Sociological Imagination*. New York: Oxford.

Misgeld, Dieter. 1976. "Critical Theory and Hermeneutics: The Debate Between Habermas and Gadamer." In John O'Neill, ed., *On Critical Theory*. New York: Seabury Press, 164–83.

Morris, Charles. 1971. *Writings on the General Theory of Signs*. The Hague: Mouton.

Morris, Robert. 1970. "Some Notes on the Phenomenology of Making." *Artforum* (April): 62–66.

Mueller, John H. 1938. "The Folkway of Art: An Analysis of the Social Theories of Art." *American Journal of Sociology* 44: 222–38.

Mukerjee, Radhakamal. 1945. "The Meaning and Evolution of Art in Society." *American Sociological Review* 10: 496–503.

Murphey, Robert F. 1971. *The Dialectics of Social Life*. New York: Basic Books.

Natanson, Maurice, ed. 1973. *Phenomenology and the Social Sciences*. Evanston, Ill.: Northwestern University Press.

——. 1970. *The Journeying Self: A Study in Philosophy and Social Role*. Reading, Mass.: Addinson-Wesley.

——. 1967. "Man as an Actor." In Erwin W. Strauss and Richard M. Griffiths, eds., *Phenomenology of the Will and Action, The Second Lexington Conference on Pure and Applied Phenomenology*. Pittsburgh: Duquesne University Press, 201–20.

——. 1962. "Causation as a Structure of the Lebenswelt." In *Literature, Philosophy and the Social Sciences*. The Hague: Nijhoff, 195–211.

Nietzsche, Friedrich. 1986. *Human, All Too Human*. Translated by R. J. Hollingdale. New York: Cambridge.

Nisbet, Robert A. 1969. *Social Change and History: Aspects of Western Theory of Development.* New York: Oxford.

———. 1962. "Sociology as an Art Form." *Pacific Sociological Review* 5, no. 2 (Fall): 67–74.

Nota, John H., S.J. 1983. *Max Scheler: The Man and His Work.* Translated by Theodore Plantinga and John H. Nota, S.J. Chicago: Fransciscan Herald Press.

O'Neill, John, ed. 1976. *On Critical Theory.* New York: Seabury Press.

———. 1972. *Sociology as Skin Trade.* New York: Harper and Row.

Osborne, Harold. 1970. *The Art of Interpretation.* London: Oxford.

Palmer, Richard. 1969. *Hermeneutics: Interpretation Theory in Scheleirmacher, Dilthey, Heidegger, and Gadamer.* Evanston, Ill.: Northwestern University Press.

Piaget, Jean. 1970. *Structuralism.* New York: Basic Books.

Plekhanov, Georgil. 1957. *Art and Social Life.* Moscow: Foreign Languages Publishing House.

Ponsetto, Antonio. 1981. *Max Horkheimer.* Bologna: Il Mulino.

Psathas, George. 1973. *Phenomenological Sociology.* New York: Wiley.

Rabinow, Paul, and William Sullivan, eds. 1979. *Interpretive Social Science: A Reader.* Berkeley: University of California Press.

———. 1948. "The Art of Social Science." *American Journal of Sociology* 54, no. 3 (November): 181–90.

Radnitzky, Gerard. 1973. *Contemporary Schools of Metascience.* Chicago: Henry Regnery.

Reisman, David. 1954. *Individualism Reconsidered.* New York: Free Press.

Rickert, Heinrich. 1913. *Die Grenzen der Naturwissenschaftlichen Begriffsbildung.* Tübingen: Mohr (Paul Siebeck).

Ricoeur, Paul. 1981. *Hermeneutics and the Human Sciences.* Cambridge: Cambridge University Press.

———. 1974. *The Conflict of Interpretations: Essays on Hermeneutics.* Evanston, Ill.: Northwestern University Press.

———. 1972. "La Metaphor et le probleme central de l'hermeneutique." *Revue Philosophique de Louvain,* 4th ser. 10, no. 5 (February): 93–112.

Rogers, Rolf E. 1969. *Max Weber's Ideal Type Theory.* New York: Philosophical Library.

Rose, Gillian. 1981. *Hegel Contra Sociology.* New Jersey: Humanities Press.

————. 1978. *The Melancholy Science.* New York: Columbia University Press.

Rosen, Michael. 1982. *Hegel's Dialectic and Its Criticism.* London: Cambridge University Press.

Roth, Guenther. 1971. "Max Weber's Comparative Approach and Historical Typology." In Ivan Vallier, ed., *Comparative Methods in Sociology.* Berkeley: University of California Press, 75–93.

Ruesch, Jurgen, and Kees Weldon. 1956. *Non-Verbal Communication.* Berkeley: University of California Press.

Sabelli, F. 1973. "Theorie du Developement et Ideologie du Developement." *16 Geneve-Afrique* XII, no. l: 83–91.

Scheflen, Albert E. 1972. *Body Language and the Social Order: Communication as Behavioral Control.* Englewood Cliffs, N.J.: Prentice-Hall.

Scheler, Max. 1993. *On Feeling, Knowing, and Valuing: Selected Writings.* Edited by Harold J. Bershady. Chicago: University of Chicago Press.

————. 1980. *Problems of a Sociology of Knowledge.* Translated by Manfred S. Frings. Edited and introduction by Kenneth W. Stikkers. London: Routledge and Kegan Paul.

————. 1973a. *Formalism in Ethics and Non-Formal Ethics of Values: A New Attempt Toward the Foundation of an Ethical Personalism.* Translated by Manfred S. Frings and Roger L. Funk. Evanston, Ill.: Northwestern University Press.

————. 1973b. "Ordo Amoris." In *Max Scheler: Selected Philosophical Essays.* Translated by David R. Lachterman. Evanston, Ill.: Northwestern University Press, 98–135.

————. 1961. *Man's Place In Nature.* Translated and introduction by Hans Meyerhoff. New York: The Noonday Press.

Schneider, Louis. 1975. *The Sociological Way of Looking at the World.* New York: McGraw-Hill.

Schutz, Alfred. 1989. *Philosophen in Exile: The Correspondence of Alfred Schutz and Aron Gurwitsch, 1939–1959.* Edited by Richard Grathoff. Translated by J. Claude Evans. Forward by Maurice Natanson. Bloomington, Ind.: Indiana University Press.

————. 1985. With Aron Gurwitsch. *Briefwechsel 1939–1959.* Mit einer Einleitung von Ludwig Landgreb. Herausgegeben von Richard Grathoff. München: W. Fink.

————. 1982a. *Das Problem der Relevanz.* Frankfurt: Suhrkamp.

————. 1982b. *Life Forms and Meaning Structures.* Translated and annotated by Helmut R. Wagner. London: Routledge and Kegan Paul.

————. 1981. *Theorie der Lebensformen: Fruhe Manuskript aus der Bergson Period.* Herausgegeben und Einleitung von Ilga Srubar. Frankfurt: Suhrkamp.

―――. 1978. *The Theory of Social Action: The Correspondence of Alfred Schutz and Talcott Parsons.* Edited by Richard Grathoff. Bloomington, Ind.: Indiana University Press.

―――. 1976. *Studies in Social Theory.* Edited and introduction by Arvid Brodersen. The Hague: Martinus Nijhoff.

―――. 1975. *Studies in Phenomenological Philosophy.* Edited by I. Schutz. Introduction by Aron Gurwitsch. The Hague: Martinus Nijhoff.

―――. 1973. *The Problem of Social Reality.* Edited and introduction by Maurice Natanson. Preface by H. L. von Breda. The Hague: Martinus Nijhoff.

―――. 1970a. *On Phenomenology and Social Relations: Selected Writings.* Edited and introduction by Helmut R. Wagner. Chicago: University of Chicago Press.

―――. 1970b. *Reflections on the Problem of Relevance.* Edited, annotated, and introduced by Richard M. Zaner. New Haven, Conn.: Yale University Press.

―――. 1967. *The Phenomenology of the Social World.* Translated by George Walsh and Frederick Lehmert. Introduction by George Walsh. Evanston, Ill.: Northwestern University Press.

―――. 1962–66. *Alfred Schutz: Collected Papers.* Edited and introduced by Maurice Natanson. Preface by H. L. van Breda. The Hague: Martinus Nijhoff.

―――. 1954. "On Multiple Realities." *Philosophy and Phenomenological Research* 5, no. 4 (June): 533–76.

Schutz, Alfred, and Thomas Luckmann. 1973. *The Structures of the Life World.* Translated by Richard M. Zanner and H. Tristram Englehardt, Jr. Evanston, Ill.: Northwestern University Press.

Seweter, A. C. 1935. "The Possibilities of a Sociology of Art." *Sociological Review* 27: 441–53.

Shills, Edward A. 1960. "Mass Society and Its Culture." *Daedalus* 89: 288–314.

Silverman, Hugh J., and Don Ihde, eds. 1985. *Hermeneutics and Deconstruction.* Albany, N.Y.: State University of New York Press.

Simmel, Georg. 1980. *Essays on Interpretation in Social Science.* Translated by Guy Oakes. Totowa, N.J.: Rowman and Littlefield.

―――. 1978. *The Philosophy of Money.* Translated by Tom Bottomore and David Frisby. London: Routledge and Kegan Paul.

―――. 1922. *Die Probleme der Geschichtsphilosophie: Eine Erkenntnistheoretische Studie.* München: Duncher and Humblot.

―――. 1918. *Lebenanschauung: Vier Metaphysische Kapital.* München und Leipzig: Duncher and Humblot.

Sixel, Friedrich W. 1976. "The Problem of Sense: Habermas v. Luhmann." In John O'Neill, ed., *On Critical Theory*. New York: Seabury Press, 184–204.

Solomon, Robert C., ed. 1980. *Nietzsche*. Notre Dame: University of Notre Dame Press.

Sontag, Susan. 1967. *Against Interpretation*. New York: Delta Books.

Sorokin, Pitirim A. 1967. *Social and Cultural Dynamics*. New York: Bedminster Press.

———. 1947. *Culture and Personality: Their Structure and Dynamics*. New York: Harper Brothers.

Spiegelberg, Herbert. 1971. "Max Scheler." In *The Phenomenological Movement: A Historical Introduction*. The Hague: Martinus Nijhoff, 228–70.

Staude, John Raphael. 1967. *Max Scheler: An Intellectual Portrait*. New York: The Free Press.

Stein, Maurice. 1963. "The Poetic Metaphor of Sociology." In Maurice Stein and Arthur Vidich, eds., *Sociology on Trial*. Englewood Cliffs, N.J.: Prentice Hall, 173–82.

Strasser, Stephan. 1963. *Phenomenology and the Human Sciences: A Contribution to a New Scientific Ideal*. Pittsburgh: Duquesne University Press.

Tiryakian, Edward. 1965. "Existential Phenomenology and the Sociological Tradition." *American Sociological Review* 30, no. 5 (October): 674–88.

———. 1962. *Sociologism and Existentialism*. Englewood Cliffs, N.J.: Prentice Hall.

Tönnies, Ferdinand. 1963. *Community and Society*. Translated by Charles P. Loomis. New York: Harper and Row.

Törnebohm, Håkan. 1964. *Information and Confirmation*. Göteborg: Elanders Boktr.

Tylor, Stephen. 1969. *Cognitive Anthropology*. New York: Holt.

Weber, Max. 1985. *The Protestant Ethic and the Spirit of Capitalism*. Translated by Talcott Parsons. Introduction by Anthony Giddens. London: Unwin Paperbacks.

———. 1975. *Roscher and Knies: the Logical Problems of Historical Economics*. Translated by Guy Oakes. New York: Free Press.

———. 1968. *Economy and Society: An Outline of Interpretive Sociology*. Translated by Ephraim Fischoff, et al. New York: Bedminister Press.

———. 1963. *The Sociology of Religion*. Translated by Ephraim Fischoff. Introduction by Talcott Parsons. Boston: Beacon Press.

———. 1958a. *Gesammelte Politische Schriften*. Tübingen: Mohr (Paul Siebech).

———. 1958b. *The Rational and Social Foundations of Music*. Translated and edited by Don Martindale, Johannes Riedel, and Gertrude Neuwirth. Carbondale, Ill.: Southern Illinois University Press.

————. 1949. *On the Methodology of the Social Sciences.* Glencoe, Ill.: Free Press.

————. 1946. *From Max Weber: Essays in Sociology.* Translated by H. H. Gerth and C. Wright Mills. New York: Oxford University Press.

————. 1927. *General Economic History.* Translated by Frank H. Knight. London: Allen and Unwin.

————. 1920–21. *Gesammelte Aufsätze zur Religionssoziologie.* Tübingen: Mohr.

Wellmer, Albrecht. 1974. *Critical Theory of Society.* New York: Seabury Press.

Wheelwright, Phil. 1968. *The Burning Fountain: A Study in the Language of Symbolism.* Bloomington: Indiana University Press.

Wilden, Anthony G. 1968. *The Language of the Self.* Baltimore: Johns Hopkins.

Wilensky, Harold L. 1964. "Mass Society and Mass Culture: Interdependence or Independence?" *American Sociological Review* 29: 173–97.

Windelband, Wilhelm. 1894. *Geschichte der Alten Philosophie, von Dr. W. Win. Nebst einem Anhang: Abriss der Geschichte der Mathematik und der Naturwissenschaften in Altertum, von Dr. Siegmund Günther.* München: C. H. Beck.

Zaner, Richard M. 1970. *The Way of Phenomenology: Criticism as a Philosophical Discipline.* New York: Pegasus.

Zimmerman, Don H., and Lawrence D. Wieder. 1970. "The Everyday World as a Phenomenon." In Jack D. Douglas, ed., *Understanding Everyday Life.* Chicago: Aldine, 80–103.

INDEX

action: affective, 24; cause/function relationship, 63–64; in community vs. in society, 24; goals of, 24; rational-instrumental, 24; traditional, 24–25; value-oriented, 24, 25–26
adequacy in sociology, 47–48
Adorno, Theodor W., xii, 127–47; on aesthetics, 128–29, 141–47, 142; *The Authoritarian Personality,* 128; on autonomy, 135; biographical sketch of, 127–28; on capitalism, 137–38; critique of Hegel, 142; critique of Marxism, 142; *Dialectic of Enlightenment,* 128, 142; on everyday life, 133–34; on the individual, 133–34, 139; *Minima Moralia,* 133–37, 140, 141; on music, 145; on negative thinking, 140; on pathological professional stupidity, 136; on postmodernism, 141, 145–47; on prophecy, 134; on sociological extra-territoriality, 134; on the subject, 142; on superstructure and infrastructure, 143
adventure, 119
aesthetic experience, 146, 179 *(see also* art); as creative and critical, 129, 132; as a model of knowledge, 129–30, 133
aesthetics: and beauty, 144; and Being, 144; as a holistic realm of life, 144; judgments of, 145; and the modern state, 143; religious connotations of, 144
application: definition of, 109; as increasing consciousness of Being, 109; and understanding, 108–9
application of text, 104, 105, 106
Archives for Social Science and Social Welfare, 12

Arieti, Silvano, 165, 167
Aristotle, 81
art *(see also* art, reproductive interpretation in): autonomy of, 130, 145; as creative and critical, 131; as everyday life, 131; in the modern world, 129–32; normative categories of, 146; political dimension of, 146; and postmodernism, 141; and production, 130; and spontaneity, 131; and style, 132; under capitalism, 130–31, 132, 145
art, reproductive interpretation in, 92–99; actuality of understanding vs. adequacy to the object, 94–97; classical, 97; postmodern, 97–98; and self-knowledge, 99; and tradition, 104–5
The Authoritarian Personality (Adorno and Horkheimer), 128
authority vs. reason, 160, 162, 165
autonomy: of art, 130, 145; and objectivity, 91–92, 93

Beethoven, Ludwig van, 97
behavior, uniformities of, 23–24 *(see also* action)
Being, 101n, 107; and aesthetics, 144; application as increasing consciousness of, 109; and knowledge, 113–14; and its objects, 113; and truth, 110
being-ready-to-hand *(Zuhandenheit),* 112
belongingness, 113–18; between subject and object, 114–15, 116; and tradition, 115
Bergson, Henri, 94
Bershady, Harold J., 85
Betti, Emilio, 89–100, 174; biographical sketch of, 89; on the interpretive